GW00976525

Beijing

WORLD BIBLIOGRAPHICAL SERIES

General Editors:
Robert G. Neville (Executive Editor)
John J. Horton

Robert A. Myers   Hans H. Wellisch
Ian Wallace   Ralph Lee Woodward, Jr.

John J. Horton is Deputy Librarian of the University of Bradford and was formerly Chairman of its Academic Board of Studies in Social Sciences. He has maintained a longstanding interest in the discipline of area studies and its associated bibliographical problems, with special reference to European Studies. In particular he has published in the field of Icelandic and of Yugoslav studies, including the two relevant volumes in the World Bibliographical Series.

Robert A. Myers is Associate Professor of Anthropology in the Division of Social Sciences and Director of Study Abroad Programs at Alfred University, Alfred, New York. He has studied post-colonial island nations of the Caribbean and has spent two years in Nigeria on a Fulbright Lectureship. His interests include international public health, historical anthropology and developing societies. In addition to *Amerindians of the Lesser Antilles: a bibliography* (1981), *A Resource Guide to Dominica, 1493-1986* (1987) and numerous articles, he has compiled the World Bibliographical Series volumes on *Dominica* (1987), *Nigeria* (1989) and *Ghana* (1991).

Ian Wallace is Professor of German at the University of Bath. A graduate of Oxford in French and German, he also studied in Tübingen, Heidelberg and Lausanne before taking teaching posts at universities in the USA, Scotland and England. He specializes in contemporary German affairs, especially literature and culture, on which he has published numerous articles and books. In 1979 he founded the journal *GDR Monitor*, which he continues to edit under its new title *German Monitor*.

Hans H. Wellisch is Professor emeritus at the College of Library and Information Services, University of Maryland. He was President of the American Society of Indexers and was a member of the International Federation for Documentation. He is the author of numerous articles and several books on indexing and abstracting, and has published *The Conversion of Scripts and Indexing and Abstracting: an International Bibliography*, and *Indexing from A to Z*. He also contributes frequently to *Journal of the American Society for Information Science*, *The Indexer* and other professional journals.

Ralph Lee Woodward, Jr. is Director of Graduate Studies at Tulane University, New Orleans. He is the author of *Central America, a Nation Divided*, 2nd ed. (1985), as well as several monographs and more than seventy scholarly articles on modern Latin America. He has also compiled volumes in the World Bibliographical Series on *Belize* (1980), *El Salvador* (1988), *Guatemala* (Rev. Ed.) (1992) and *Nicaragua* (Rev. Ed.) (1994). Dr. Woodward edited the Central American section of the *Research Guide to Central America and the Caribbean* (1985) and is currently associate editor of Scribner's *Encyclopedia of Latin American History*.

VOLUME 226

Beijing

J. E. Hoare
and
Susan Pares

Compilers

CLIO PRESS
OXFORD, ENGLAND · SANTA BARBARA, CALIFORNIA
DENVER, COLORADO

British Library Cataloguing in Publication Data

Hoare, James
Beijing. – (World bibliographical series; v. 226)
1. Peking (China) – Bibliography
I. Title II. Pares, Susan
016.9′51156

ISBN 1–85109–299–4

ABC-CLIO Ltd,
Old Clarendon Ironworks,
35A Great Clarendon Street,
Oxford OX2 6AT, England.

—————————

ABC-CLIO Inc.,
130 Cremona Drive,
Santa Barbara,
CA 93117, USA

Designed by Bernard Crossland.
Typeset by ABC-CLIO Ltd, Oxford, England.
Printed and bound in Great Britain by print in black, Midsomer Norton.

THE WORLD BIBLIOGRAPHICAL SERIES

This series, which is principally designed for the English speaker, will eventually cover every country (and some of the world's principal regions and cities), each in a separate volume comprising annotated entries on works dealing with its history, geography, economy and politics; and with its people, their culture, customs, religion and social organization. Attention will also be paid to current living conditions – housing, education, newspapers, clothing, etc. – that are all too often ignored in standard bibliographies; and to those particular aspects relevant to individual countries. Each volume seeks to achieve, by use of careful selectivity and critical assessment of the literature, an expression of the country and an appreciation of its nature and national aspirations, to guide the reader towards an understanding of its importance. The keynote of the series is to provide, in a uniform format, an interpretation of each country that will express its culture, its place in the world, and the qualities and background that make it unique. The views expressed in individual volumes, however, are not necessarily those of the publisher.

VOLUMES IN THE SERIES

Contents

Contents

Introduction

The Beijing that both of us first knew in the 1970s has largely disappeared. Then, as the Cultural Revolution came to an end, it was a drab and subdued place. Its citizens avoided contact with foreigners, and the once vibrant life of the city was hidden under a pall of Maoist rectitude.

Mao and his planners had irrevocably changed an older Beijing which had so charmed Western visitors and residents from the mid-19th century onwards and until the Second World War had led them to describe it in glowing terms. After the proclamation of the People's Republic of China from Tiananmen, the Gate of Heavenly Peace of the old imperial palace, on 1 October 1949, China's new rulers progressively changed the face of the city in a way that had not been done since the third Ming emperor moved his capital from Nanjing in the south in 1421 and began a massive construction programme to create a new imperial city. Now, 'revolutionary buildings' replaced the grey courtyards of the past. Imitating, but exceeding, Moscow's Red Square, the new regime created a huge open space in front of Tiananmen. It was bordered by monumental buildings, including the Great Hall of the People, where China's National Assembly would meet, and the foremost museum of the revolution. The massive city walls, once the city's most remarkable feature, were demolished to meet what were seen as the urgent needs of a then almost non-existent traffic. The onset of the Cultural Revolution in 1966 led to ten years when revolutionary posters were everywhere and to paint one's front door was considered bourgeois. The city steadily became drabber and drabber.

Now, in its place, there has re-emerged a bustling, bright and noisy city, more reminiscent of Hong Kong or Seoul than Chairman Mao's revolutionary capital. Newly refurbished for the fiftieth anniversary of the founding of 'New China' in 1949, the capital of the People's Republic is now described as a 'garden city', the envy of all Asia. The keen Beijing householder can now choose from a variety of paints to brighten up doors and walls. Most inhabitants of the city, however, live in apartment blocks,

Introduction

which, whatever their interior comfort in these days of relative affluence, present a bleak aspect to the outside world. In compensation, especially in spring and summer, the city now has a mass of street-side restaurants, beer gardens, and markets large and small. Where people once went to bed by ten o'clock, they now revel until the early hours. China, and with it Beijing, has changed.

Beijing: the city

Location, climate, economy and people

Beijing – the name means Northern Capital – lies at 39.6° latitude and 116.2° longitude at the northern end of the North China plain, in the angle of several ranges of mountains that enclose it to the north, northeast, northwest and west. Three main passes, Nankou, Gubeikou and Shanhaiguan, link the Beijing region with the northern parts of the country. To the south the land is flat, stretching down towards the Yellow River. The Bay of Bohai, opening on to the East China Sea, lies about 160 km (100 miles) to the east and southeast of Beijing. The city does not stand on a river, but several rivers, the most important of which are the Yongding and the Chaobai, water the surrounding countryside, and Beijing is linked to the northern end of the Grand Canal. The first attempts at canalization date from the 4th century BC. Work on the southern stretches of the canal was resumed in the 7th century under the Sui dynasty. In the 13th century the Yuan dynasty extended it from Hangzhou in Zhejiang province as far north as the Beijing-Tianjin area. The chief purpose of the canal was to facilitate the transport of grain from the rich agricultural areas of central-south China to the north, to meet the needs of the imperial capital. It functioned thus until the mid-19th century, when, in 1855, the Yellow River, which crosses the canal, changed its course as a result of severe flooding and resumed its old bed to reach the sea north of the Shandong peninsula instead of south of it. One consequence was a heavy reduction in the flow of water in the northern stretches of the Grand Canal.

Although relatively near the sea, the city has a continental monsoon climate, with a short spring, humid and rainy summer, sunny autumn and cold, dry winter. Temperatures range from around -4°C in January to an average of 26°C in July. During spring, the winds blowing eastwards from the loess plateau of northwest China bring clouds of fine yellow dust to the capital, which used to combine with the local dust to create gritty sandstorms. Programmes of planting trees, shrubs and grass and of careful landscaping seem now to have reduced the hazard of these spring duststorms and of soil erosion in general. Most of the annual rainfall comes during the summer months of July and August. As elsewhere in East Asia, autumn in

Beijing is cherished as the most agreeable season, with bright skies and fine colours. Winter brings very little precipitation. The whole of the Beijing region suffers from a low average rainfall of around 635 mm, and the amount falling each year can vary enormously. Shortage of adequate water supplies has always plagued the capital. The Yongding river, with a course to the west of Beijing, generally remains a sandy riverbed under the Marco Polo bridge (Lugouqiao) that spans it, and serves as an exercise ground for young men riding their horses. In Qing times a system of pipes brought water from springs in the Western Hills outside of Beijing into the capital, where it alimented the series of lakes flowing from north to south just west of the Forbidden City. In more recent times reservoirs have been constructed on the upper reaches of the Yongding at Guanting to the northwest of Beijing and on the upper stretches of the Bai river at Miyun northeast of Beijing, supplemented by a reservoir near the Ming tombs. These help to relieve the perennial shortfall in water, and the Guanting and Ming tombs reservoirs also provide hydroelectric power for the city.

The metropolitan region of Beijing has traditionally extended over a large area. The siting of the Forbidden City within the Imperial City constituted a core, embodying the authority of the emperor, around which the larger city could radiate. For as long as the imperial system continued, such a concentric arrangement held its value and its rationale. The present municipality, as finally established in 1961, still radiates out from the central point of Tiananmen, and now covers a total of 16,808 square km (6,489.5 square miles); to provide a comparison, this is roughly half the land area of Belgium. The city is one of the three centrally administered municipalities of China – the other two being Shanghai and Tianjin. Such status puts it on a par with a province. The greater part of the municipality is occupied by eight rural counties, mountainous to the north and west, flatter to the south and east. Beijing proper takes in four districts, which are surrounded by four inner and two outer suburban districts. The Beijing Municipal People's Congress holds responsibility at the decision-making level, while the Beijing People's Government acts as the executive organ under the leadership of the city mayor, potentially a powerful political post. Authority descends through district or, in the rural areas, township administrations down to street committees and neighbourhood or residents' associations. The administrative structure is matched by a party political hierarchy. The population of the municipality at the end of the 20th century exceeded ten million.

As the capital of succeeding dynasties, Beijing functioned primarily as the seat of the emperor's power and administrative centre of the empire, housing government offices and their attendant bureaucracy. The final examinations in the regular search for new officials to man the civil service were held in Beijing. Commercial activity was less esteemed, but the production of handicrafts and luxury goods was encouraged, largely for use at the court. In line with a long tradition of state control of the manufacture of such goods, workshops installed inside the Forbidden City in the 17th-18th centuries turned out porcelain, cloisonné, glassware, textiles and other costly products for imperial use. The Qing emperors, who were from the minority Manchu race, prevented their Manchu followers from engaging in any other than civil or military duties. Commerce was kept for the Han Chinese, that is, the subordinate race. Beijing under the Qing was divided by walls into an area enveloping the Imperial City which was reserved for Manchu and Chinese officials, and an area to the south inhabited by the ordinary Chinese. In economic terms, the capital's northerly districts were generally unproductive, while the southerly district housed such commerce as existed and was also a centre for entertainment. Beijing was, in short, a city of consumption, sustained by a flow of goods from other parts of the country that arrived first of all by canal or sea and later by rail.

The new Communist regime of 1949 took vigorous steps to turn Beijing into a centre of production. Self-sufficiency in food supplies was aimed at through the incorporation of rural counties within the boundaries of the municipality; these continue to provide a wide range of foodstuffs. Beijing was to contribute, moreover, to the national wealth. Building on such industry as had started up in the region earlier in the century, the new regime constructed steel works, machine-building plants and textile factories during the 1950s and 1960s. Petrochemical processing was added in the 1970s. A high-tech industry has grown up since the late 1980s, specializing in research and production of electrical and electronic goods and with officially backed plans for expansion. At the same time the traditional handicrafts industry has been maintained.

One effect of the post-1978 reforms in the economy, research and education has been a growing awareness of environmental issues. The deleterious impact of polluting industries on the health of the city's population and on the fabric of its buildings has been gradually acknowledged. In 1980 the Party Central Committee proposed a master plan for Beijing that would seek to control the growth of heavy industry and instead re-emphasize the political, educational and cultural importance of the capital.

The Communist regime that came to power in 1949 had always acknowledged these roles for Beijing and took the decision to develop the city's resources in higher education and research. The northwest district around Haidian, where the former Yanjing University had been established in 1916 by Western missionaries, was chosen as the centre for a host of universities, colleges and research institutes. The foremost universities are Beijing and Qinghua, the latter renowned as a technical institute. Academics and research cadres, augmented by museum and library curators, thus make up one element in the population. Beijing's rich cultural life – music, opera, painting and crafts – is yet another strand; the banking and finance sectors are important; and in keeping with Beijing's role as the seat of party control and national administration, many of the large buildings in the capital are party and government departments, employing sizeable numbers of cadres and civil servants. Although the term is used very cautiously, a small middle class is slowly re-emerging in Beijing, alongside the greater numbers of factory and office workers and shop and stall keepers. One element in this new group is formed by those who have benefited as entrepreneurs from the post-1978 liberalization of the economy. They work particularly in the expanding service industries of retailing, catering and tourism. Many are self-employed and enjoy far higher incomes than those in fixed-salary employment.

The population of Beijing has always been mixed. The installation of alien dynasties that had sprung from one or other of the tribes to the north of China brought new elements into the city to exist alongside the native Han Chinese. Beijing is said to have had a Moslem population from the 10th century. This is now centred around the Niujie – Ox Street – mosque in the southwest corner of the inner city, but is also present throughout the municipality, as signalled by the mosques in the rural counties. The city also has inhabitants from the Mongol, Uighur, Kazakh, Korean and Tibetan minorities, some of whom have congregated in certain areas. Since 1949 the population of Beijing has been growing continuously, although large-scale immigration into the city was for a long time controlled by strict residence qualifications. These have been loosened in recent years and Beijing has received heavy influxes of itinerant workers who arrive in the capital in search of employment.

To introduce more flexibility into housing and to encourage those who have sufficient funds to buy their own, the municipality has eased the provision and allocation of accommodation. Formerly this was built and administered through work units – that is, the units of employment, be they factory, office, college, government department, military unit or other – which constructed housing, generally large blocks of apartments, near the place of work and rented it at very subsidized rates to their employees. Now, although the state still initiates all housing construction and much is still bought by work units to rent to their employees, albeit at higher rates than formerly, the possibility of buying one's own property exists. Since the economic and other reforms of 1978 and after, efforts have been made to meet the needs of a growing population, to assist the clearing and rehabilitation of old quarters in the inner city and to accommodate the new businesses that have settled in the capital. From two ring roads the city now stretches out to four, with a fifth mooted, swallowing up much arable land that once lay around the perimeter. Satellite towns are planned. New construction is almost all in tower blocks, which contrive to ensure a southerly orientation – the favoured outlook – and more living space per inhabitant. An average of 15 square metres (161.5 square feet) per person was claimed at the end of 1999. Many new estates, some very large, have been laid out. The old heart of the city, the area of *hutong* or narrow lanes of one-storey courtyard dwellings or *siheyuan*, that extended east, west and north of the Imperial City and to its south in the Chinese city, is coming under continuous attack. Such housing, once intended for single, multi-generational families, was subdivided among many separate families in the years after 1949. Nonetheless, it still represents a lavish use of land at a time of high demand for office space and housing and for better living standards. The municipality has designated some of the finest examples of courtyard and *hutong* housing as conservation areas in the inner city, and has renovated some of the other old stock. The small towns out in the rural areas of Beijing municipality are built in a mixture of styles. Farmers' houses in the villages and countryside are generally of the traditional single-storey pattern, orientated to face south.

Beijing still keeps its image as a city of bicycles and cyclists still weave their interlocking routes at junctions, although they are now confined to their own lanes along the main thoroughfares. Buses and trolley-buses and two metro lines provide public transport, all of it heavily used. Extensions of the underground system and a massive programme of road building are envisaged. Mini-buses, taxis and, increasingly, private and business cars and commercial vehicles are adding to congestion on the roads and to levels of street pollution. The quality of air in Beijing remains poor. Airborne dust blows off the many building sites; industrial pollution remains severe; and the winter atmosphere is still made heavy by the fumes of coal-fired heating. Twenty-eight million tons of coal are consumed annually. The municipality is encouraging the use of cleaner domestic and vehicle fuels, and has taken steps to improve the quality of the local groundwater system.

The city's religious life has declined considerably under the impact of half a century of Communist rule and many of its religious buildings have been given over to secular uses or retained as tourist sites, such as the many fine temples in the Western Hills to the northwest of Beijing and the Tibetan-style temples at the former summer resort of Chengde. Of the large number of Buddhist temples, which include those of Lama Buddhism, only a handful maintain religious communities and perform services. The best known are the Yonghegong or 'Lama temple' and the Guanghua, Guangji and Fayuan temples and Tongjiao convent. Other temples have had the offices and workshops that had been installed in their grounds removed and have been restored as visitors' sites. Yet others remain untouched as the cost of reclaiming and renovating them is considerable. There is a large Daoist temple, the Baiyun or White Cloud temple. Of the former altars and shrines at which ceremonies were held, sometimes by the emperor himself, to honour the ancestors or the natural elements, most now form the centrepieces of public parks. The 'Temple of Heaven' with its two round vaulted halls, the Qiniandian and the Huangqiongyu, and the Altar of Heaven form a favourite landmark in the southern part of the inner city. Moslem worship has been more tenacious, perhaps because its adherents have a recognized status as the Hui national minority. The Christian churches, Catholic and Protestant, have often come under suspicion in the past because of their foreign associations, and their buildings, such as the Southern (Nantang) and Northern (Beitang) Catholic cathedrals stand out because of their openly Western design. Catholicism has been represented on and off in Beijing since the 14th century and still has a modest congregation in the city, though, like most of the Catholic community in China, it is regarded by the Vatican as schismatic. In the second quarter of the 18th century a Russian church mission was permitted to establish itself in the capital, while from 1860 a foreign Western community gradually grew up within the confines of succeeding diplomatic quarters.

Linguistically, the Chinese spoken by the educated population of the Beijing region has been taken as the model for *putonghua*, the 'common language' or form of Chinese adopted as standard throughout China. Beijing itself, however, has its own dialect, a subdivision of the Chinese spoken in Hebei province, itself one of the northern forms of the language. It is characterized chiefly by 'erization', the addition of an 'er' sound to the end of many words. A lively exchange in Beijing dialect forms the core of the two-man cross-talk so popular in the capital. This was one of the acts at the Beijing teahouses along with conjuring and juggling. Peking opera is probably the best known art form associated with the city, and is a blend of music, singing, recitation, acting and acrobatics performed by gorgeously costumed and made-up actors and actresses. Training for the opera is rigorous and starts in childhood. Musical skills in both Chinese and Western classical music are also promoted through concerts. The city's cultural life is rich and enjoys the participation of many sections of society.

History

Beijing has been the capital city of a unified China for the greater part of seven and a half centuries, a comparatively short span when set against the country's long history. Archaeological evidence of this history currently extends back into the Pleistocene period (which is estimated to have begun about 1.8 million years ago and ended some 10,000 years ago); the first use of written records is attributed to the Zhou dynasty, founded in about 1050 BC. Nevertheless, the Beijing region is associated with the discovery and identification of some of the earliest human remains to be found in China.

Introduction

These are skulls and bones of early human beings dated to varying periods and since named, some *Sinanthropus pekinensis* or Peking Man, others Upper Cave Man. They were all discovered in caves at Zhoukoudian, 55 km (34 miles) southwest of Beijing, in the course of excavations undertaken, following local advice, by Western and Chinese archaeologists throughout the 1920s and 1930s. The advent of hostilities between China and Japan in the Beijing area forced an end to the excavations in 1937. Plans were made to ship the fossils so far unearthed, including the skullcaps, to the United States for safekeeping, but in the confusion of war they disappeared in 1941 after being packed in crates and have never been seen since. Plaster casts, photographs and detailed drawings survived, as did some other fossils excavated at the Zhoukoudian caves. The dating of Peking Man has been put at *c.* 500,000 BC, that is, the mid-Pleistocene period, but a revised, later dating of *c.* 17,000-16,000 BC, representing the later Pleistocene period, has also been advanced on the basis of radiocarbon dating, presumably of surviving fossils.

The area at the head of the North China plain and at the foot of mountains that demarcated the plain from the higher land to the north was clearly favourable for settlement. It remained, however, at the edge of the territory covered by the ancient kingdoms of Shang (*c.* 1500-*c.* 1050 BC), Zhou (*c.* 1050-221 BC) and succeeding imperial dynasties. For many centuries the core of Chinese civilization and authority lay to the south and west, along the valleys of the Yellow and Wei rivers and of the Yangzi River further south. Settlements in the area covering present-day Beijing and Tianjin had the status of provincial towns or semi-independent states. During the Eastern Zhou (770-221 BC) the powerful state of Yan (a name that is still associated with Beijing) existed in a feudal relationship with the dynasty, for which it acted as a bulwark against the tribes living further to the northeast. Yan built a capital, Ji, at some distance to the east of modern Beijing. When the Zhou dynasty disintegrated, a multitude of small states, including Yan, emerged which fought constantly among themselves for supremacy. The state of Qin was the victor and in 221 BC its king succeeded in unifying what was considered the heartland of China. He styled himself Qin Shihuangdi. Yan was incorporated into his empire as one of thirty-six administrative units and its capital of Ji was destroyed. To demarcate and protect the Chinese empire, the centre of civilization, from the barbarians to the north and northeast, Qin Shihuangdi sought to link up and extend sections of already existing wall into a longer defensive barrier, the Great Wall. His proud claims to have established an empire for all time fell apart, however, after his death in 210 BC and by 206 BC a new dynasty, the Han, had established itself.

The Han initially kept the former state of Yan within their territory. The name Yan itself was transferred to a new provincial town, which acquired strategic importance as the Han struggled to hold off the incursions of northern tribes such as the Xiongnu. With the end of the Han dynasty in AD 220 China largely lost any central administration for over three hundred years as fleeting dynasties and kingdoms formed and dissolved. The northern parts of the country, which included the Beijing area, were divided among various invaders who maintained shortlived states. Eventually, in AD 581, a new dynasty, the Sui, succeeded in restoring cohesion to China and in rehabilitating the empire. They were followed by the Tang (AD 618-907), who brought the northern area around Beijing back under imperial Chinese control. The city was re-established as Yuzhou and again became important as a frontier post against northern tribes, among them the Khitan.

In a repetition of past patterns, Tang power faded and the Khitan moved into the Yuzhou region. In AD 947 they established themselves within their northern territories as the Liao dynasty (the Chinese heartland itself passed in AD 960 under the Song dynasty) and built a new city on the site of Yuzhou, naming it Nanjing, 'southern capital', to distinguish it from their four other more northerly capitals. Taking as their model the concepts of Chinese city planning (the northern invaders were generally, if not invariably, quick to absorb Chinese political and cultural influences), the Liao surrounded Nanjing by a square wall pierced by eight gates and built a palace in the centre. By the mid-12th century, yet another northern tribe, the Jurchen, which had elevated itself into the Jin dynasty in 1115, had broken Liao power and moved south to capture the Song capital of Kaifeng in 1126 and seize the Emperor Huizong and the imperial family. The remnants of the dynasty fled south to re-establish itself in Hangzhou as the Southern Song (1126-1279), leaving the Jin to hold the north. In 1153 the Jin built their capital on the site of the former Liao Nanjing, enlarging it and naming it Zhongdu, 'central capital'. It was the first time a city on that site had functioned as a capital city. Its status was terminated, however, when, under escalating pressure from the Mongols, the Jin moved their capital south from Zhongdu to Kaifeng. The Mongols, under their leader Genghis Khan, captured and destroyed Zhongdu in 1215.

Genghis remained preoccupied with maintaining order in his extensive territories, and the final conquest of the Song and re-unification of China was the work of his grandson, Kublai Khan (1215-94). In 1271 Kublai had established his dynasty as the Yuan (it lasted as the ruling dynasty of China from 1279 to 1368) and in 1264 had moved his capital from the city of Karakoram in Mongolia to a site slightly to the northeast of the old Liao capital of Zhongdu. In 1272 he named the new city Dadu, 'great capital'. It was also widely known as Khanbaliq, a word of Turkish origin signifying 'city of the Khan', which name, distorted into Cambalec or Cambaluc, was used by Western travellers to China. Mongol domination of vast stretches of territory ranging from China across Central Asia to the Black Sea allowed these areas to be pacified under a single authority. This in turn created a favourable environment for lengthy travels by Arabs and Europeans into China. Some of the latter, such as John of Plano Carpini and William of Rubeck, got as far as the earlier Mongol capital of Karakoram (Plano Carpini in 1246 and Rubeck between 1253 and 1255). Others reached the new capital of Dadu, the best known among them being the Venetian Marco Polo (1254-1324), whose account of his experiences was both popular and influential. (Lugouqiao, the fine bridge to the southwest of the city over the Yongding river, bears the name of 'Marco Polo bridge', since it is said it was already in place by the time of his visit and that he described it.) Polo claimed to have spent the years from 1275 to 1292 in China, some of them in the service of the Khan, as Kublai was known. Doubt has been cast on the veracity of his account, but it is still frequently quoted for its descriptions of the size and splendour of Dadu, with its walls and gates and imperial palace within. The city was modelled on the traditional square of Chinese town planning, with twelve gates giving access to the town through walls 18 miles (29 km) in circumference made of pounded earth. (Small lengths of the Yuan wall are still visible in the northern part of modern Beijing.) The Mongols took care never to become sinicized and retained many of the customs of their nomadic days, such as the practice of sleeping in tents or in curtain-hung rooms, even within the imperial quarters. To ease the passage of essential supplies of rice from the south, they extended the Grand Canal north and constructed a connecting canal that allowed boats to come into one of the lakes that lay inside the Imperial City.

Whatever the truth of Marco Polo's claims that he was in the Khan's service, it appears that Kublai did employ a number of foreigners as experts and advisers rather than turn to his Han Chinese subjects. Muslims seem in particular to have been favoured, as architects, doctors, astronomers and traders. Kublai himself eventually came to support Buddhism in its Tibetan Lamaist form, but he was tolerant of many religions, including Christianity. His lenient policies were followed by his successors to the extent of permitting Catholic Franciscan friars to settle and proselytize in Dadu. One of them, the Italian John of Montecorvino, was even appointed Archbishop of Cambeluc by the Pope in about 1307 and given a complement of clergy. Other Catholic priests such as Odoric of Pordenone and John Marignolli visited Dadu in the first half of the 14th century and stayed for several years, probably ministering in the churches founded by Montecorvino. However, this Christian community did not survive the fall of the Yuan dynasty in 1368. The accounts left by these temporary residents in Dadu and by the Arab traveller Ibn Battuta are still valuable for the information, sometimes firsthand, sometimes hearsay, they give of the Yuan capital.

With the installation of the Ming (1368-1644), imperial authority reverted to a Han Chinese dynasty. The first Ming emperor established his capital at Nanjing in the south on the Yangzi river, renaming Dadu as Beiping, 'northern peace', and placing it under the charge of his fourth son as prince of Yan. In 1402 this prince usurped the power of the second Ming emperor, the grandson of the first emperor, and ruled thereafter as the Yongle emperor (1403-24). He brought the capital back to the north in 1421, naming it Beijing. Hostile tribes continued to threaten the new dynasty from the north and the city's strategic position commanding the passes leading south from the mountains was again in its favour. Between 1406 and 1421 Yongle undertook a further reconstruction of the city and imperial palace. The Ming capital was sited somewhat to the south of the Yuan city, which was largely demolished. New walls were built, faced with brick, the magnificent Forbidden City, surrounded by moats, was constructed and the city was laid out on a strict north-south axis. Until the demolition of the city walls in the second half of the 20th century, Beijing retained the appearance and layout it had been given by the Ming. The Ming were also responsible for the present stretch of the Great Wall in the vicinity of Beijing, on which work started in 1566, and for the thirteen imperial tombs constructed from the early 15th century to the northwest of the city. Although the capital does not appear to have supported the same cosmopolitan society that the Yuan did in Dadu, by the first quarter of the 16th century European traders and diplomats, such as the Portuguese, were seeking to establish contact with China and to gain permission to travel as far as Beijing to petition the emperor. Catholic missionaries in the form of the Jesuits joined them. They were more successful, and in 1601 the Italian Matteo Ricci was permitted to settle in the capital. The Jesuits were tolerated for the scientific knowledge they were able to offer in astronomy, weaponry and other skills. The old observatory, first constructed under the Yuan, was added to by two Jesuit directors, Adam Schall von Bell and Ferdinand Verbiest. Across Siberia the Russians made their first contact with the Chinese empire in 1618.

By the first half of the 17th century the Ming were faltering under the pressure of domestic insurrection and increased incursions by the Manchu, another northern tribe descended from the Jurchen (who had earlier ruled the north of China as the Jin dynasty: see above). Faced by the imminent prospect of defeat at the hands of the Han Chinese rebel Li Zicheng, the Ming Chongzhen emperor, the last of his dynasty, committed suicide by hanging himself from a tree still pointed out on the hill behind the Forbidden City. The Chinese rebels, split by dissension, at once lost ground to the Manchu invaders, who in 1644 installed themselves in Beijing as the Qing dynasty (1644-1911). The Manchu had already created a base in northeast China around their capital at Shenyang, where their early leaders had built up a Chinese style of administration. They transferred their capital to Beijing, where they made little physical alteration to the Ming city with its massive walls and palaces, but changed its social organization. The northern half of the capital, containing the Forbidden City within the Imperial City, was largely inhabited by Manchu and Chinese officials and military and was known as the Inner City or, among foreigners, as the 'Tartar City'. To the south lay the Outer City inhabited by the Han Chinese population and known popularly as the 'Chinese City'. The two parts of the capital were separated by a wall, pierced by three gates, and walls surrounded the Inner and Outer Cities. The walls of the Inner City measured 23.7 km (14.7 miles) in circumference and were 12 m (40 ft) high, 18.6 m (62 ft) wide at the base and 10.2 m (34 ft) wide at the top. Those surrounding the Outer City were less imposing, standing only 9 m (30 ft) high and with a width at the base of 7.5 m (25 ft). Including the three gates between the Inner and Outer Cities, Beijing under the Ming and Qing had sixteen gates. Two of the early Qing rulers, the Kangxi (reigned 1661-1722) and Qianlong (reigned 1736-95) emperors, laid out and extended a series of parks, gardens and palaces to the northwest of Beijing, of which the most splendid was the Yuanmingyuan, known as the 'Summer Palace'. Further from Beijing and to the northeast was the summer resort of Chengde (known formerly as Jehol or Rehe), where a smaller palace was laid out in extensive hunting grounds and a number of Buddhist temples built in Tibetan and Chinese style.

The foreign contacts initiated by the Ming were tolerated and even at times encouraged by the early Qing emperors. The Jesuits in particular maintained a prominent presence in Beijing, where members of the order served Kangxi and Qianlong as artists or as advisers in diplomatic matters, astronomy, metal casting, architecture, garden construction, hydraulics and other technical skills. The ultimate hope of the missionaries, of course, was conversions at the highest level of Qing society, but their success in that direction was slight. Their most famous contributions to the fabric of Beijing were the intricate palaces, gardens and fountains in European style which they designed for the Summer Palace and the Catholic churches constructed in the capital. Their letters and drawings sent back to Europe gave valuable information on Qing practice and style, spread a knowledge of China and helped to promote the taste for chinoiserie.

The Europeans were joined early on by Russians. Following the Treaty of Nerchinsk of 1689, designed to stabilize the Sino-Russian border in Siberia after a period of fighting between the Russians and the Qing, Russia was in 1693 permitted to send a trade mission every three years to Beijing. The Treaty of Kiakhta (1727) some thirty years later sought to further regulate border and trade matters, but also agreed to the establishment of a permanent Russian ecclesiastical mission in Beijing, where Russian students were allowed to learn Chinese in order to act as interpreters in dealings between the two sides. (In negotiating both these treaties the Chinese were assisted by Jesuit advisers.) From the end of the 17th century Russia thus had a foothold in Beijing in the form of permanent residences and institutions that was denied to other foreigners until 1860. For long the oldest Western building in Beijing was said to be the small stone structure on the site of the old Russian, later Soviet, legation, itself on the site of an earlier Russian hostel, in the former legation quarter. This building was supposed to have been the church of the early ecclesiastical mission. In 1991 it was demolished in the course of constructing the Supreme Court.

Western attempts to secure the right to be permanently represented in Beijing were repeatedly rebuffed by the Qing. At the end of the 18th century the British sent a diplomatic mission headed by Lord Macartney, seeking to open up trade with China. The delegation was received by the Qianlong emperor in 1793 at the summer resort of Chengde, but had to return without securing any concessions. Relations in the following century became very strained between China and various Western powers as the latter sought to force China to accept trading and diplomatic links. Hostilities broke out which did not at first threaten Beijing, though a British fleet menaced the port of Tianjin southeast of Beijing on the coast. However, when China failed to ratify the 1858 Treaty of Tianjin, aimed at opening up the country to foreign diplomatic and commercial activity, and tried to prevent the arrival in the capital of diplomatic representatives of Britain and France, these two countries sent a punitive force against the Chinese which seized Tianjin and eventually fought its way into Beijing in 1860. The emperor and his court had fled to Chengde. The Anglo-French troops, as a reprisal against Chinese maltreatment of British and French prisoners (including the British consular officer Harry Parkes), then looted the Yuanmingyuan, the Summer Palace, carrying off its treasures and setting fire to the buildings, including the gardens designed by the Jesuits. All that is now left of the formerly magnificent palace are a few ruins. China capitulated in face of this show of force and in 1860 signed the Convention of Beijing, whereby permanent diplomatic missions were permitted in the capital and the interior of the country was opened up to consular, trade and missionary activities. Within the capital foreign diplomats were allowed to settle in a small area in the southeastern corner of the Inner City, and in 1861 British and French diplomatic missions were installed. They were followed by the Japanese and other Western nations and by the establishment of hospitals, schools and research institutes. Some of the earliest foreign-language studies of Beijing's topography and history date from this period.

Chinese resentment at foreign demands and the presence of foreigners on Chinese soil continued, exemplified in the Tianjin massacre of 1870, when a number of foreigners were killed. It came to a head in the last years of the 19th century. Political confrontation within the government between those anxious to push through reforms in public administration, education and the economy and the conservative faction headed by the Dowager Empress Cixi reflected the Qing dynasty's difficulties in confronting change. In the provinces the activities of foreign Christian missionaries and such radical innovations as the construction of railways antagonized the peasantry. Prolonged drought in northern China exacerbated other tensions. A popular, loosely organized movement known as the Yihetuan or 'Boxers' gathered momentum first in Shandong province, then throughout north China. Its followers, who enjoyed Cixi's backing, advanced on Beijing and from June to August 1900 besieged the legation quarter. An eight-power allied force managed to break through from Tianjin to relieve the siege. It occupied Beijing, among scenes of further looting. The events of 1900 yielded many firsthand accounts by foreign participants in the siege.

The growing tide of anger over China's inability to resist foreign predations, coupled with the perceived refusal of the Qing to countenance reform or cope with change led in 1911 to the downfall of the dynasty and a rejection of the imperial principle. Political parties emerged and a Nationalist government was formed under Chiang Kai-shek. Beijing remained a political centre. It provided the rallying point for the demonstrations of 4 May 1919 when protesters, many of them students, met at Tiananmen to denounce the failure of the Paris Peace Conference of early 1919 to restore to China former German concessions in Shandong province, which had instead been handed to the Japanese. The renewed infringement of sovereignty that sparked off the demonstrations provoked a widespread surge of nationalist feeling in which issues of modernization, new ideologies and new political and social forms were all discussed. The May Fourth movement also represented a great literary ferment and a renewal of the Chinese language itself when classical Chinese was passed over in favour of the vernacular.

Beijing was not always under the control of the Nationalists, who were stronger in the south of the country, where they were centred on Canton. From 1916 to 1928 Beijing was administered by a series of warlords. In 1928 the Nationalist government decided to transfer the national capital from Beijing to Nanjing on the Yangzi. Beijing lost its appellation of 'capital' – *jing* – and reverted to an earlier name, Beiping, meaning 'northern peace'. It retained a foreign community. By 1931 a new danger threatened the city when Japan, eager to extend its hold on the mainland of northeast Asia, occupied the northeastern provinces of China, the homeland of the Manchu. Japan revived the area under the name of Manzhouguo (Manchukuo) or Manchuria. In 1933 it created a buffer zone in the area around Chengde between Manchuria and China. In 1937 a contrived incident at Lugouqiao or Marco Polo bridge southwest of Beiping led to the outbreak of war between Japan and China and to the Japanese occupation of the city. By the time the war against Japan had ended in 1945, the Communist forces that had been increasingly pitted against the Nationalists since the 1920s had grown in strength and organization to the point where they could take on the Nationalists in civil war. Beiping and Tianjin fell to the Communists in January 1949, and in October 1949 the Communist leader Mao Zedong proclaimed the establishment of the People's Republic of China and reinstated Beijing as the capital of China. The new government, while acknowledging the city's pre-eminent role in national life, insisted that it must modernize and transform itself economically. Its encircling walls and gates were almost all demolished in the two decades following 1949. The second ring road still follows the former line of the walls; the third and fourth ring roads repeat the same pattern at a greater distance. A vast square flanked by enormous public buildings was constructed in front of Tiananmen for the tenth anniversary in 1959 of the founding of the new China. As part of the programme to reclaim the centre of Beijing for the new regime, the foreign diplomatic community was eased out of the old legation quarter beside Tiananmen Square and resettled in two foreigners' enclaves at Jianguomenwai and Sanlitun, both in the eastern section of the city that lay outside the line of the old city wall.

Beijing as national capital and the seat of party and government headquarters has often played a leading role in the political campaigns that have marked the half-century since the advent of Communist rule. (Sometimes, if the situation in the capital was judged unfavourable, the new campaign might be initiated elsewhere. This was so with the Cultural Revolution [1966-76]; the impetus came from Shanghai, though the first big-character poster bearing criticism was put up at Beijing University.) Beijing has also been the site of the most dramatic of the unofficial movements that have drawn together protest against leaders or policies. Such were the April 1976 rallies in Tiananmen Square to commemorate the deceased premier Zhou Enlai, the pro-democracy campaign of wall-posters and unofficial publications in 1978-79 and the six-week-long occupation of Tiananmen Square from April to June 1989.

Economic reform has brought many changes to the material and social fabric of Beijing. The opening up of China in general has brought increasing numbers of domestic and foreign tourists to the capital. Foreign students are now a common sight in the university area. There are ambitious plans to develop Beijing as an 'international metropolis'. Its renewed exposure to the outside world means that the number of books and reports written about it in English and other foreign languages looks set to remain high.

The Bibliography

This book follows the general pattern of other city volumes in the ABC-CLIO series. As usual, its aim is to meet the needs of the general, non-specialist, English-reading enquirer, rather than those of the scholar, and we have excluded all books in Chinese or other Asian languages. The reader should be aware, however, that the Chinese have been writing and printing

Introduction

books for a long time and there is a vast corpus of works in Chinese on all aspects of Beijing. The Japanese too have produced an extensive literature, very little of which has been translated, on Beijing and its surroundings. We have included several works in French and a few in German, either where there is nothing equivalent in English or where the work in question covers new ground.

In the second half of the 19th century, largely under the impetus of foreigners living in the concessions, Tianjin emerged as the port for Beijing and Beidaihe as a seaside resort. Beijing has a number of surrounding, sometimes outlying, places associated with it. For this reason this bibliography includes a section of books on Tianjin, Beidaihe, Chengde, the Great Wall, the Ming and Qing tombs and the Grand Canal, since such works have a more or less close relationship with the greater number devoted to Beijing.

The history of Beijing since the 17th century has had its effect on the production of books about the city. The 18th century, thanks to the Jesuits and to the members of a number of visiting diplomatic missions, produced a remarkable number of works relating to Beijing. From the mid-1790s onwards came a tailing away, as the Qing government increasingly limited access to the city. Only with the opening of the capital to resident diplomatic missions in 1860-61 was there a revival, which continued at a steady pace until China descended into warlordism and confusion in the 1920s. The loss of the city's status as the country's capital also affected the number of books about it. The Communists' victory in 1949 saw another period of eclipse, for like the Qing before them, China's new rulers kept foreigners either at bay altogether or on a very tight rein. Beijing features in books by visitors, but there is a remarkable sameness about their accounts of visits to primary schools and factories, and meals in a small number of grand restaurants. The Cultural Revolution produced some Western writing, but it was only with the gradual opening up of China from around 1972 onwards that new guidebooks and histories of the city made their appearance. Since Deng Xiaoping's reforms of 1978 and the two decades of opening to the outside world that followed, there has been a torrent of new books about Beijing, including a growing number of academic studies, while new access has allowed novelists to draw on the city as material for their work. All these fluctuating phases are reflected in this bibliography, sometimes, of course, by the absence of publications.

Bibliographies about capitals can easily fall into the trap of becoming bibliographies about the country. The shorthand use of 'Beijing' or 'Washington' to describe the government and people of a country in a book title, while perhaps reflecting the importance of the capital in decision-making, often does not provide the reader with any information about or understanding of the history, life and work of the city itself. For example,

P'yongyang between Peking and Moscow is not concerned with the three cities, but with the diplomacy conducted by the three governments; in such a title 'North Korea, China and the Soviet Union' could equally be used. We have tried to exclude such works, concerning ourselves with books that inform the reader in one way or another about Beijing, the place and its people. That said, no doubt others would have included some that we have excluded, and vice versa. We can only plead that constraints of space and especially time have limited what we could do. We are confident that all the items covered here add something to our knowledge of Beijing, its people and their lives, or the role that the city has played in the history of China.

Most of the categories are obvious, and the reason for including a particular book or article in one section rather than another is equally obvious. There is some difficulty about older guidebooks, however. Often these are still of use as guides to at least some aspects of Beijing and its surrounding area, and therefore seem naturally to belong in the guidebook section. Others are now more historical in their value, and so have been placed in the history section. The distinction between memoirs and history is another tricky area. We have not satisfactorily solved the problem, and one could argue that some items placed in the memoirs section really belong under history, or vice versa. Within each section, works are listed alphabetically, not by date of publication. Only where two or more books have the same title have we listed them by date.

While neither of us subscribes to the idea that the book, or the printed article, is finished, there is no doubt that the world of publishing is changing in the face of the spread of computers, the World Wide Web and other electronic methods. Older technologies such as microfilm and the microfiche are also more readily available than they were twenty years ago. We have therefore indicated where we know that journals or newspapers are available on line, or where material has been published on CD-ROM or in microform, although we have not spent much time pursuing these sources. Those who wish to do so can profitably check the catalogues of such companies as Cheng & Tsui of Boston, Massachusetts (www.cheng-tsui.com), Norman Ross Publishing Inc. of New York (www.nross.com), or Inter Documentation Company bv, of Leiden, Netherlands (P.O.Box 11205, 2301 EE, Leiden, The Netherlands). Such publishing methods have made available far more widely than once seemed possible many of the rare books on China and Beijing published before the 1860s.

As well as our own private collection of books on China built up over the last forty years, we have been able to call on the resources of many libraries for help with this work. Of particular importance has been the library of the School of Oriental and African Studies (University of London). In addition, between us we have made use of the resources of the British Library, the Foreign and Commonwealth Office Library and Information Services, the

Introduction

Great Britain-China Centre, the Mitchell Library, Sydney, and, via the internet, the Library of Congress and the Bodleian Library. Booksellers and their catalogues around the world have proved most useful. Barnes and Noble in the United States, together with many other bookstores scattered around various parts of the east coast; the Old Book Room in Canberra; Waterstones, Dillons and Fine Books Oriental, amongst others, in London; the Friendship Store and numerous hotel bookshops in Beijing and elsewhere in China; and Kelly and Walsh and the South China Morning Post bookshops in Hong Kong have all contributed, as have on-line booksellers such as Amazon.com. To all these, and to those friends and contacts who have allowed us to sit in their reading rooms or private studies, we are most grateful. We are also grateful for the help and encouragement of the staff of ABC-CLIO, especially Julia Goddard and Bob Neville in Oxford, even if they perhaps have placed too great a reliance on our ever-optimistic delivery dates.

When transcribing from Chinese, we have generally used pinyin, the system favoured by the People's Republic of China since the mid-1970s. However, older books and even many modern academic works still use the Wade-Giles system, which dates from the late 19th century, and even pinyin is not without its variations. Authors' names are given as those concerned have preferred to cite them, even though this may occasionally seem confusing. Anybody hoping to learn about China will quickly find that it is necessary to master more than one method of transcription, even today. In addition, we have, as do most educated Chinese when using English, decided that 'Peking Man', 'Peking duck' and 'Peking opera' are too well established to need transforming into their pinyin versions. Many Chinese-speaking English now also extend this usage to 'Peking university' or to the 'Peking Union Medical College'. We have generally followed the widespread practice in Asia of putting the family name first. Thus Mao Zedong, is Mr Mao, not Mr Zedong. Where a person has a Western given name, however, we follow the Western practice. Professor Jerome Ch'en, therefore, is listed in that form.

As always, errors and mistakes are our responsibility.

Jim Hoare and Susan Pares
London, April 2000

Chronology

DATE	CHINA	BEIJING
c. 1,800,000- c. 8000 BC	Pleistocene	'Peking Man', dated variously to between c. 500,000 BC and c. 17,000-16,000 BC
c. 6000- c. 1700 BC	Neolithic	
c. 1500- c. 1050 BC	Shang dynasty	
c. 1050-221 BC	Zhou dynasty	State of Yan in area of modern Beijing, Eastern Zhou (770-221 BC); capital Ji
770-475 BC	Spring and Autumn period	Yan emerges as an independent state
475-221 BC	Warring States period	
221-206 BC	Qin dynasty	Yan incorporated into Qin empire; Ji destroyed
206 BC-AD 220	Han dynasty	Yan retained on NE border, name transferred to city
AD 221-280	Three Kingdoms	Beijing area under control of succeeding invaders
AD 265-589	Southern Dynasties	
AD 386-581	Northern Dynasties	
AD 581-618	Sui dynasty	
AD 618-907	Tang dynasty	Beijing area brought back under imperial control; city of Yuzhou founded
AD 907-960	Five Dynasties and Ten Kingdoms	

907-1125	Liao dynasty (Khitan)	Liao establish Nanjing on site of Yuzhou as 'southern capital' of Khitan
1115-1234	Jin dynasty (Jurchen)	Jin establish their capital, Zhongdu, on site of former Nanjing 1215: Zhongdu captured and destroyed by Mongols
960-1279	Song dynasty (held central, then southern China)	
1279-1368	Yuan dynasty (Mongols)	Mid-1260s: Mongols move their capital to Beijing area, name it Dadu (also known as Khanbaliq or Cambeluc). Said to have been visited by Marco Polo between 1275 and 1292 1280s-1290s: Yuan extend Grand Canal north to Dadu c. 1307: John of Montecorvino appointed Bishop of Cambeluc First half of 14th century: visits by Odoric of Pordenone and John Marignolli
1368-1644	Ming dynasty	Ming establish first capital in southern city of Nanjing, call former Dadu Beiping 1421: capital returned to north, named Beijing 1406-21: construction of Forbidden City. Work starts at same time on Changling, first of Ming tombs 1420: construction of Temple of Heaven 1566: work starts on rebuilding of Great Wall in Beijing area

1644-1911	Qing dynasty (Manchu)	1601: Jesuit Matteo Ricci founds mission in Beijing
		1644: Manchu transfer their capital to Beijing
		1693: Russian trade missions to Beijing permitted
		1727: permanent Russian ecclesiastical mission permitted in Beijing
		17th-18th centuries: gardens and palaces created to northwest of Beijing, some with technical help of Jesuits, and summer resort built at Chengde
		1793: Macartney mission to Beijing and Chengde
		1860: Anglo-French force captures Tianjin, enters Beijing, loots Summer Palace. Permanent foreign diplomatic missions permitted in Beijing
		1870: massacre of foreigners in Tianjin
		1900: Boxer siege of diplomatic legations at Beijing
1911-49	Republic of China	1919: May Fourth demonstrations in Beijing
		1916-28: Beijing ruled by warlords
		1928: Nationalist government transfers capital to Nanjing, Beijing renamed Beiping
		1937: 'Marco Polo bridge' incident, start of Sino-Japanese war. Japanese occupy Beiping
1949-	People's Republic of China	1949: Communists seize Beiping and Tianjin, Beijing restored as capital

Chronology

1950s: extensive demolition
and rebuilding of Beijing
1989: Tiananmen
demonstrations in Beijing
1990: Asian Games in Beijing

Beijing and Its People

General

1   Beijing.
Deborah Kent.   New York: Children's Press, 1996. 64p. maps. (Cities of the World Series).

A brief account, aimed at 9-12 year olds, of the history of Beijing, together with a description of the life and work of its inhabitants, with many illustrations, some in colour. The author is a well-known writer of non-fiction books for children. In a somewhat similar format, also aimed at the same age group, is *Daily life in ancient and modern Beijing*, by Robert F. Baldwin, illustrated by Ray Webb (Minneapolis, Minnesota: Runestone Press, 1999. 64p. bibliog. [Cities Through Time Series]).

2   Beijing: an ancient city.
Edited by the Foreign Languages Press.   Beijing: Foreign Languages Press, 1988. 18p. (China – Facts & Figures Series).

Part of a collection meant to be handed out at Chinese embassies overseas and readily available in hotels and shops in many Chinese cities. It is a simple account of the capital and its salient features, together with some badly reproduced photographs of the main attractions of traditional Beijing and what the authorities clearly think will appeal to a modern audience. There is no index but the booklet itself is so short that it is easily skimmed.

3   Beijing: the nature and planning of a Chinese capital city.
Victor F. S. Sit.   Chichester, England; New York; Brisbane, Australia; Toronto; Singapore: John Wiley & Sons, 1995. 389p. maps. (Belhaven World Cities Series).

A stimulating and informative analysis of the genesis and history of China's capital, which makes an important contribution to the study of modern Beijing. By discussing his subject in terms of Chinese, rather than Western, criteria, Sit obliges his non-Chinese readers to re-evaluate their understanding of the role and functioning of a capital city. He argues that the city now called Beijing evolved to meet philosophical and spiritual needs as the setting for the point of contact between heaven and earth in the person of the emperor. This role allowed it to serve as a model for other Chinese cities. The Communist government of 1949 applied different, Soviet-inspired criteria that required Beijing to become a centre of production as well as the seat of central government. Investment in the infrastructure was restricted and environmental issues hardly addressed. Sit shares the general view that Beijing has suffered greatly under such a regime. He ends with a lengthy discussion of a number of separate issues affecting the city's health. The book has no bibliography, but the chapter references are very full.

4 Beijing superlatives.
Li Xingjian, translated by Ma Shiyu.   Hong Kong: Hai Feng Publishing Co. Ltd, 1989. 142p.

A collection of 'oldest, biggest and best' stories about China's capital, which supplements some of the material to be found in ordinary guidebooks. The stories themselves are quite well told, and many of them are accompanied by some rather small black-and-white photographs. The absence of maps means that it is of little use as an ordinary guidebook, though it might serve as a useful supplement to such a book, perhaps to be read after a visit. It will also delight quiz setters.

5 Beijing: yesterday, today and tomorrow.
Zhang Jinggan.   In: *Urbanization in Asia: spatial dimensions and policy issues.*   Edited by Frank J. Costa, Ashok K. Dutt, Laurence J. C. Ma, Allen G. Noble.   Honolulu, Hawaii: University of Hawaii Press, 1989, p. 227-45. maps.

Zhang's short essay, produced like the others in this book for an academic conference held in 1985, falls into two parts. The first provides an overview of Beijing's history since the city became the capital of the Yuan dynasty in 1267, though Zhang also links the Mongols' 'Dadu' to previous cities on or near the site. Good maps show the way in which Beijing has developed since the Mongols, emphasizing the role of the Imperial court in determining the layout of the city. The second part examines how the city has changed since the Communist victory in 1949, so that it could become the showcase for China's new rulers. Zhang notes that in the process, much of what gave old Beijing its charm had disappeared, although he concedes that some effort has been made to preserve a little of the heritage. However, new demands, as a result of massive economic and social change since the reforms of 1978, are beginning to change the city even more drastically.

6 The Chan's great continent: China in western minds.
Jonathan Spence.   London: Allen Lane: The Penguin Press, 1998. 279p.

Although Jonathan Spence is concerned with all China, and not just its capital, the reality is that most of those whose works he examines in this entertaining and witty book have been concerned with Beijing and the sense of power which the city evoked. He traces the Western fascination with things Chinese from the writings of William of Rubeck through Marco Polo and the Jesuits, down to the presentation of the capital and those who ruled there in the writings of 20th-century authors as different as Karl Wittfogel, Henry Kissinger and Jorge Luis Borges. With Spence, it is essentially the Beijing of the imagination that the reader meets, but it is a useful and entertaining way to begin the approach to the city.

7   China.
Qin Shi.   Beijing: New Star Publications, 1993; 2nd ed., 1997. 248p. map.

This is not a guidebook, but rather a small encyclopaedia of general information about all aspects of China today, as seen from a Chinese point of view. There is an abundance of facts and figures, with accounts of organizations, cultural developments, government structures and a host of other material. As with all such books, the capital features prominently, not least in the many coloured photographs found throughout the book.

8   China ABC.
New World Press.   Beijing: New World Press, 1985. 238p. map.

Although concerned with all of China, this little collection of important information about China in the mid-1980s inevitably contains much about Beijing and its role as the national capital. Specific Beijing entries are few, but the capital features in section such as administrative division, newspapers and religion. Some of the claims, though well-known, have long since been discounted – for example, you cannot see the Great Wall from the moon – but others remain true. Confusingly, despite the title, the entries are not in alphabetical order!

9   China: a cultural and historical dictionary.
Edited by Michael Dillon.   Richmond, England: Curzon Press, 1998. 450p. maps.

A valuable addition to the existing dictionaries and encyclopaedias, part of a series produced by staff of the University of Durham. There is much on Beijing and its role as a cultural and political capital, supplementing older works such as that by Couling (see item no. 19).

10   China: a literary companion.
A. C. Grayling, Susan Whitfield.   London: John Murray, 1994. 289p. map.

Neither guidebook nor history, this book of extracts with linking passages by the authors is designed to introduce the reader painlessly to aspects of China and its culture as encountered in a variety of Western and Chinese sources. Beijing features prominently, whether in Marco Polo's disputed account or Harold Acton's intoxicated description of 1932. There are descriptions of ceremonies in the capital under the emperors, of great processions and funerals. Beijing's ghosts and gardens feature, as does the city's vicissitudes in modern warfare. The result is a pleasing and entertaining compendium. There is a small collection of illustrations, several of them relating to Beijing.

11   China through the sliding door: reporting three decades of change.
John Gittings.   London: Touchstone, 1999. 280p. map.

Gittings, East Asia correspondent of the London newspaper *The Guardian*, has reported on China since the 1960s, originally from Hong Kong, and first visited the country in

1971. Although this anthology of his reporting goes far beyond events and occasions in the capital, Gittings, who has a strong sense of the political, returns again and again to the centre of Chinese political life. The result is a series of vignettes of the main events in Beijing from the last phase of the Cultural Revolution to the era of reform and opening to the outside world which marked the 1990s. In addition, there are sketches of the lives of ordinary people, whether on bicycles or paraded by the roadside for the visit of Queen Elizabeth II in 1986. Gittings' clear style, with the occasional barb as a reminder of his radical past, make this an entertaining and informative introduction to late 20th-century China and its capital city.

12   Chinese cities: the growth of the metropolis since 1949.
Edited by Victor F. S. Sit.   Oxford; New York; Hong Kong: Oxford University Press, 1985. 239p. maps.

The role of large cities in China and the process of urbanization have concerned the Communist leadership since 1949, as the editor observes in his introduction. The government has at times intervened in the movement and location of regional populations and has encouraged the transformation of large cities from centres of consumption into production bases through the installation of industry, while they continued to act as centres for higher education, medical and cultural services. The emphasis on industrialization, however, has led to underfunding of the service sector and to poor housing and transport. Chapter 2, on Beijing, by Dong Liming, suggests that Beijing has suffered from being constrained to turn itself into a modern industrial base and that it should be allowed to resume its former role as an administrative and cultural centre and form part of a Beijing/Tianjin/Tangshan economic region. Imbalanced distribution of population, housing and industry throughout the municipality has increased its problems. Dong sees hope for the city in the achievement of the municipality's official targets for the year 2000. This is one of the first books on city planning with a strong input from mainland Chinese scholars.

13   The Chinese empire illustrated: being a series of views from original sketches, displaying the scenery, architecture, social habits, etc., of that ancient and exclusive nation.
Thomas Allom, G. N. Wright, adapted and abridged by D. J. M. Tate. Hong Kong: John Nicholson Ltd, 1988. 125p. maps.

The 60 plates reproduced here have been chosen from the 143 comprising the original edition of *The Chinese Empire Illustrated*. This appeared in 1843, shortly after the First Opium War (1839-42), and a new edition was published in 1858 (London; New York: London Printing and Publishing Co. Ltd, 1858. 2 vols. in 1). T. N. Allom, as D. J. M. Tate explains, was a talented draughtsman and architect, who, however, apparently never visited China. He based his drawings largely on those made by William Alexander (see item no. 24), who travelled in Lord Macartney's party to China in 1793, and on the work of others. The commentaries accompanying the engravings were by G. N. Wright, a Protestant missionary to China; they have been abridged and adapted here for a modern readership. Several of the engravings reproduced, particularly those in section 1 on 'Imperial China', show scenes of Beijing and Chengde. Allom's drawings were based on sketches made on the spot, and therefore it can be assumed they are reasonably accurate; they nonetheless convey a very European view of exotic scenes.

14   Chinese profiles.
Zhang Xinxin, Sang Ye.   Beijing: Panda Books, 1986, second
printing 1987. 376p.

This appeared in Chinese as *Beijingren* (which can be translated either as Beijingers or as Peking Man), and is a similar, though slightly earlier, collection to *Portraits of ordinary Chinese* (q.v.), supposedly based on the work of the American writer, Studs Terkel. Although the book covers all of China, and the original title apparently refers to the common ancestor of all Chinese, 'Peking man', there is some concentration on people living in the capital region. While there is perhaps not much depth to many of the interviews, the real interest is that such a stress on the role of the individual is now accepted by a party and state that until very recently emphasized the need for the suppression of such individual needs and wishes. Another version of this work, edited by William J. Jenner, Delia Davin, translated by the editors and Cheng Lingfeng, Gladys Yang, Judy Burrows, Jeffrey C. Kinkley, Geremie Barmé, foreword by Studs Terkel, is *Chinese lives: an oral history of contemporary China* (London: Macmillan London Ltd; New York: Panthenon Books, 1987. 368p. map).

15   Chinese roundabout: essays in history and culture.
Jonathan D. Spence.   New York; London: W. W. Norton & Co.,
1992. 400p.

Spence is a distinguished historian of China, whose work ranges widely across the whole spectrum of Chinese history from the foundation of the Ming dynasty to the present. This collection of historical essays of varying lengths demonstrates that breadth of scholarship. Several of the essays relate to Beijing. They include 'Matteo Ricci and the ascent to Peking', describing the long years Ricci spent trying to reach China and his joy at getting there; 'Gamble in China', an account of the social scientist and photographer Sidney Gamble, which includes some of his photographs taken in Beijing in the 1920s; and a long essay on 'Tiananmen', placing the square and the events of 1989 in the context of the city's history. Many of the other essays throw up useful facts or interpretations about all aspects of Beijing life, from the rituals of the court to food and medicine, all presented in elegant language.

16   Chinese shadows.
Simon Leys.   New York: Viking, 1977; Harmondsworth, England:
Penguin Books, 1978. 220p.

Simon Leys is the pen-name of a Belgian scholar (and sometime diplomat), Pierre Ryckmans, who teaches at the Australian National University. This collection of essays, originally published in French as *Ombres Chinoises* (Paris: Union Générale d'Editions, 1974. 312p. [Bibliothèque Asiatique]), is typical of his downbeat approach to contemporary China, partly born out of his experiences in the Cultural Revolution. Caustic descriptions of Beijing feature more frequently in this set of essays than they do in various other collections he has published in French and English, which is why it is included. However, readers may find the excessively negative tone rather wearisome.

17 The city in modern Chinese literature and film: configurations of space, time, and gender.
Zhang Yingjin.   Stanford, California: Stanford University Press, 1996. 390p. bibliog.

This study examines the way in which cities are portrayed in modern Chinese literature, and, to a much lesser extent, in film. Zhang shows how important small towns were in late Qing and early Republican literature, and how gradually the big cities, especially Shanghai and Beijing, came to play a more important role. He argues that small towns and cities were seen as places that trapped their inhabitants, who therefore wished to escape, but having done so, the small town became an important source of roots and knowledge. The imperial capital, Beijing, and the economic and cosmopolitan capital, Shanghai, provided different opportunities. Beijing represented tradition and culture, Shanghai diversity and modernity. Yet at the same time, both offer seductive ways of life to the newcomer.

18 A companion to China.
Frances Wood.   London: Weidenfeld & Nicholson, 1988. 222p. map. bibliog.

Wood heads the China Section at the British Library in London. As well as being a professional Sinologist, she is also an accomplished guide for foreign tourists; both aspects feature in this guide, which provides the non-specialist reader with a good introduction to many aspects of China. There is a chapter on 'travel essentials', similar to those found in conventional guidebooks, followed by chapters on town and countryside, history, contemporary China, food, language, literature, religion, art and architecture, and science and inventions. There is also an historical chronology. Together, they add up to a painless way of beginning to understand China. Beijing – which she prefers to call Peking, reflecting a long, romantic attachment with the city – features in many of the sections, both as a tourist destination in its own right, and because of its importance in Chinese history. There are numerous black-and-white photographs, as well as several delightful line drawings culled from Chinese sources.

19 The encyclopaedia sinica.
Samuel Couling.   Shanghai: Kelly & Walsh, 1917. Reprinted, with an introduction by H. J. Lethbridge, Hong Kong; Oxford; New York; Melbourne: Oxford University Press, 1983. 633p. bibliog.

Couling was an English Baptist missionary who arrived in China in 1885, and remained there until his death in 1922. His *Encyclopaedia*, in dense double column pages, is packed with information on all aspects of China as seen by a sympathetic foreigner in the years after the fall of the Qing dynasty. Beijing features in many entries, and many references help to cast light on the city's importance both as the administrative centre of Imperial China and as a major cultural force in the country. There are entries about Chinese and foreigners connected with the city, from the emperors and court dignitaries, through to the missionaries and the diplomats. There are also frequent entries relating to particular parts of the city and associated areas such as the Great Wall and the Imperial Tombs. As well as the short bibliography attached to the introduction, many of the entries have their own bibliography of works available to Couling; some of these are quite comprehensive. Much new information has become available since Couling wrote his work, but there are few who would not benefit from looking at it. Lethbridge's introduction sets Couling and his book in context.

20 Encyclopedia of China today.
Frederic M. Kaplan, Julian M. Sobin, introduction by John S. Service.
London; Basingstoke, England: Macmillan Publishing Ltd, 1979; 3rd
ed., revised and expanded, 1982. 446p. maps. bibliog.
A useful basic reference work, as much guidebook as encyclopaedia, produced by two
non-academic China specialists. It covers all aspects of modern China, with a strong
emphasis on the period since 1949. There are essay-length sections on land and
population; government, law and politics; the economic system; doing business with the
People's Republic of China; the educational system; health and related matters; art and
culture; and travel and tourism. In addition, one chapter gives short biographies of leading
personalities in modern China, and another provides both an extensive bibliography and
a discussion about publishing in China. Numerous charts, tables and chronologies add to
its usefulness. Much of the information relates to Beijing, and while inevitably some of it
is out of date, this encyclopaedia is still worth consulting.

21 A glossary of reference on subjects connected with the Far East.
Herbert A. Giles.   Shanghai: Kelly & Walsh Ltd, 3rd ed. 1900. 328p.
Giles, who produced this useful compendium of information, served in the British
consular service in China and was later Professor of Chinese at the University of
Cambridge. He was also the co-deviser, with Sir Thomas Wade, of the Wade-Giles system
for transcribing Chinese that was the most widely used method until the 1970s, and which
can still be found in many academic publications today. The glossary covers much more
than just China, but it is a useful quick guide to most aspects of Chinese history and
culture. It supplements works such as that by Couling (see item no. 19), and contains
useful information about Beijing. Wherever appropriate, Giles gives the Chinese
characters for the term or concept discussed.

22 The great China earthquake.
Qian Gang, translated by Nichola Ellis, Cathy Silber.   Beijing:
Foreign Languages Press, 1989. 354p.
On 28 July 1976, a massive earthquake measuring some 7.8 on the Richter scale struck
the industrial city of Tangshan. The earthquake demolished 97 per cent of the city's
buildings and killed some 240,000. A much wider area was also affected, including both
Beijing and Tianjian. Although the damage was not nearly so great, as late as October-
November 1976, people were still living in makeshift dwellings on the streets of Beijing
rather than risk returning to their earthquake-damaged houses. In this book, translated
from a Chinese one of the same title published in 1986, Qian Gang tells the story of the
devastation and the clear-up afterwards. Inevitably, it is Tangshan that occupies centre
stage, but there are occasional insights into what happened elsewhere in both the Beijing
and the Tianjin municipal areas.

23 Home tuning.
Susan Pares. *Building Design* (London), no. 1063 (17 January
1992), p. 12-13.
An article on new housing estates and renovation projects in old neighbourhoods in
Beijing in the late 1980s. It discusses architecture and design as well as financing,
allocation and management of new and renovated properties.

24   Image of China: William Alexander.
Susan Legouix.   London: Jupiter Books Publishers, 1980. 96p.
bibliog.

The English artist William Alexander (1767-1816) accompanied Lord Macartney as 'draughtsman', or official artist, on his embassy to China in 1792-93. Western interest in Chinese style and design encouraged the inclusion of artists in Macartney's entourage and Alexander was able to take advantage of his trip to produce several collections of drawings and prints. Other artists, moreover, made use of his original studies (see item no. 13). In the event, Macartney did not take Alexander with him to his audience with the Qianlong emperor in Rehe (Jehol – now Chengde), and Alexander's record of the meeting is reconstructed on the basis of eye-witness accounts. Despite its title, this book covers more than Alexander's studies of Chinese subjects and those reproductions depicting scenes in Beijing and Tianjin have to be sought out. The bibliography and two appendices detailing written sources and the location of drawings and sketches by Alexander nonetheless make this a useful work of reference.

25   McDonald's in Beijing: the localization of Americana.
Ya Yunxiang.   In: *Golden arches east: McDonald's in East Asia.*
Edited by James L. Watson.   Stanford, California: Stanford
University Press, 1997, p. 39-76. bibliog.

The enormous popularity of the hamburger chain McDonald's in Beijing is here examined in minute detail by Professor Yan Yunxiang, an anthropologist from the University of California at Los Angeles. For the residents of Beijing who frequent the McDonald's restaurants in the capital, including the world's largest, Yan concludes that the restaurant is a symbol of affluence and modernization. He argues that while for children, perhaps, it is the food that counts, for older people, it is the ambience, the sense of being in an 'American' establishment. Yet he also argues that in subtle ways, McDonald's in Beijing has adapted to the local ambience. The restaurants, therefore, are no longer fast-food outlets, but places to absorb American culture. All in all, this is a fascinating study of how Beijing is changing under the influence of foreign companies and pressures.

26   Modern China: a chronology from 1842 to the present.
Colin Mackerras, with the assistance of Robert Chan.   London:
Thames & Hudson, 1982. 703p. maps.

This most useful aid will be of interest to all those concerned with China, whether specialists or generalists. For each year from the eve of the Treaty of Nanjing, which effectively opened China to foreigners, until 1980, when Deng Xiaoping's 1978 economic reforms began to make an impact, Mackerras provides a detailed list of developments in politics, economics, official appointments, cultural and social affairs, publications and of the major births and deaths of each year. While the main thrust of the work is obviously all-China matters, Beijing, and events and people associated with the capital, figure prominently throughout Mackerras's text.

27 **'Neue perspectiven' für die stadtplanung Beijings: übersetzung und kommentar.** ('New perspectives' for city planning in Beijing: translation and commentary.)
Ch. Peisert, Wu Liangyong. Berlin: Verlag Ute Schiller, 1985. 44p. maps. bibliog. (Culture and Development in Asia, Discussion Papers No. 6/7).

In May 1980, the Central Committee of the Chinese Communist Party issued a four-point proposal to guide the future development of Beijing which heralded a much wider view of the functions and role of the capital than had previously been tolerated. Wu Liangyong, dean of the faculty of architecture at Qinghua University, was one of those who had been contributing to the debate on new criteria for the capital. This discussion paper introduces some of his observations, traces the effects of earlier policies, details the problems facing Beijing and discusses new approaches. The text is in German throughout and the bibliography lists works in Chinese or German.

28 **No dogs and not many Chinese: treaty port life in China 1843-1943.**
Frances Wood. London: John Murray, 1998. 368p. map. bibliog.

Wood, head of the Chinese collection at the British Library, having demolished Marco Polo's claim to have visited China (see item no. 188), here turns to those who undoubtedly did visit, even if they kept China firmly at bay. The foreign residents of the treaty ports and cities that existed from the end of the First Opium War until the Second World War probably did not put up notices saying 'No dogs and no Chinese', though many Chinese believe that there was such as notice in Shanghai, but they did live their own lives, imitating life-styles in Paris or New York. Although Beijing, well inland and not on a major waterway, was not a 'treaty port' in strict terms, its social life was not unlike that of the ports proper, and it features frequently in this book, as does its neighbour Tianjin. Wood notes how most foreigners were captivated by Beijing, with its great walls and complex alleyways. There is a useful glossary of place-names, which are given in the 'Post Office' form, Wade-Giles and modern pinyin, and a chronology.

29 **Old Peking: city of the ruler of the world.**
Selected and edited by Chris Elder. Hong Kong; Oxford; London: Oxford University Press, 1997. 302p. map. bibliog.

This anthology, compiled by a New Zealand diplomat who was his country's ambassador to Beijing in 1993, draws on the observations of a wide range of writers, Arab, Persian, European and American, from Marco Polo to Arnold Toynbee. Some were travellers, others resided in the city as diplomatic or religious emissaries or for business. Their writings, for the most part personal and informal, reveal one or other of the two common responses to the city: enthusiasm or distaste. Elder has made a judicious and on the whole well-balanced choice from his sources to give the authentic flavour of foreigners' reactions to a city that many judged to be without comparison in its splendour, if not squalor. The anthology ends with the Japanese occupation of Beijing in 1937. The bibliography gives details of sources.

30 Peking.
David Bonavia, editors of Time-Life Books, photographs by Peter
John Griffiths. Amsterdam: Time-Life International (Nederland) B.
V., 1978. 200p. maps. bibliog. (The Great Cities).

This book, with text by David Bonavia, the respected Beijing correspondent of the
London *Times* from 1972 to 1976, and illustrated with photographs taken by fellow
journalist Peter Griffiths, can be enjoyed as a fine example of Bonavia's wit and writing,
but also as a now nostalgic reminder of how life was in the Chinese capital for both native
inhabitants and foreign residents in the last years of Mao's life. Despite the almost total
bar on contact between Chinese and foreigners, it was possible, as Bonavia shows, to
discover something of the daily life of the city. Griffiths' photographs show a population
of uniformly dressed inhabitants, near-empty streets and horse-pulled carts on main
thoroughfares – now barely imaginable. This is a book to enjoy for its 'period' flavour.

31 Peking.
Felix Greene, photographs by Felix Greene and Yu Ma. London:
Jonathan Cape, 1978. 162p. map.

The journalist and film-maker Felix Greene made several trips to China, reporting on the
Maoist revolution in films and books in positive terms. This book is no exception. It
records a visit that he and his wife made to Peking in the late 1970s, just before Deng
Xiaoping's reforms began to sweep away much of the Maoist legacy. The book is
handsomely produced and full of excellent photographs, but it recalls a world that was on
the brink of disappearing. This is particularly true of the section on 'rural Beijing', the
area made up of the communes that surrounded and supplied the city. Greene also
includes an account of a May Seventh Cadre School that appears to be identical to that
described by James C. F. Wang (see item no. 304). He concludes on an upbeat note,
claiming that China is approaching a classless society, and that the people of Beijing,
though poor, are more content than their richer counterparts elsewhere.

32 Peking.
Encyclopaedia Britannica. Chicago, Illinois: Encyclopaedia
Britannica Inc., 1997- . CD-ROM annually updated. maps. bibliog.

With the spread of electronic publishing, the Encyclopaedia Britannica CD-ROM or
Internet version are likely to be an increasingly used resource for those wishing to find
general information about Beijing. They will be well served by linked sections covering
subjects such as physical and human geography, landscape, climate, plant life, the people,
and industry and commerce. Each section is short and readable, and packed with
information. Surprisingly, the editors have chosen to use the Wade-Giles system of
transliteration, which is now likely to confuse readers who are more familiar with the
pinyin system. The bibliography is also thin, but this is a good introduction for the non-
specialist.

33 **Peking: a historical and intimate description of its chief places of interest.**
Juliet Bredon. Shanghai: Kelly & Walsh 1919, 3rd ed., revised and enlarged, 1931. Reprinted, with an introduction by H. J. Lethbridge, Hong Kong; Oxford; New York; Tokyo: Oxford University Press, 1982. 571p. maps. bibliog.

Juliet Bredon was the only daughter of Sir Robert Bredon, a member of the Chinese Imperial Maritime Customs, and brother-in-law of its late 19th-century head, Sir Robert Hart (see item no. 223). She spent most of her life in Beijing, for her husband was also an employee of the Chinese government, and this book is a tribute to her love affair with the city. In some ways it is a conventional guidebook, including information about areas such as the legation quarter and other foreign haunts. But it is much more than that, for it is full of unusual information of all aspects of Beijing and its history, from one who knew it intimately, and at street level. Lethbridge's short introduction fills in the background on Juliet and the world in which she lived, and there are many maps and plans, as well as some rather indistinct photographs.

34 **Portraits of ordinary Chinese.**
Edited by Liu Bingwen, Xiong Lei, with in-house editor Tong Xiuying. Beijing: Foreign Languages Press, 1990. 483p.

Some seventy individual Chinese feature in this book of reportage. Not all are from Beijing, but a sufficient number either live, study or work in the capital to make it an important guide to the lives of ordinary Beijing citizens. They include a former cadre (official), now retired from the Central Conservatory of Music, who tells of the difficulties facing the elderly; students both past and present; a prison warder; a housemaid; a pop star; and various others.

35 **Rehabilitating the old city of Beijing.**
Wu Liangyong, foreword by Peter G. Rowe, preface by Aprodicio A. Laquian. Vancouver, Canada: University of British Columbia Press, 1999. 246p. maps. bibliog.

One aspect of the economic reforms implemented in China since 1978 has been an overhaul of the housing sector. This has led to the demolition of much old stock and to new construction and new systems of financing, allocating and managing housing in place of the former state provision of accommodation through work units. In Beijing attempts have also been made since 1987 to renovate old *hutong* housing. Wu Liangyong's scheme at Ju'er Hutong in the northeastern sector of the old inner city is the subject of this book, which is illustrated with architectural drawings and photographs of the finished project. The book should appeal to those interested in urban history, planning, architecture and conservation.

36 Things Chinese; or, notes connected with China.
James Dyer Ball.   London: Sampson Low, 1892. 5th ed., revised by
E. Chalmers Werner, Shanghai: Kelly & Walsh, 1925. Reprinted, with
an introduction by H. J. Lethbridge, Hong Kong; Oxford; New York;
Toronto: Oxford University Press, 1982. 766p.

This vast compendium of information covers all aspects of Chinese life, customs and
history, though it was not the intention of the author to produce an encyclopaedia. Dyer
Ball was born in Guangzhou of missionary parents and spent most of his life in Hong
Kong. Much of the information he collected therefore relates to southern China, but he
was careful to cover the north as well, while Werner, who edited the 1925 edition, lived
in Beijing. There is information on subjects such as language and religion and other
matters that relate to the capital. It remains a valuable source of general background
reading.

37 Western images of China.
Colin Mackerras.   Hong Kong; Oxford; New York: Oxford
University Press, 1989. 337p. bibliog.

Colin Mackerras examines the way in which China has been portrayed in Western books,
newspapers and films. He notes how China has sometimes been seen sympathetically, and
sometimes with hostility, yet those doing so often draw on the same material. Thus
'unchanging China' is good for some, bad for others, yet 'changing China', especially
after 1949, is seen in exactly the same way. There is much about Beijing and events in the
capital, such as the Boxer uprising, since these have played an important part in creating
the images of China. Similar themes, again with much about the role of Beijing, are
examined in Raymond Dawson, *The Chinese chameleon: an analysis of European
conceptions of Chinese civilization* (London; New York; Toronto: Oxford University
Press, 1967. 235p. bibliog.).

Books of photographs

38 Beijing hutongs: 101 photos.
Xu Yong.   [s.l.]: Zhejiang Photograph Publishing House, 1990.
117p.

A selection of outstanding black-and-white photographic studies of *hutongs* or lanes in
the old parts of Beijing, taken between early summer 1989 and spring 1990. These are
primarily studies of *hutong* design, architecture and decoration. Although there is plenty
of evidence of human activity, only one plate shows a group of people. Perhaps because
of the absence of human beings on the lanes, a common enough phenomenon as one
passes through a *hutong* district, these photographs convey the sense of enclosure, privacy
and near mystery of the Beijing *hutongs*. Not all of the scenes are identified in the English
captions, and the poor standard of English in the preface and captions is the only jarring
note in this fine volume.

39 Beijing photos.
Bethsabée Süssmann, Roland Süssmann.   New York: Adama Books, 1987. 128p.

A photographic record, mostly in colour with some black-and-white plates, of the authors' visit to Beijing. Many of the groups of people shown have evidently posed for the photographers, and the effect is sometimes stilted.

40 Chasing rickshaws.
Text by Tony Wheeler, photographs by Richard l'Anson. Melbourne; Oakland, California; London, Paris: Lonely Planet Publications, 1998. 190p. map. bibliog.

The original rickshaws were developed in late 19th-century Japan by a Western missionary, and the name derives from the Japanese *jinrikisha*, or 'man-pulled cart'. Few rickshaws are pulled today though they are still propelled by human effort. In most of Asia, the bicycle or, more accurately, tricycle, has been adapted to provide a cheap and efficient means of transport. Beijing is no exception. Rickshaws first caught on in the 1920s and survived into the early years of the Communist government. They then vanished, as unacceptable evidence of man's exploitation of man, only to reappear in the wake of the 1978 economic reforms. During the tragic events of 4 June 1989, the rickshaws and their brave drivers played an heroic role in removing the dead and injured from the army's attack. Here the various styles of vehicle and their sturdy drivers are shown in a delightful collection of photographs, together with a drawing to show the construction. A short bibliographical note gives details of books and films that have featured rickshaws.

41 China.
Series editor Vitaly Naumkin, compiled by Andrei V. Subbotin, introduction by Calina V. Dluzhnevskaya, consultant editor Frances Wood.   Reading, England: Garnet Publishing Limited, 1993. 162p. maps. (Series Caught in Time: Great Photographic Archives).

This album, one in a series of selections of 19th-century and very early 20th-century photographs held in St Petersburg archives, presents the travels of 'The Russian Research and Trading Expedition' of 1874-75, which undertook the journey from St Petersburg across Russia and Mongolia to Beijing, Shanghai and Hangzhou, then back to Russia through northwest China, with the aim of investigating possible trade and access into China. A photographer, A. E. Boyarsky, accompanied the expedition, working with glass plates under considerable difficulties, and 160 of the 200 or so plates he took are reproduced here. Dr P. Y. Pyasetsky, responsible for the scientific side of the expedition, kept a diary, extracts from which form the basis of the notes to the photographs. Plates 6-33 are of Beijing, and plate 34 is of Tianjin. Between them they offer a glimpse of these two Chinese cities with their mix of ancient monuments and the buildings of the early foreign settlements.

42   China: land of mystery.
Photographs by Fritz Dressler, Kai Ulrich, text by Johnny Erling,
translated by Monica Bloxham.   London: Tauris Parke Books, 1997.
180p. maps.
This is essentially a picture book, originally published in German by C. J. Bucher Verlag
(Munich, Germany: 1995), with descriptive text, together with a few longer passages
describing particular aspects of China. These include vignettes on Beijing and on the
Forbidden City. The text is informative, and is well-translated, but what makes the book
stand out are the excellent photographs. Beijing and the area around it, including the
Great Wall and Chengde, take up about one third of the book. There are good maps and
diagrams.

43   The Chinese century: a photographic history.
Jonathan Spence; Chin Annping, photographic research by Jonathan
Spence, Chin Annping, Colin Jacobson, Annabel Merullo.   London:
HarperCollins Publishers, 1996. 264p. map.
The text of this handsomely produced volume provides a good history of China from the
1911 revolution to the 1990s, but what makes the book are the black-and-white
photographs, collected from a wide range of sources. They cover all aspects of 20th-
century China, from war, revolution and invasion, through social and economic
developments. Many of them are horrific; there are pictures of executions and the
consequences of war that require a strong stomach. Although the book deals with the
whole country, the central importance of Beijing to so many aspects of life and modern
Chinese history mean that the capital and its inhabitants feature in many of the pictures.
There are good shots of the city's walls, for example, and of the funeral of the Empress
Dowager Cixi in 1908.

**44   The face of China as seen by photographers & travelers 1860-
1912.**
L. Carrington Goodrich, Nigel Cameron.   New York: Aperture
Books; London: Gordon Fraser, 1978. 159p.
The London edition is a case-bound version of the catalogue for an exhibition held at
various places in the United States in 1978. It provides a good selection of the work of
Western photographers in China from the opening of Beijing to foreign residence in 1860-
61 to the end of the Manchu empire. While the photographs come from all over China, or
are of people, a large number were taken in and around the capital. They include pictures
of the Old Summer Palace soon after its sack by British and French forces in 1860, views
of the Great Wall, Tianjin, the capture of the nearby Dagu forts in 1860, Beijing at the
time of the Boxers in 1900, and various views of the walls and gates of the capital. There
are short essays on the historical background, on Westerners in China and on early
photographers. There is no bibliography as such, but there is a note on both the literary
and photographic sources.

14

45   A golden souvenir of Beijing.
Photographs by Magnus Bartlett, Anthony Cassidy, China Photo
Library, Pat Lam *et al.*, text by May Holdsworth.   Hong Kong: The
Guidebook Company Limited, 1988. 79p. map.

This selective but nonetheless attractive choice of photographs of the best-known
monuments in and around Beijing is preceded by a short discussion of the history and
development of the city up to the present time. Scenes of the streets, markets and people
of Beijing, studies of Peking opera artistes and shots of some of the actors who appeared
in Bernardo Bertolucci's *The Last Emperor* extend the range of the book.

46   Indien und China: meisterwerke der baukunst und plastik. (India
and China: masterpieces of architecture and sculpture.)
Ernst Alfred Nawrath.   Vienna: Anton Schroll & Co., 1938. 64p.
map.

Nawrath's chief interest in his travels to Asia (and perhaps his reason for going) was
clearly photography. He describes the difficulties of taking satisfactory photographs in
extremes of temperature and light and appends technical information on each of the 208
black-and-white plates reproduced. In China he appears to have visited only Beijing (or
Peiping, as it was known at the time of his stay, in the mid-1930s) and its immediate
surroundings. The rest of the book is given over to Burma, Sri Lanka (Ceylon) and India.
His introductory paragraphs on China and the notes on the sites he photographed in
Beijing are slight. His plates of the city (nos. 1-43), by contrast, are outstandingly good
as well as being of historical interest and constitute the true value of this book.

47   John Thomson: China and its people.
Foreword by Andrea Rose, introduction by William Schupbach.
London: The British Council, 1991. 68p. bibliog.

Prepared as a catalogue to accompany an exhibition of Thomson's photographs organized
by the British Council. Thomson (1837-1921) was a professional photographer who
travelled extensively to South and Southeast Asia and, from 1868-72, to Hong Kong and
China. A trip in 1871-72 took him to northern China, and the plates in section 4 of the
catalogue are devoted to Beijing and its environs. His photographs, taken with the wet
collodion process, are marvellously sharp. They depict a wide range of Chinese society
and occupations. Thomson took many negatives, of which only a selection is presented
here, drawn from the Thomson archive in the Wellcome Institute for the History of
Medicine in London. Other plates were reproduced by Thomson in his *Illustrations of
China and its peoples* (London: Sampson Low, Marston, Low & Searle, 1873-74. 4 vols.),
republished as *China: the land and its people* (Hong Kong: J. Warner Publications, 1979.
160p. bibliog.) and as *China and its people in early photographs: an unabridged reprint
of the classic 1873-74 work* (New York: Dover Publications, 1982. 272p.); and in
Through China with a camera (London: A. Constable & Co., 1898).

48   Life in hutongs: through intricate alleyways in Beijing.
Text by Shen Yantai, photographs by Shen Yantai, Wang Changping, translated by Huang Youyi, edited by Liao Pin, designed by Cai Rong.   Beijing: Foreign Languages Press, 1997. 190p.

Beijing's lanes, or *hutongs* – the word has passed into general usage among Beijing's Western community and is no longer regarded as a purely Chinese term – are what traditionally gave the city much of its charm. These narrow alleyways, with their high walls enclosing a variety of courtyard houses, often had exotic names, and always conveyed an air of mystery. Viewed from the city walls, they revealed much more of their life than they did from the street, which added to their charm. Unfortunately, many of the houses in the *hutongs*, which were built of brick, were badly damaged by the 1976 Tangshan earthquake, and had to be pulled down either then or later. Rapid modern development has led to the destruction of many others, and by the late 1990s, only a small number of *hutongs* and their unique houses remained in Beijing. This photographic essay by two Chinese photographers records both the beauty and the poverty of those that survive, and the varieties of social life which occurred in them, as well as the destruction underway as Beijing modernizes. There is a small amount of explanatory text in English and Chinese, but generally the photographs are allowed to speak for themselves.

49   Marc Riboud in China: forty years of photography.
Photographs by Marc Riboud, preface by Jean Daniel, translated by Aaron Asher.   London: Thames & Hudson, in association with Barbican Art Gallery, 1996. 175p.

This album of 134 black-and-white plates by the French photographer Marc Riboud was produced for the exhibition 'Marc Riboud in China', held at the Barbican Art Gallery, London, June-August 1997, and shown in Paris, May-August 1996, at the Centre National de la Photographie, with an accompanying book, *Quarante ans de photographie en Chine* (Forty years of photography in China) (Paris: Editions Nathan, 1996). The photographs, taken between 1957 and 1995, are roughly divided into: those depicting life in the first decade of Communist rule; those taken during the agitated years before and during the Cultural Revolution (1966-76); and those illustrating the economic and social changes of the 'new China' of the early 1990s. Some of the most memorable photographs are of Beijing, but the collection does not focus exclusively on the capital. Riboud has not set out to record social change, but through his perceptive and engaged studies over four decades of the Chinese scene, which has in itself changed, he is able to illuminate those shifts.

50   Old Beijing in panorama.
Fu Gongyue, Zhang Hongjie, Yuan Tiancai, English translation by Chen Dezhen, Fang Zhiyun, Feng Caoxiu.   Beijing: People's China Publishing Company, 1992. 315p. map.

This album, with text and captions in Chinese and English, presents over 600 black-and-white photographs of Beijing taken from the later period of the Qing to the Japanese occupation of 1937. The material is arranged in eleven sections covering: the construction and function of buildings; places of interest; popular trades and activities; the city's occupation by the Eight-Power Allied Forces in 1900; and portraits of prominent figures. The captions are generally precise, but the quantity of photographs and the poor quality of reproduction of some of them create a confusing impression. The book takes an uncompromising line over the events of 1900, recording the foreigners' revenge on the Boxers but omitting reference to the siege of the legations that precipitated it. This exposition of the Chinese view of events is valuable. The choice of 'prominent figures' is fairly wide and the captions are generally cautious. All in all this is a fascinating album, but it is less coherent than the earlier *Old photos of Beijing* (q.v.).

51   Old Peking: the city and its people.

Part 1 by Qi Fang, part 2 by Qi Jiren, translated by Hu Shi Ping. Hong Kong: Hai Feng Publishing Company, 1993. 146p. map.

An excellent collection, well-reproduced, of all aspects of life in the capital in the early 20th century, from the markets of the Chinese city, through the splendours of the grand buildings, to the Victorian suburbia of the legation quarter. Many of the photographs come from little-known sources, and have not been seen before.

52   Old photos of Beijing.

Fu Gongyue, English translation by Yu Meijiang, Japanese translation by Lu Lang, Gao Po, foreword by Zhu Jiajin.   Beijing: People's Fine Arts Publishing House, 1989. unnumbered.

This appears to be an earlier version of *Old Beijing in panorama* (q.v.), following a similar arrangement of themes and drawing on the same range of photographs but incorporating a smaller selection. Reproduction is better than in the 1992 volume, but the captions are less precise and the pages too crowded with pictures, captions and comment in three languages to make for easy viewing. This earlier version omits the two sections on the Eight-Power Allied Forces and on prominent figures. In his foreword, Zhu Jiajin writes lovingly about the Beijing he knew as a child in the early decades of the 20th century and again immediately after liberation from the Japanese in 1945. Although he does not spell it out, it is clear that he regrets, as other older Chinese do, the destruction of the city walls and of other ancient fabric. One can share Mr Zhu's regrets.

53   Peking.

Photographs and text by Hubert Eichheim.   Augsburg, Germany: Brigg Verlag, [n.d.]. unnumbered.

The photographs, in black-and-white, in this attractive album of Beijing were taken in the months of April to July 1977 and show the Chinese capital at a time before modernization was launched in 1978. As such the album has considerable value as a record of the still unchanged and humble life of the city. It is somewhat self-conscious in its search of the picturesque, but contains some beautiful studies of the natural scene.

54   Peking/Pékin.

Text by Zeng Nian, Charles Goddard, photographs by Zeng Nian, edited by Ian Lambot, foreword by Ian Lambot, translations (into Chinese and French) by Yuen Yin Ching, Marine Valette, Janice Wickeri, Catherine Capdeville, Marianne Cantacuzène.   Hong Kong: Studio Publications, 1990. 120p.

Zeng Nian took the black-and-white photographs in this album between 1987 and 1989. The final section consists of fifteen photographs of events in the capital between 19 April and 6 June 1989 and thus constitute one record of the Tiananmen demonstrations and their aftermath. Zeng left China in June 1989 after the suppression of the students' campaign to live in France with his French wife. His earlier studies are marvellously vivid and perceptive in the way they seize the essence of a scene, and give a penetrating and evocative view of Beijing life in the late 1980s. The text and captions are in Chinese, English and French.

55 A photographer in old Peking.
Text and photographs by Hedda Morrison, foreword by Wang Gungwu.   Oxford; Hong Kong; New York: Oxford University Press, 1985. 266p. maps. bibliog.

The photographer Hedda Morrison, who as Hedda Hammer arrived in Beijing in 1933 to manage Hartungs Photo Studios, has left an amazingly beautiful and varied corpus of work. She managed to remain in Beijing throughout the war years until she left in 1946 on her marriage to Alastair Morrison, son of the famous *Times* correspondent, G. E. Morrison (see item nos. 209 and 231). Most of her photographs (all black-and-white plates, largely taken with Rolleiflex cameras) were of scenes and people in and around Beijing in the last years of the old pre-Communist era. She clearly had a good rapport with those she photographed, and her plates are full of humour and sympathy. As valuable and interesting are her descriptions of places and activities, some of which have disappeared for good, and of life in Beijing where she got to know many of her fellow long-term foreign residents. A useful bibliographic note is attached. Her forays into the wider Beijing area and further afield are recorded in *Travels of a Photographer in China 1933-1946* (q.v.).

56 Tianqiao of old Beijing.
Editorial Committee of *Tianqiao of old Beijing*.   Beijing: Beijing Publishing House, 1990. 152p. maps.

Tianqiao (Bridge of Heaven) in Xuanwu district was, and to some extent still is, the popular entertainment area of Beijing. It is situated in the southern part of Beijing in what was known formerly as the Chinese City, where shops and theatres were tolerated by the Manchu Qing administration. The photographs assembled in this album show the amazing range of entertainers who made a living in Tianqiao and the variety of shops, but also the general poverty of the area and the seedier side of prostitution and opium-taking. The compilers see their task as a serious one of gathering and preserving material – photographs and interviews – on a place that fostered folk arts and skills. Modern painters and calligraphers have contributed to the volume. Publisher's notes, a postscript and section headings in English supply basic information, but the detailed notes on the illustrations are accessible only to readers of Chinese.

57 Travels of a photographer in China 1933-1946.
Hedda Morrison.   Oxford; Hong Kong; New York: Oxford University Press, 1987. 246p. maps. bibliog.

Hedda Morrison managed to escape from time to time from her long working week into the area surrounding Beijing and, on holidays, to go even further afield. This volume, a sequel to her *A photographer in Old Peking* (q.v.), reveals her talents as a photographer of the natural scene and of architectural detail as well as of people. Within the Beijing area she visited the former imperial mountain resort at Chengde (these plates include two of the explorer Sven Hedin, the author of an important book on Chengde, or Jehol, as it was known to Westerners). There are also views of Shanhaiguan and Beidaihe.

58 Vistas of China.
Chief editor Qian Hao, editors Zhang Yunlei, Zheng Guanghua, text by Zheng Guanghua, Qian Hao, translated by Jiang Weining, photographs by Ding Hong and 161 others.   Beijing: China Pictorial Publishing Company, 1987. 283p. map.

This large and sumptuously produced book covers the whole of China. Several sections carry views of Beijing: 'Imperial and private gardens and parks'; 'Imposing ancient architectural complexes'; and 'Notable architecture at historical sites', featuring palaces, temples and tombs in and near Beijing. The photographs are superb. Text and captions are in Chinese and English.

Geography

General

59 Beijing and Tianjin: towards a millennial megalopolis.
Edited by Brian Hook.   Hong Kong; Oxford; New York: Oxford
University Press, 1998. 179p. maps. (Regional Development in China
Series).

Based on the assumption that the Beijing-Tianjin region will steadily become a more
integrated whole as time passes, and assuming that to be the present course of Chinese
economic development, this book examines the likely outcome. The scene is set by an
introductory chapter by Colin Mackerras on the history and culture of what has long been
the capital of a unified China. Even when briefly dethroned from that position, Beijing
has continued to exercise a fascination for the rest of the country because of its past and
the grandeur of its buildings. Jane Duckett then shows how local leaders in these two
cities have tried to develop and expand their own political base, as a means of advancing
the special needs of the region against the overarching demands of the nation's capital.
The remaining essays tackle the theoretical main theme of the book, looking at the trends
in economic development in recent years, and trying to estimate how far they can be
expected to continue. There are clearly difficulties ahead for the area, as it faces both
competition from other economic centres such as Shanghai and Guangzhou, and
problems such as the general decline in water supplies in North China.

60 Beijing today.
Chinese editor: Rao Fengqi; English editors: Wang Xin, Wang
Rongfang, Ren Ying, Zhu Weie, Zhang Siying; photographic editor:
Tian Lihua; layout designer: Hen Fengze.   Beijing: New Star Press,
1990. 83p. maps. (What's New in China, no. 41).

Although apparently designed with visitors to the 1990 Asian Games in mind, and while
it does incorporate some guidebook features, this is more of a descriptive account of the
way Beijing has developed in recent years than a guidebook proper. There is therefore
much stress on the modern side of the city. Rather dull black-and-white photographs, and

somewhat indifferent English reduce its value to all but the most dedicated collector of such publications.

61 Geography.
China Handbook Editorial Committee, translated by Liang Liangxing. Beijing: Foreign Languages Press, 1983. 260p. maps. (China Handbook Series).

This book was designed as the first in a series of ten on aspects of modern China, the intention being to combine all ten sections into a single *China Handbook*. The statistics presented in *Geography* are valid for 1980. Chapter 5, on the provinces, municipalities and autonomous regions of China, discusses Beijing on p. 131-39, Tianjin on p. 139-42 and Hebei province, which surrounds both these municipalities, on p. 142-46. Topics dealt with include topography, climate, industry, agriculture, culture, communications and administrative divisions.

62 Native place, migration and the emergence of peasant enclaves in Beijing.
Laurence J. C. Ma, Biao Xiang. *China Quarterly*, no. 155 (September 1998), p. 546-81.

As the former tight controls on internal migration within China have been relaxed over the years since the reform process began in 1978, there has been a steady influx of people from the countryside to the cities. There was always some movement in the past, but not on the current scale, when more efficient farming methods are creating surplus farm labour, and when the cities seem to offer so much more, at least from a distance. In some cities, this 'floating population' can account for up to a quarter of the total population. The authors claim that in Beijing this movement has led to the development of separate enclaves, where the people from a particular province or ethnic group gather together. Thus there are areas where Uighurs from Xinjiang settle, and which have become known as 'Xinjiang villages'. Other groups also gather in similar communities, but they are not as well organized as the Uighurs. The emergence of these *laoxiang*, or native place 'villages', are matched by the emergence of speciality 'villages', where carpenters or other skilled craftsmen gather. This is a useful snapshot of what is clearly going to be an increasing feature of Chinese life.

Maps

63 Aerial image map of the Palace Museum.
Edited by Zhong Shi'an, Chen Ligen, photographs by Zong Tongchang. Beijing: China Map Publishing Co., 1987. Two-sided single sheet.

This carries on one side an aerial view of the Palace Museum, which is fascinating in the detail it shows, and on the other a text in Chinese and English giving a brief introduction together with a small map and photographs of details. The maps are intended for tourists, and are widely available in and around the area of the museum, but can also serve as souvenir posters.

64 Atlas of Beijing.
Supervising editors Huang Jicheng, Xuan Xiangliu, Cui Fengxia, chief editor Dong Yiguo, Chinese text compiled by Liu Fuchai, Yin Junke, edited by Zhang Dayou, Jin Guangqun, Zhang Jinggan, English translation by Mai Yangzeng, Chen Gengtao, Zhou Lifang, Chun Baohui, Wu Jigan, Liu Bingwen, Sun Lebing, Li Huaixian, English text edited by Wang Pinyu, foreword by Hou Renzhi. Beijing: Surveying and Mapping Publishing House, 1994. 273p. maps.
This comprehensive atlas of Beijing was compiled by the Beijing Surveying and Mapping Institute under an editorial committee established in September 1991 under the chairmanship of Chen Xitong, the then mayor of Beijing. Most of the statistical data selected were released in 1990, with some available for the end of 1992. The atlas incorporates over 200 maps, 100 charts and 400 remote-sensing images and colour photographs. The text is in English; maps are annotated in characters with some pinyin romanization. The material is divided into ten sections: an introduction on the 'capital of China'; administrative divisions; population and nationalities; construction; science, education, culture and public health; tourism; socioeconomics; natural resources; historical changes; and overall planning. The emphasis, in keeping with more recent views on the role of Beijing, is on its significance as the country's political, cultural and educational centre. Both layout and text are well presented, but the generally small type makes the information sometimes difficult to read.

65 Beijing street directory & map.
8 Dragons Publishing. Hong Kong: 8 Dragons Publishing & Cultural Services, 1990. 50p.
It is hard to convey the pleasure among foreigners and Chinese alike at the appearance of this little book in 1990. What is taken for granted in most of the world's major cities, namely a set of maps with a street directory, had long been missing in Beijing (and often still is for other major Chinese cities). This multicoloured and bilingual guide has proved a godsend to many a traveller in difficulties. For those who can read the very tiny print, it can also serve as a rudimentary guidebook, with sections on a few of Beijing's attractions. But its main value is to identify streets and to show them clearly on the maps. A detachable bus, trolleybus, and underground railway guide is equally useful for those who wish or have to use the city's public transport.

66 Beijing street guide.
United States Central Intelligence Agency. Washington, DC: Central Intelligence Agency, 1985. 241p. maps.
The name of the United States Central Intelligence Agency (CIA) does not appear on this compilation of maps of Beijing streets, nor did it appear on the earlier *Peking Street Guide* (Washington, DC: Central Intelligence Agency, 1978. 53p. maps), but both are widely believed to be CIA products, and are so listed in the Library of Congress catalogue. The layout of the sites shown suggests the maps originated in an aerial survey. The 'landmark'

principle operates in some of the identification: 'chimney', 'prison', 'industrial area', but monuments, institutions, government ministries, etc. are fully labelled. Naming is in a mixture of English and pinyin romanization. The atlases cover the whole of the inner urban area of Beijing and parts of the suburban districts immediately surrounding it. The 1985 atlas includes the airport and some tourist areas to the north. Now probably somewhat dated, especially in the peripheral sections, this is nonetheless an extremely detailed and helpful guide for foreign residents of Beijing.

67 Beijing tourist map.
Cartographic Publishing House. Beijing: Cartographic Publishing House, 1982, regularly reprinted. 2 sides.

The appearance of this excellent multi-coloured map of Beijing in the early 1980s did much to help foreign residents and tourists to explore the city. Its clear layout and semi-pictorial style was much more in keeping with tourist maps elsewhere than anything hitherto available in China. As well as the central city area, smaller maps show the Forbidden City, the Beihai Park, the Summer Palace, the Great Wall at Badaling, and the Temple of Heaven. The reverse gives detailed descriptions of the main tourist sites, and some guidance about hotels, restaurants, shopping and entertainment. The rapid pace of development in Beijing means that it is essential to find as up-to-date an edition as possible.

68 The contemporary atlas of China.
Editorial board Professor Nathan Sivin, Frances Wood, Penny Brooke, Colin Ronan, editor Jinny Johnson, art director John Bigg. London: Weidenfeld & Nicholson Ltd, 1988. 200p. maps.

The maps in this atlas, reproduced in sections according to cartographic conventions, were prepared by the Cartographic Publishing House, China, and their partners, Esselte Map Service AB, Sweden. Place-names are given in pinyin romanization and in Chinese transliteration of non-Chinese names. There is a detailed index to the maps. The maps are followed by short essays contributed by twenty-three specialists writing on the regions of China, its history, society and culture and on China today. Beijing has an entry to itself (p. 54-55), as does the Great Wall (p. 62-65). Although some of the sections are by now a little dated, many of the others offer useful information on many aspects of Chinese achievements and history. A great deal of information about Beijing and its surroundings can also be derived from Robert Benewick, Stephanie Donald, *The state of China atlas: a dramatic visual survey of the world's fastest growing economy* (London: Penguin Books Ltd, 1999. 128p. maps. bibliog.).

69 Tour map Beijing.
China Travel and Tourism Press. Beijing: China Travel and Tourism Press, 1988. 1p. 54 x 49 cm.

A single sheet, multi-coloured map, showing tourist sites, streets, parks, palaces, hotels, bus routes and other information useful for tourists. As is often the case with Chinese maps, no scale is shown, which can lead the unwary into thinking that distances are comparatively short!

70 Tourist atlas of Beijing.
Editor in chief, Qian Jinkai.   Beijing: Science Press, 1990. 88p.
maps.

Until China began to open up to the outside world in the late 1970s, it was often extremely difficult to find maps of the country or of individual cities. This was as true of the capital as it was of other cities, even though Beijing had always had a number of foreign visitors. Although the situation began to improve in the 1980s, the publication of this atlas still marked a major breakthrough. It not only provides good, clear maps of Beijing and the surrounding countryside, but it also includes detailed plans of some of the more prominent shopping and tourist areas of the city, as well as bird's-eye views of some of the monuments. Several pages provide descriptions of temples and other buildings. On top of all this, details are given of embassies, internal transport systems, train and air connections to the capital, and some brief notes about tourist sites elsewhere in China. The city's rapid expansion since its first publication has made some of the information dated, but nothing has been published which could replace it.

Guidebooks

71 Beijing.
William Lindesay, Wu Qi.   Hong Kong: The Guidebook Company
Ltd; Lincolnwood, Illinois: Passport Books, 1st ed. 1988, 5th ed.
1999. 203p. maps. bibliog.

This is a well-produced general guidebook, which many visitors are likely to come across
bound up in special hotel editions. It covers the city proper and the surrounding areas,
with accounts of the Great Wall and the Ming Tombs, together with suggested itineraries
for one to four-day visits. There is a guide to the pronunciation of Chinese names, a list
of useful addresses, including hotels, airlines, banks, embassies and other facilities, a
detailed fifteen-page section on restaurants, and a note on the growing club and general
night life scene. There are good photographs, including some historic ones, together with
extracts from novels and other books about the city.

72 Beijing.
Zhang Ming, Zhang Peigen, edited by Liang Hua, book design by
Zhu Penghe.   Beijing: New World Press, 1989. 120p. maps.
(Discover China's Cities).

Similar in size to a Michelin Green Guide, this useful guidebook covers all the usual
tourist requirements from details of hotels and restaurants to where to shop and what to
see, including museums and galleries. In addition, however, it also includes details of
somewhat more unusual tourist destinations, such as prominent educational institutes and
the various official religious bodies.

73 Beijing.
Produced by Manfred Morgenstern, Heinz Vestner, photography by
Bodo Bondzio, Manfred Morgenstern, Erhard Pansegrau, and others,
edited by Dieter Vogel, 3rd ed. created and directed by Hans Höfer,
update editor Ron Spurling, executive editor Scott Rutherford,
editorial director Brian Bell. Hong Kong: APA Publications, 1989.
3rd ed. 1997. 265p. maps. (Insight Cityguides).

This volume in the Insight series meets the very high standards set by the series in terms
of text and, particularly, illustrations. The formula is a well-tried one; a series of essays
on various aspects of the city is well illustrated with specially taken photographs, and
occasional other pictures. The essays are informative and draw on up-to-date academic
work for background as well as more obvious popular sources, making the book useful
for the scholarly reader as well as the traveller. It is perhaps likely to be especially useful
at the planning stage, and for following up after a visit, but, despite its size, it is also a
practical guide for day-to-day use. The essays cover all aspects of the city proper, and
there are short chapters on the Great Wall, the Ming Tombs and Chengde. There is also a
section, regularly updated, on practical matters such as hotels and restaurants. Beijing
also features, though clearly not in as much detail, in the same publishers' *Insight Guides:
China*, edited by Tim Larimer (Hong Kong: APA Publications, 3rd ed. 1997. 402p. maps).

74 Beijing.
Xu Mingqiang. Beijing: Foreign Languages Press, 1997. 291p.
maps. (China Travel Kit Series).

The editor of this high-quality guidebook has worked for many years with the Foreign
Languages Press, and his command of English is impressive. The book covers the city in
all its aspects, and also brings in the surrounding areas such as Chengde, the Great Wall
and so on, as well as the usual lists of hotels, embassies and useful telephone numbers.
The text is clear and straightforward, and it is modelled on Western guidebooks, though
perhaps more on the Insight Guides than on the Lonely Planet guides, with plentiful
illustrations reproduced on high-quality paper.

75 Beijing: bird's-eye views.
Editor-in-charge Zhang Zhaoji, text in Chinese and English, with a
foreword by Lou Cheng and 'Random Notes on Aerial Photographing
of Beijing' by Wang Lixing, English translation by Mai Yangzeng.
Beijing: Beijing Publishing House, 1990. 91p.

This album of aerial views of urban and rural sites in Beijing Municipality, taken by a
team of ten photographers, offers unusual and at times thrilling perspectives on the chief
monuments and scenic spots of the capital. It includes shots of some of the modern
buildings of Beijing, several of which hold their own with the more ancient ones, and
gives a flavour of the new development of the city.

76 Beijing official guide.
Edited by Beijing This Month. Beijing: Beijing This Month, 12th
ed., 1999. 136p. maps.

This small-format guidebook is issued under the auspices of the Information Office of the
Beijing Municipal Government, the Beijing Tourism Administration and the monthly

magazine *Beijing This Month*. It appears twice a year, but much of the information is constant, making it less a periodical publication and more of a standard guidebook. The frequent publication ensures that much of its information will be more up-to-date than that in more conventional guides, but its main entries are fairly short and the discerning tourist will wish to seek out something more detailed. As well as the monthly *Beijing This Month*, the same company also produces the bi-monthly *Business Beijing*.

77   Beijing old and new: a historical guide to places of interest, with descriptions of famous sights within one day's journey of Beijing.
Zhou Shachen.   Beijing: New World Press, 1984. 2nd printing, 1987. 404p. maps.

A much-thumbed personal copy certifies to the usefulness of this Chinese-produced guidebook, which is packed full of information about the capital and its surroundings. Some of the descriptions are a little barbed; that on the legation quarter, for example, ignores anything that happened before 1900, and assumes that the foreign troops just came along and took over an area to which they had taken a fancy. However, it does include many out-of-the-way places, such as temples in the hills and explains much that is often taken for granted in Chinese-produced guidebooks. Similar, but perhaps slightly more scholarly and with a good selection of illustrations, is Liu Junwen's *Beijing: China's ancient and modern capital* (Beijing: Foreign Languages Press, 1984; 2nd ed. 1991. 254p. maps).

78   Beijing-Tianjin.
Editor-in-charge and cover design, Zhang Zongyao.   Beijing: China Photographic Publishing House, Orient Publishing House, 1990. 98p. maps.

This pocket-size guidebook, packed with fifty-four maps and much information crammed into a rather small type-face, is good on both Beijing and Tianjin, and on the vast municipal areas attached to both cities. The desire to be as comprehensive as possible means that some of the entries are very short, almost note-like in their brevity, but the coverage is impressive. Beijing and the surrounding area accounts for three-quarters of the book, but the section devoted to Tianjin does reasonable justice to the city and its attractions. The original photographs were clearly very good, the reproductions less so. Nevertheless, this is still a useful addition to available guidebooks.

79   Beijing walks.
Don J. Cohn, Zhang Jingqing.   Hong Kong: Odyssey Publications, 1992, reprinted 1993. 270p. maps. bibliog. (The Henry Holt Walks Series).

Beijing is a city of broad avenues and considerable distances, which, together with growing traffic congestion and a high pollution level, make it at first sight an unattractive prospect for walkers. But there are areas which are made for the visitor on foot, and this book captures a number of them. As well as traditional tourist spots such as Tiananmen Square and the Forbidden City, it covers more interesting walking areas such as the old legation quarter and – a favourite with many foreigners for its feel of old Beijing – the Beihai park and the rear lakes areas. Each of the walks is described in some detail, with a good collection of interesting anecdotes, and is illustrated with maps and photographs.

In addition, there are all the usual guidebook features, including lists of hotels, restaurants and a series of useful telephone numbers.

80 Beijing wine and dine guidebook.
Executive editors, Jiang Cheng An, Du Juan.   Beijing: Morning Glory Publishers, 1997. 253p. maps.

This book is a further indication of how much Beijing has changed since the 1970s. It describes over 300 restaurants and 100 pubs, covering all styles of cooking and establishments both grand and modest. There are lists of addresses and speciality dishes, making it a welcome addition to specialist guidebooks for the city.

81 Biking Beijing.
Diana B. Kingsbury.   San Francisco: China Books & Periodicals Inc., 1994. 213p. maps.

Given that Beijing is renowned for its bicycles, and that most foreigners who stay in the city for any length of time tend to acquire a bicycle, it is surprising that this appears to be the first guidebook on how to see the city by bicycle. Much of the text is standard guidebook material, with details of places to stay and places to eat – the author has done her research and found many interesting places often little known to residents. There are also descriptive passages about cycling through the streets and the sort of incidents one is likely to encounter at such a level. In addition, there are plenty of clear sketch-maps, making this a useful guide for those on foot as well as those cycling.

82 China.
Pamela Youde.   London: B. T. Batsford Ltd, 1982. 176p. maps. bibliog.

This is a general guide to China, written by the wife of a former British ambassador to Beijing. Although the practical information has long since dated, the descriptive accounts are still worth reading. Beijing is included in a chapter on 'China's capitals', which also has a substantive section on the summer capital of Chengde. There are also shorter entries on the Great Wall and the Imperial Tombs, and a brief account of Tianjin, which confines itself to the city proper rather than the wider municipality. The book is well illustrated by colour and black-and-white photographs, many of them taken by the author. A similar work by another British diplomatic spouse is Evelyne Garside's *China companion: a guide to 100 cities, resorts and places of interest in the People's Republic* (New York: Farrar-Strauss-Giroux, first American edition, 1982. 276p. maps. bibliog.). Again, while some of the practical information is dated, the text in general is still useful. The section on Beijing and the surrounding areas, and the clear maps and diagrams which accompany it, are comprehensive.

83 China bound: a guide to academic life and work in the PRC: revised.
Anne F. Thurston, with Karen Turner-Gottschang, Linda A. Reed, for the Committee on Scholarly Communication with China.
Washington, DC: National Academic Press, 1981, 1st rev. ed. 1987, 2nd rev. ed. 1994. 252p. map. bibliog.

While this handbook deals with all of China, there is inevitably much information on Beijing, not only reflecting the capital's importance in educational and cultural terms, but also the fact that most long-term visitors to China, whether academics or not, arrive in the capital and will probably need to go there from time to time. Much of the information will be of interest to other longer-term residents in China, such as those engaged in business, while advice on shopping and behaviour may be of interest even to those on tourist visits. The bibliography, which appears somewhat oddly as Appendix M, lists several works of interest to those going to Beijing.

84 China: five famous cities: Beijing, Shanghai, Guangzhou, Guilin, Xi'an.
Edited by Lu Niangao, Li Teifei, art designer Ma Yulian. Beijing: China Tourism and Travel Press, 1986. 199p. maps.

Beijing occupies slightly over a quarter of this short guidebook, which is intended to meet the needs of the short-term traveller to China's most popular resorts. It is clearly written, with good coverage of the main tourist sites, hotels and restaurants, as well as notes on special local products.

85 China: a tourist guide.
Qi Xing. Beijing: Foreign Languages Press, 1989. 469p. maps.

A very detailed Chinese-produced guide, which covers all of China, including comprehensive sections on Beijing and Tianjian, as well as general tourist information. It includes lists of tourist offices, airlines and embassies, as well as much general information for the visitor. There are numerous rather poor black-and-white illustrations, and a somewhat better colour section, showing the main tourist attractions. A very similar publication, but with the possible advantage that it is bilingual, is Shen Caibin, editor-in-chief, *China tourist guide* (Beijing: China Social Sciences Publishing House, 1988. 419p. maps).

86 China's historical sites.
Zhao Hua Book and Picture House. Hong Kong: China Foreign Publishing Co. (HK) Ltd, 1987. 235p. maps.

This compact, narrow-format guide opens with sections on Beijing and Tianjin municipalities and Hebei province, which surrounds the first two. Descriptions are very brief, the maps show no lines of transport and no information is given on how to reach a particular site, though the location of each is stated fairly fully. Nonetheless, the selection of sites is surprisingly wide and in Beijing includes places not always mentioned in other guides, such as the caves at Fangshan containing engraved Buddhist scriptures, Miaoying temple, Zhihua monastery, Zhoukoudian (site of 'Peking Man'), the Huangshicheng Imperial Archives and Prince Gong's mansion and gardens. The guide would be helpful in planning visits.

Guidebooks

87 Exploring Beijing illustrated.
Editor in chief Shen Honglei.   Beijing: People's China Publishing
House, 1997. 104p. maps.

This well-produced book shows the tourist how to visit Beijing and the surrounding areas through a series of cartoon impressions. There are also a number of spectacular photographs, especially of the Great Wall. These features, and its handy pocket format, make it a very useful addition to the available guidebooks to Beijing. It covers many areas which, while familiar to foreign residents of the capital, are often missed by more transient visitors. There are also German and French editions.

88 Guide de Pékin.
Odile Cail.   Paris: Denoël, 1973. 266p. maps.

A clear and comprehensive guidebook to all aspects of Beijing, originally published in London 1971, with illustrations by Peter Thomson, but now very dated. It is well illustrated with colour plates and line drawings.

89 A guide to the former imperial palaces.
Edited by the Palace Museum.   Beijing: Palace Museum, [n.d.]
(c. 1975). 32p. map.

This little booklet is worth searching out, if only to see what guidebooks used to be like in the People's Republic of China before the 1978 reforms changed the face of publishing along with so much else. The style is heavily political, with links to the campaigns under way in China in the early 1970s, together with a somewhat heavy-handed Marxist explanation of how the Imperial Palace – despite the title, it is only concerned with the Forbidden City – was the product of the labouring masses. That said, the map, and the minimalist information provided about the main buildings, did allow the visitor to understand something of the grandeur of Beijing's most famous monument.

90 Guide-book to Beijing.
Compiled and designed by Qin Yin Pan.   Xian, China: Xi'an
Cartographic Publishing House, [n.d.] (c.1988). 68p. maps.

Until the 1980s, Chinese-produced guidebooks were generally hard to come by, and those that were available often consisted of pictures with somewhat uninformative captions. As China opened up to tourism, this began to change, and this little book was one of the better products to appear. Despite some spelling idiosyncrasies and occasional quaint language, it provides good, clear information about the major tourist attractions of Beijing and the surrounding region, together with maps and lists of hotels, restaurants, arts and crafts outlets, theatres, cinemas and museums. Its bilingual listings makes it useful for those who do not speak Chinese, and although the city has altered much since it first appeared, it is still a useful supplement to more recent guides. In similar format, the *Tourist atlas of China*, chief editor Zhao Xilin (Shanghai: Cartographic Publishing House, 1985. 99p. maps), also includes some twenty pages covering Beijing, Tianjin, the Great Wall, Chengde and Beidaihe.

91   Illustrated guide to Beijing.
Zhao Mingde, illustrated by Lin Hua.   Beijing: China Today Press,
1990. 231p. maps.

This is as much a language aid as it is a guidebook. While most of the major sights of the capital are listed, there is little in the way of information about them apart from their names. The main purpose of the book is to provide bilingual Chinese-English listings of places foreigners are likely to visit, with a breakdown, also bilingual, of what should be seen at each, and lists of things they are likely to need, from shampoo to film. The intention is a good one, but one needs to have good eyesight to be able to find what one requires among the very small print chosen for the text.

92   In search of old Peking.
L. C. Arlington, William Lewisohn.   Beiping [Beijing]: Henry
Vetch, 1935. Reprinted with an introduction by Geremie Barmé,
Hong Kong; Oxford; New York: Oxford University Press, 1987,
reissued 1991. 382p. maps.

This comprehensive guidebook, by two long-term residents of Beijing/Beiping, provides detailed accounts of the palaces and temples in and around Beijing as they were in the mid-1930s. They therefore record much that has long since disappeared, and yet there is also a fair amount still remaining, making this guide still usable after some sixty years. In any case, it is full of interesting and obscure anecdotes, bringing life to the dead bricks of the Imperial city. Baramé's introduction brings the story up to date, drawing attention to some of the more recent losses.

93   Peiping.
Edited by members of the American Red Cross, Beiping, with
contributions by Lt. V. R. Schuyler Cammann, USN, Madame Dan
Pao Tchao, Hedda Hammer, H. Y. Lowe, Stuart Mitchell, Dr E.
Margaret Phillips, photographs by Hedda Hammer.   Beiping
[Beijing]: No publisher given, 1946. 129p. maps. bibliog.

This guide was prepared in 1946 by the American Red Cross for the benefit of US troops stationed in what at that time was the former capital of China. Publication details are unclear, but the book refers to the 'cooperation of the Topographic Company of the Third Amphibious Corps' of the US armed forces, which made publication possible. It draws on the knowledge of Dan Pao Tchao, a former lady-in-waiting to the Dowager Empress Cixi, and of Westerners long resident in Beijing or expert in Chinese art. The result is a distillation of foreign or foreign-orientated writing on Beijing shortly before the installation of the Communist regime brought new perspectives. More than a simple guide to Beijing and its region, it offers essays on famous Chinese historical personalities, on Chinese religion, on symbols in Chinese art and architecture and on annual festivals and craft workers and guilds in the city, as well as one hundred popular proverbs and information on temple fairs and markets. Line drawings and the beautiful black-and-white photographs of the talented Hedda Morrison (Hammer) add to the attractions of this book.

94 Pékin. (Peking.)
Chantal Gressier.   Paris: Seuil, 1981. 125p. maps. bibliog.
(Collections Microcosme, Petite Planète/Villes, no. 107).

Serves both as a guide and an introduction to Beijing. The city's history is outlined and more recent developments are presented. Several itineraries are suggested. The author is anxious to give some of the flavour of life in the Chinese capital. The information and illustrations relate, however, to the Beijing that was emerging from the Maoist era, which had ended only in 1976, into the new order of the post-1978 economic reforms. The guide's main appeal thus resides in its portrayal of a rather tentative period in Beijing's recent history.

95 Pékin au centre de l'univers. (Peking at the centre of the universe.)
Ulysse, no. 47 (March-April 1996).

This issue of the travel journal *Ulysse*, edited by Philippe Boitel, is devoted to Beijing. Eleven articles discuss: the history of the city and of the imperial dynasties that occupied it; the spatial principles of its construction; the Great Wall; the Forbidden City; the Yonghegong or Lama temple; Fahai temple to the west of the capital; the Summer Palace; the imperial Ming Tombs; the modern economy of Beijing; pleasures of the table; and practical details of travel, accommodation and sightseeing. By its very nature outdated in some of its information, this issue of *Ulysse* is nonetheless worth seeking out, if only for its report on the little-visited Buddhist temple of Fahai with its fine wall-paintings.

96 Peking.
Ando Hikotaro.   London; Sydney: Ward Lock & Co., Ltd, 1968.
150p. maps. (This Beautiful World).

Between 1949 and 1979, there were relatively few guidebooks available for China or for Beijing in particular. China under Mao Zedong was not a conventional tourist destination, and few except those on official visits, or as students, managed to reach it. When this book appeared, therefore, it was something of a breakthrough. Based on his experience of living in Beijing from 1964 to 1966, the author, a Japanese professor from Waseda University, described the city as it was on the eve of the Cultural Revolution. The historical and political context is given in an essay that originally appeared in the Japanese-language edition of the book, published by Kodansha, and was reprinted in an article in the *Japan Quarterly*. The rest of the book is devoted to describing the city, and it is fully illustrated. Many of the pictures now have an historical interest, so great are the changes in Beijing since the late 1970s.

97 Shopping in China: arts, crafts & the unusual.
Roberta Helmer Stalberg.   San Francisco, California: China Books
& Periodicals, 1986. 230p. maps.

By 1986, China seemed well embarked on the capitalist road, with many elements of the free market emerging in the main cities. For foreigners, shopping then became more difficult, since the choice was no longer confined to the local friendship store. Now, foreigners could go to Chinese shops and markets, haggle and discuss, and, perhaps, find a bargain. Even if that was not possible, there was still a lot of fun to be had poking around in the many markets that spring up in Beijing and other major Chinese cities. Stalberg is not concerned with much beyond the advantages that superior purchasing power gives foreigners, and some of her information is inevitably dated. But she provides what is still a valid guide to what to look for in China, and where it might be found. Some fifty pages are devoted to Beijing, and there is a useful chapter on craft terms and techniques.

98 The Summer Palace.
Geng Liutong, edited by Huang Zhuan, layout by Huang Zhongjun, Ma Jiangyan, translated by Deng Xin, photographs by Ru Shichu and twenty-five others.   Beijing: China Pictorial Publishing Co., 1987. 2nd ed. 1989. 127p. map. (Beijing Scenes Series).

The Summer Palace in Beijing is one of the showpieces of late Qing architecture and is today a favourite spot for Chinese and foreigners in both summer and winter. Once the complex was much larger, but foreign sackings in 1860 and 1900 destroyed much. In addition, Chinese farmers ploughed up the land, destroying archaeological evidence, and took stones for building, damaging what remained of the palace. An extensive area still survives, however, and this guidebook gives a brief history, explaining in particular the affection of the Empress Dowager, Cixi, for the Palace, which she did much to restore, and drawing attention to the major features of the complex. The book is illustrated with numerous colour photographs.

99 The Summer Palace long corridor pictures – a collection of stories portrayed by them.
Xin Wensheng, translated by Li Nianpei, finalized by Qiu Ke'an. Beijing: China Travel & Tourism Press, 1985. 509p.

One of the features of the Summer Palace on the outskirts of Beijing is a magnificent long open-air corridor, designed to link the many complexes of buildings on the site, to provide views over the Kunming lake, and to offer an area to walk in during bad weather. Originally constructed in 1750, it was destroyed by British and French forces in 1860, and restored in the 1880s. As well as enjoying spectacular views over the lake, the 728-metre corridor has a series of pictures painted at regular intervals on the ceilings and on the crossbeams and side pillars that divide the corridor into 273 separate sections. In all there are 14,000 paintings. Some feature landscapes, but the majority deal with scenes from Chinese history and mythology. This book explains the stories behind 187 of the pictures, some of which are reproduced in rather faint black-and-white reproductions. The stories covered are divided roughly between the two categories, and the book thus provides a guide to much traditional Chinese story-telling, as well as helping to explain an interesting facet of the Summer Palace.

100 Through the moon gate: a guide to China's historic monuments.
Chief compilers Luo Zhewen, Shen Peng, translated by Wang Mingjie, Carole Murray, Li Chunjia, edited by the China People's Publishing House of Fine Arts.   Hong Kong; Oxford; New York: Oxford University Press, 1986. 313p. maps.

This fine volume, edited by the China People's Publishing House of Fine Arts, covers the whole of China and includes Taiwan. It lists one hundred sites of historical interest, providing historical and descriptive notes, sketch maps where helpful, and detailing locations. Black-and-white photographs and colour plates complement the text. The first three sections deal with Beijing and Tianjin municipalities (pages 1-36) and Hebei province (pages 37-56). In and around Beijing, the following are described: Zhoukoudian

('Peking Man'), the Lugou (or 'Marco Polo') bridge, Beihai and the Round City, the White Dagoba and Miaoying temple, the Palace Museum, the Ming mausolea or tombs, the Altar of Heaven, the ancient observatory, the Great Wall at Badaling, and the Summer Palace. Also described are Dule temple in Jixian in Tianjin municipality, and in Hebei, the Eastern Qing mausolea or tombs to the east of Beijing, as well as Chengde and two of its temples.

101   Top 10 guide to Beijing: the top 10 things to do, see, enjoy & experience, for the on the go traveller.
Li Sun, Yi Yang, Serena Hao Pao.   Boston, Massachusetts: New Internationalist, 1999. 200p. maps. (Top Ten Travel Guides).
The authors are three women from Beijing, all experienced as business executives or guides. They provide information, in a somewhat relentless style, on what to do, where to eat and where to be seen in contemporary Beijing, usually in the form of lists of the 'ten best night-spots, ten best restaurants, or ten best things to do with kids'. As well as being sold through conventional outlets as a paperback, it can also be downloaded from the Internet in PDF format.

102   Touring in Beijing.
Editors in chief: Li Shentao, Guo Changjian, Zhang Ming; executive editor: Zhang Dan; articles: Zhang Ming, Zhang Peigen; designer: Chan Chor Keung.   Hong Kong: Hong Kong Man Hai Language Publication, 1988. 189p. maps.
This is a fairly run-of-the-mill guidebook, produced in Hong Kong, and therefore likely to be picked up at the airport or in one of the bookshops by those on the way to China. Its maps are clear with good instructions on how to reach tourists spots, hotels and restaurants by public transport, and there are useful lists of addresses and telephone numbers for embassies, shops and restaurants. Since many of these change rather rapidly as new commercial centres open in Beijing, it is important to seek out the most recent edition.

103   Tourist guide to China.
Edited by China International Travel Service, Foreign Languages Press.   Beijing: Foreign Languages Press, 1974. 194p. map.
This guide, with a large number of photographs, is now chiefly of historical interest as an example of the pre-1978, Maoist approach to visiting China and of the different order of priorities that prevailed in China at the time. The emphasis is on the 'creative ability' of the working people, on the achievements of the Cultural Revolution and on the benefits of Mao's leadership. Beijing is praised for its revolutionary traditions, Tianjin for its contribution to the economy.

Encyclopedia of China today.
See item no. 20.

Pékin: ses palais, ses temples, & ses environs: guide touristique illustré.
See item no. 267.

Memoirs and Travellers' Accounts

Pre-Qing (pre-1644)

104   Cathay and the way thither: being a collection of medieval notices of China.
Translated and edited by Henry Y. Yule.   London: Hakluyt Society, 1866; new edition, revised throughout in the light of recent discoveries, by Henri Cordier, London: Hakluyt Society, 1914-15. Reprinted, Taipei: Ch'eng wen, 1972; New Delhi, Munshiram Manoharlal Publishers Pvt. Ltd, 1998. 4 vols. maps. bibliog.

A magnificent collection of early material on China, derived from Arab and Western accounts, and copiously annotated. Here will be found the earliest accounts of Beijing, or rather of its Mongol predecessor, Dadu or Cambalac. Some are surprisingly detailed, with descriptions of wall-building, street layouts and other aspects of the city that are instantly recognizable; others are disappointing in their brevity. But the collection as a whole is fascinating. The bibliographies are still of use in identifying rare sources for the history of Beijing.

105   The travels of Marco Polo the Venetian.
Edited with an introduction by John Masefield.   London; Toronto: J. M. Dent & Sons; New York: E. P. Dutton & Co., 1908, reprinted 1918. 461p. (Everyman's Library no. 306).

Whether or not Marco Polo ever did go to China, there can be no doubt that his description of the capital of the Great Khan, Cambalac (Khanbalik), and the new capital of Dadu (modern Beijing) built nearby, has since the first appearance of the book describing his travels featured in all accounts of China. The great palaces, the courtyard houses and the many lanes all feature in the Polo account, as does the life of the court and of the city. This is not a particularly good edition, although its notes are comprehensive and draw attention to the various texts available, but it is likely to be widely found. Other editions include: *Marco Polo: the description of the world*, edited and translated by A. C. Moule, Paul Pelliot (London: Routledge, 1938. Reprinted, New York: AMS Press, 1976.

2 vols. maps. bibliog.); *The book of Ser Marco Polo, the Venetian, concerning the kingdoms and marvels of the East, translated and edited by Henry Yule* (London: John Murray, 3rd ed., revised by Henri Cordier, 1903. Reprinted, under the title *The travels of Marco Polo: the complete Yule-Cordier edition; including the unabridged third edition of Henry Yule's annotated translations, as revised by Henri Cordier, together with Cordier's later volume of notes and addenda (1920)*, New York: Dover Books, 1993; and under the original title, New Delhi: Munshiram Manoharlal Publishers Pvt. Ltd, 1998. 2 vols.), probably the most scholarly; and Ronald Latham, *Travels of Marco Polo* (Harmondsworth, England: Penguin Books, 167. 380p.).

Qing (1644-1911)

106 The attaché at Peking.
Algernon Bertram Freeman-Mitford.   London; New York: Macmillan, 1900. 386p.

Algernon Freeman-Mitford, later Lord Redesdale, joined the British Foreign Office in 1858, and spent time as an attaché in Beijing (1865-66) and Tokyo (1866-70). This book, based on letters home, gives an interesting and informative account both of the work of a diplomat in Beijing soon after the capital was first opened to diplomats in 1861, and of the city and its surroundings. Unlike some of his colleagues, Mitford was not wholly enchanted by Beijing or the British legation, but he seems to have enjoyed the Chinese countryside. There are good descriptions of the major buildings of the city, and of the temples that foreigners used in the hills. Mitford returned to his time in Beijing, and added to his earlier account, in his autobiography: Lord Redesdale, *Memories* (London: Hutchinson & Co., 1915), chapter XV.

107 The diaries and letters of Sir Ernest Mason Satow (1843-1929): a scholar-diplomat in East Asia.
Selected, edited and annotated by Ian C. Ruxton.   Lewiston, New York; Queenston, Canada; Lampeter, Wales: The Edwin Mellen Press, 1998. 511p. bibliog.

Sir Ernest Satow is perhaps best known for his time as a British official in Japan between 1861 to 1900, but he also had connections with Beijing. He spent some time there in 1861 on his way to Japan, and from 1900 to 1905 he was British Minister in Beijing. Short sections of this volume therefore cover his time in China. Most of the later material is concerned with diplomatic negotiations immediately after the Boxer affair, but there are also occasional insights into diplomatic life in Beijing, while the copious notes provide details about people Satow met or those with whom he corresponded.

UL: RE. 9.30 // N Fr. Fl.4

108   A diary of the siege of the legations in Peking, during the summer of 1900.

Nigel Oliphant.   London; New York: Longmans, Green & Co., 1901. 227p. maps.

Among the monuments now preserved in the grounds of the British ambassador's residence in Beijing is one for those killed in the Boxer incident of 1900. The names include that of David Oliphant, of the British consular service, whose brother Nigel wrote this account of the siege. It is a fresh and lively account of the events of the summer of 1900 in Beijing seen through the eyes of a young and rather idealistic young man, saddened by the awful events through which he lived.

109   A diplomatist's wife in many lands.

Mrs Hugh Fraser.   London: Hutchinson & Co., 1911. 2 vols.

Mrs Fraser was the wife of a British diplomat, Hugh Fraser, who served in both China and Japan, and who died as British minister to Tokyo in 1895. She wrote an entertaining account of their life in Tokyo, and followed it up with recollections of their earlier diplomatic life together, including, in the second volume, just under one hundred pages on life in the legation quarter in Beijing in the 1870s. She describes that peculiar enclave, very much in but not of the city, in which she was quite happy to spend long periods, rarely venturing beyond it at first. There are accounts of summer in the Western Hills, of visits to the sights of Beijing, and of the day-to-day preoccupations of foreigners. While the world of the legations has long since gone, Mrs Fraser can still, after all these years, bring it alive.

110   Emperor of China: self-portrait of K'ang-hsi.

Jonathan D. Spence.   London: Jonathan Cape; New York: Alfred A. Knopf, 1974. Reprinted, New York: Vintage Books, 1988. 218p. map.

In this unusual book, Spence draws on the public and private letters of the Kangxi Emperor (reigned 1661-1722), to provide an account of life at court in Beijing as the Manchu conquerors were gradually transformed into Chinese emperors. Thanks to Spence, we have a unique insight into life at the top in Beijing when the Manchu empire was at its height. Here we can read what the emperor thought about a wide range of subjects, from hunting, to suitable medicines for old people with dysentery, and the problems of selecting an heir. There is an extensive bibliography as well as notes, and some delightful illustrations. There are no other comparable imperial memoirs, but there is an interesting examination of how the Qianlong emperor (reigned 1736-96) viewed his role, which also casts much light on the imperial way of life in Beijing, in Harold L. Kahn, *Monarchy in the emperor's eyes: image and reality in the Ch'ien-lung reign* (Cambridge, Massachusetts: Harvard University Press, 1971. 314p. bibliog. [Harvard East Asian Series, no. 59]).

111 From Belfast to Peking 1866-69: a young Irishman in China.
Francis Knowles Porter, edited with an introduction, by J. L. McCraken.   Dublin: Irish Academic Press, 1996. 160p. map. bibliog.

Frank Porter, a member of the British consular service in China, was twenty-three-and-a-half when he drowned at the treaty port of Ningpo in May 1869. He had been at Ningpo only since the end of 1868. Before that he had spent two years as a student interpreter in the British legation in Beijing, studying Chinese under Thomas Wade. After his death, his father transcribed his letters, written mostly to his mother, as a memorial to his sons, and these letters are reproduced here. Many of them are preoccupied with family affairs, but others give a fresh and interesting account of life in the British legation some five years after its establishment, and of Beijing just as it was becoming known again to foreigners after many years of seclusion. There are several illustrations showing the city, mostly taken from the *Illustrated London News*.

112 My Chinese notebook.   UL: NA.6.73 (Rarebook)
Lady Susan Townley.   London: Metheun & Co., 1904. 338p.

Susan Townley was the wife of the secretary of legation (number two officer after the minister) in the British legation in Beijing just after the Boxer rebellion. Despite its title, much of the book is given up to a potted history of China, together with an account of the then recent siege. However, there are also some chapters describing the city and its monuments as they were around 1902, and some describing travel outside Beijing. Of most interest, however, is the section dealing with the visit to the Forbidden City by a number of foreign ladies to meet the Empress Dowager, Cixi, soon after her return from exile in Manchuria. Both parties were clearly fascinated by each other, and, to Susan Townley's evident surprise, found a lot in common.   W. Fun nds.

113 With the empress dowager of China. UL: 1989.9.883
Katherine Augusta Carl.   New York: Century Co., 1905. Reprinted, with an introduction by Kaori O'Connor, London; New York: KPI Ltd, 1986. 306p. (Pacific Basin Books).

The Empress Dowager Cixi (T'zu-hsi in the Wade-Giles transliteration) exercised a great fascination on foreigners in late 19th-century China, a fascination that greatly increased as a result of her alleged role in the Boxer incident and the siege of the legations in 1900. Cixi became better known after 1900, in that she received foreigners in the Forbidden City, but she still seemed aloof and distant to most foreigners. Katherine Carl was different, for at the instigation of the American minister's wife, Sarah Conger, she was employed in 1903 to paint the empress's portrait. As a result, she spent some nine months in the Forbidden City, the only Westerner to do so until Reginald Johnston became tutor to the last emperor (see item no. 121). She thus gives a unique insight into court life in Beijing on the eve of its disappearance. The book is full of detail about the palaces of Beijing and their myriad inhabitants, illustrated with contemporary photographs and sketches by the author.

Republic of China (1912-49)

114 American diplomat in China.
Paul Samuel Reinsch.   Gardon City, New York; Toronto:
Doubleday, Page & Co., 1922. 396p.

A fairly standard diplomatic memoir by the United States minister in China at the time of the First World War, who played an important role in encouraging the Chinese to adopt their own policies, rather than follow those of the West. Reinsch is generally credited with encouraging the Chinese government to stand up to Japan, even though his proposals were not necessarily in line with those of Washington. In addition to diplomatic manoeuvrings, his memoirs contain pen pictures of some of his diplomatic colleagues in the Beijing of 1914 and give an account of life in the legation quarter at that time.

115 China bound: a fifty-year memoir.
John King Fairbank.   New York; Cambridge, Massachusetts;
Philadelphia; San Francisco; London; Mexico City; Sao Paulo,
Brazil; Sydney: Harper Colophon Books, 1983. 480p. maps.

John Fairbank, the doyen of American scholars of China, recorded in this delightful memoir how he first became involved with things Chinese at the University of Oxford from the late 1920s, through his time as a student in Beijing in the 1930s, to wartime service and his long years as a Harvard professor. For those interested in Beijing, it is the account of his life there in the years before the Sino-Japanese War that will be of most interest. Like many others, Fairbank fell in love with the city, and at the same time met foreigners such as Agnes Smedley and Harold Isaacs who opened his eyes to a very different China from the privileged enclaves of the foreign communities. The book is full of amusing stories and profound insights, and it would be hard not to enjoy it.

**116 It's been a marvellous party! The personal and diplomatic
reminiscences of Berkeley Gage.**
Berkeley Everard Foley Gage.   London: Printed for the author,
1994. 256p.

Sir Berkeley Gage ended his career as British ambassador to Thailand (1954-57) and Peru (1958-63), but began it in Beijing in the 1930s. These memoirs, privately printed but available in major British libraries, very much reflect the title; there is more on drinking and picnics than there is on diplomacy, especially in the China section. Nevertheless, they provide an amusing account of one aspect of expatriate life in Beijing in the 1930s. Another account from the same period, which also deals with the arrival of the Chinese Red Army in Beijing in 1948-49, can be found in the text of a lecture given to the China Society in London: *China through one pair of eyes: reminiscences of a consular officer 1929-50* by Walter Gerald Cloete Graham (London: The China Society, 1984. 13p.).

117 Laughing diplomat.
Daniele Varè.   London: John Murray; New York: Doubleday, Doran
& Co. Inc., 1938. 455p.

Varè was an Italian diplomat who served twice in China, between 1912 and 1920, and from 1927 to 1931. During the latter period he was to become Italian minister to Chiang

Kai-shek's government. He clearly enjoyed the years he spent in China, and these light-hearted reminiscences contain many interesting vignettes about his life as a member of the diplomatic corps, together with sketches of his colleagues. They include a famous account of the British minister, Sir John Jordan, found dining alone in the Western Hills by Varè one summer's night; despite the heat, and the absence of an audience, Sir John was impeccably dressed in full evening wear. There have been German (1938), Italian (1942) and Dutch (1944) editions of the book. Varè also wrote a series of amusing stories of Beijing life, and a biography of the last empress, which are still of interest (see item nos. 215 and 366).

118 Life in China: from the letters of Dr Nancy Bywaters.
Compiled and edited by Grace E. Woods.   Braunton, England: Merlin Books Ltd, 1992. 243p. map.

Nancy Bywaters, a British doctor, worked in China from the end of 1946 to mid-1951 for the Baptist Missionary Society. She was eventually encouraged to write up her frequent letters home into a longer account. The task, unfinished at her death, was completed by Dr Grace Woods. Dr Bywaters was in China during and after the period of civil war that culminated in Communist victory in 1949, and she relates the increasing difficulties of working as a foreign medical missionary. She spent most of 1948 in 'Peiping' (Beijing) in language training. The chief interest of the letters she wrote then lies in the atmosphere of uncertainty and confusion they convey. In 1977 Dr Bywaters and Dr Woods returned to China with a delegation and visited Beijing as part of their tour, related in Part 2. Four of her pencil sketches of the Chinese countryside decorate the book.

119 Old madam Yin: a memoir of Peking life.
Ida Pruitt.   Stanford, California: Stanford University Press, 1980. 129p.

Ida Pruitt, born 1888, was the daughter of American missionaries. From 1918 to 1938, she was head of the social services department at the Peking Union Medical College. This work, written long after the period in which she lived in China, is an artless but interesting account of a world that has vanished. While one may discount the total recall of conversations from sixty years ago, there is plenty here on foreigners' lives in Beijing, on the attractions of the city to those who lived there, and on the Chinese she met and clearly loved, to make this still an important book.

120 Peking diary: 1948-1949, a year of revolution.
Derk Bodde.   New York: Henry Schuman Inc., 1950. Reprinted, New York: Fawcett World Library, 1967; Octagon Books, 1976. 292p.

Bodde, a renowned American scholar of Chinese philosophy, spent a year in Beijing from August 1948 to August 1949 as the first beneficiary under the Fulbright scheme, which was established in 1947 to send students and researchers to China. He, his wife, and young son thus witnesssed the final year of Nationalist rule in the capital as the Communists closed in on the city, subjecting it to siege and gradually installing their new regime. His diary, translated also into German by Max Muller as *Peking tagebuch: ein jahr revolution in China* (Wiesbaden, Germany: Eberhard Brockhaus, 1952. 334p.), describes vividly the effects of war, inflation and shortages and the uncertain atmosphere in the capital as it awaited a new order. Bodde writes objectively and with sympathy about the enormous changes taking place and leaves a valuable account of an important period.

121 Twilight in the Forbidden City.
Reginald F. Johnston, foreword by the Emperor Pu Yi. London: Victor Gollanz Ltd, 1934. Reprinted, with an introduction by Pamela Atwell, Hong Kong; Oxford; New York: Oxford University Press, 1987. 486p. maps.

Reginald Johnston, a British colonial administrator, was from 1919 to 1924 the tutor to the boy emperor, Aisin-Gioro Pu Yi, in Beijing's Forbidden City. Although the imperial monarchy had been overthrown in 1910-11, the emperor's writ still ran within the confines of the Forbidden City and much continued as it had during the last years of the Qing dynasty. Johnston describes the life of the young man who has become known as the 'last emperor' and the small world in which he lived. There are good descriptions of the Forbidden City, including accounts of sections that have long since disappeared, and of the Summer Palace, as well as much information about personalities and politics in Republican China. Johnston ends his account with Pu Yi's transformation into the Emperor of the Japanese puppet state of 'Manzhouguo' in 1932. Johnston's subsequent career, as administrator of the leased territory of Weihaiwei, can be traced in Pamela Atwell, foreword by N. J. Miners, *British mandarins and Chinese reformers: the British administration of Weihaiwei (1898-1930) and the territory's return to Chinese rule* (Hong Kong; Oxford; New York: Oxford University Press, 1985. 302p. maps. bibliog.).

122 Vanished China: Far Eastern banking memoirs.
W. H. Evans Thomas. London: Thorsons Publishers, [1952]. 350p.

A set of reminiscences about life in Beijing and Tianjian from the author's arrival in Tianjin in January 1911 until his final departure at the end of 1946. While he describes some of the political developments of those years, much of the book is taken up with the activities of the foreign community. Here indeed, is the raw material from which Ann Bridge drew the characters and events described in *Peking picnic* and *The ginger griffin* (qq.v.), though perhaps told in somewhat less lively prose. Nevertheless, Thomas provides much useful information on the communities within which he lived, and ably describes their cares and concerns.

123 The years that were fat: Peking 1933-40.
George N. Kates. New York: Harper Brothers, 1952. Reprinted, with an introduction by Pamela Atwell, Hong Kong; Oxford; New York: Oxford University Press, 1988. 268p. maps.

An affectionate account by a sympathetic American, of life in Beijing during the city's twilight years, which goes a long way to explain the attraction that Beijing had for many Westerners. From 1927, Beijing had ceased to be the capital, and as the 1930s progressed, it became increasingly affected by the conflict with Japan. Kates' concerns were less with these major developments, however, but more with the way life continued for many as it had always done. He seeks to explain Chinese motivation, delighting in the quirks and idiosyncrasies of the scholar and the coolie alike. He also provides much information about the palaces, temples and other grand edifices of the city. There are some good photographs, which have unfortunately not been well reproduced.

Hermit of Peking: the hidden life of Sir Edmund Backhouse.
See item no. 261.

People's Republic of China (1949-)

124 All the emperor's horses.
David Kidd. London: John Murray, 1961. 190p.

At the time of the Communist take-over of Beijing in 1949, the American David Kidd was teaching at Qinghua University. All but one of these stories, part fact, part fiction, originally appeared in the *New Yorker*, and the style reflects that magazine. In light-hearted fashion, they tell of his life with his Chinese wife, Aimee, and her extended family, in one of the grand old mansions of the city, in the early months of the Communist occupation, before the formal establishment of the People's Republic. There is no particular depth, or great political insight in them; rather, Kidd aims to tell a good story about a way of life that has now long since vanished.

125 An American in China: thirty years in the People's Republic.
Sidney Shapiro. Beijing: New World Press, 1979. 281p.

Sidney Shapiro learnt some Chinese in the Second World War, and in 1947 found himself in Shanghai. He was to remain in China without a break until 1971, working for the Foreign Languages Press and becoming a fervent supporter of the Maoist regime. This autobiography offers a fascinating, if uncritical, view of life in Beijing for a foreigner working for the Chinese government and party from 1949 to the end of the Cultural Revolution. Shapiro appears to have swayed with every wind and supported every campaign, always convinced that Chairman Mao was in the right.

126 At 90: memoirs of my China years: an autobiography of Rewi Alley.
Rewi Alley. Beijing: New World Press, 1986. 365p.

Rewi Alley, a New Zealander by birth, lived in China from 1927. He worked first of all in Shanghai and later ran agricultural co-operatives in the Chinese countryside, which brought him into contact with the Chinese Communists. In 1953 he moved to Beijing from the provinces, and became an avid supporter of the new China, writing many books and articles praising developments under the People's Republic. About a third of this book describes his life after 1949, and there are accounts of other foreign supporters of the Communist regime. However, he is careful to stick to the orthodox view of politics. Other books by Alley, all of which display the same characteristics, and all of which contain some information about life and work in Beijing, include: *Yo banfa!* (We *have* a way!), edited by Shirley Barton, foreword by Joseph Needham (Shanghai: China Monthly Review, 1952. 193p.); *Human China: a diary with poems* (Christchurch, New Zealand: New Zealand Peace Council, 1957. 147p.); and *Travels in China 1966-71* (Beijing: New World Press, 1973. 588p. map).

127 Behind the forbidden door: China inside out.
Tiziano Terzani, originally published as *The forbidden door*. Hong Kong: Asia 2000, 1985; republished London: Allen & Unwin, 1986; republished London: Counterpoint (Unwin Paperbacks), 1987. 270p. map.

Terzani was Beijing correspondent for the German news magazine *Der Spiegel* from 1980 until 1984. In 1984, he was arrested by the Beijing Public Security Bureau (the police), held for a month, and eventually expelled from China for a variety of 'crimes', including stealing cultural relics. His real crime, however, was probably his unsympathetic reporting of China in the early 1980s, some of which is repeated in this book. There is much incidental information about life for a foreigner in Beijing, albeit one who tried as far as possible to live as a Chinese, including sending his children to Chinese schools. In addition, he provides a detailed chapter in which he attacks the destruction of old Beijing by the Communist regime, as well as drawing attention to the way in which officials of the new regime imitate those of imperial days; according to Terzani's wife, Angela, who has also written an account of her experiences in China, this may have been one of the reasons for his arrest (see item no. 131).

128 Behind the wall.
Colin Thubron. London: William Heinemann, 1987. Republished, London; New York; Ringwood, Australia; Markham, Canada; Auckland: Penguin Books, 1988. 307p. map.

Based on two journeys to China, though there is no separation of the material, this account by a well-known writer has been highly praised for the picture it gives of life in China. Two chapters deal with Beijing, and are remarkable for the detailed conversations that the author, with relatively little Chinese, managed to have with a wide range of people. Similar conversations can be found, though there is less on Beijing, in another highly-praised book by another well-known travel writer, Paul Theroux, in *Riding the iron rooster: by train through China* (London: Hamish Hamilton, 1988. 494p. map).

129 Beijing diary: an east-west love story.
Bess Spero Li. Chicago, Illinois: Bonus Books, 1989. 197p.

Bess Spero was a student at the Beijing Shifan (Normal, i.e. teacher training) University from September 1982 to May 1983, and again from August 1983 to March 1984. Her diary tells, in somewhat repetitive style and much slang, of her life, loves and studies during that period, ending with her marriage to Li Ruoxin in 1985, and their eventual decision to settle in the United States.

130 China diary.
Stephen Spender, David Hockney. London: Thames & Hudson, 1982. 250p. map.

A record of a visit to China in May-June 1981 by two British artists of international repute. The text is by Spender, the poet, and the illustrations, a mixture of drawings, paintings and photographs, by Hockney, the painter. About one third of the book is concerned with their time in and around Beijing. The result is a pretty standard tourist account, which adds little to others of the genre, although some of the illustrations are interesting as examples of what catches an artist's eye.

131 Chinese days.
Angela Terzani, translated from the Italian by Kirsten Marnane
Romano. Hong Kong: Odyssey Productions Ltd, 1988. 338p.
maps.

Angela Terzani is the wife of the Italian journalist Tiziano Terzani (see item no. 127).
While in China from 1980 to 1983, she kept a diary, parts of which are reproduced here.
She describes Beijing as it was during the early 1980s and many of its foreign and
Chinese inhabitants and their respective lives with a clear and perceptive eye, and there
are excellent photographs taken by her husband. The book was originally published in
Germany (Hamburg: Hoffmann und Campe, 1986).

**132 The empty throne: the quest for an imperial heir in the People's
Republic of China.**
Tony Scotland. London: Viking, 1993. 186p. map. bibliog.

Tony Scotland, a former BBC reporter, and now a freelance writer, first visited China in
1981, just as Deng Xiaoping's economic reforms were beginning to make an impact. In
1991, he returned with a quest in mind. Since, he claims, somewhat inaccurately, the
profound political changes in Eastern Europe had led some to believe that the old
monarchies might be restored, why not see if the same was possible in China after June
1989? The result is a somewhat jokey travelogue, as he pursues the family of the last
emperor around Beijing and other parts of China. He adds much incidental information
about the imperial court and its capital, but most readers will be left unsatisfied. His habit
of translating Chinese names into 'amusing' English ones, and the odd romanization, are
likely to jar with some readers. The illustrations are fascinating, but there is no index.

133 En Chine avec Lady Hopson. (In China with Lady Hopson.)
Denise Hardy. Paris: André Bonne, 1969. 235p.

An account, by the French wife of the British chargé d'affaires, of the events leading up
to the sack of the British mission in Beijing during the height of the Cultural Revolution
in 1967. At the time of its publication, this book gave the most comprehensive and
detailed account of the sack of the mission, but it has long been superseded by others such
as that by Sir Percy Cradock (see item no. 135). Nevertheless, it is still worth reading for
the insights it gives into the Cultural Revolution as seen by foreigners.

134 Eyewitness in China.
Hugh Portisch, translated by Michael Glenny. London; Sydney;
Toronto: The Bodley Head, 1966. 323p. maps. (Background Books).

Portisch, editor-in-chief of *Kurier*, at the time Austria's largest circulation daily
newspaper, visited China in 1964, on the eve of the Cultural Revolution. The result is a
well-written but not very profound travelogue, which records the usual visits to
communes, factories and other places shown regularly to the pre-1978 visitor. There are
good descriptions of Beijing and its peoples, the latter going about their business and
praising the revolution, with little indication of the catastrophe that was about to hit them.

135 Experiences of China.
Percy Cradock.   London: John Murray, 1994; new and enlarged ed., 1999. 319p.

When this book by the former foreign policy adviser to the British Prime Minister Margaret Thatcher first appeared in 1994, most reviews focused on the author's views on Hong Kong, and in particular the policies of the last British governor of Hong Kong, Chris Patten. Cradock, however, had also served two spells in Britain's Beijing embassy, the first as head of chancery (head of the political section and embassy number two) during the Cultural Revolution, the second as ambassador from 1978 to 1982. During the first period, the British mission (not then an embassy) was burnt down in August 1967 by red guards. Cradock's description of these events, and his later experience of a calmer Beijing as the Deng reforms began, are written in elegant and smooth prose that is a delight to read.

136 From emperor to citizen: the autobiography of Aisin-Gioro Pu Yi.
Aisin-Gioro Pu Yi, translated by William J. F. Jenner.   Beijing: Foreign Languages Press, 1964, second printing 1983. 2 vols.

This is the 'last emperor's' own account of his life and times, from his birth in Beijing in 1906 to the days immediately following his release from prison as a war criminal in 1959. Written at the behest of the Chinese Communist Party, it tells of his life in Beijing's Forbidden City both before the 1911 revolution and afterwards until he and his remaining family members were expelled in November 1924. Thereafter, the focus shifts from Beijing, as the former emperor fled first to the Japanese legation, then to the Japanese concession in Tianjin, eventually ending up as the Japanese puppet emperor of Manzhouguo. Only at the end of the second volume, after his release from prison in 1959, does he return to Beijing. The last chapter of the second volume describes his feelings at exploring the new Beijing created after 1949. The same story is told, with additional material, by the journalist Edward Behr, in *The last emperor* (Toronto; New York: Bantam Books; London; Sydney: MacDonald & Co., 1987. 335p. map. bibliog.), illustrated with a mixture of original photographs and stills from the film of the same name, which also appeared in 1987.

137 Hostage in Peking.
Anthony Grey.   London: Michael Joseph, 1970. Reprinted, London: Weidenfeld & Nicholson, 1988. 343p.

It was Anthony Grey's misfortune to arrive in Beijing in March 1967, to be the sixth person to head the Reuters News Agency Bureau in that city since it opened in 1956. The Cultural Revolution was by then well under way, and soon after Grey arrived, events in Hong Kong involving pro-Chinese journalists turned the fury of the red guards against the British. By late summer 1967, the British mission in Beijing was a smoking ruin and Grey was subjected to a particularly unpleasant form of house arrest. Confined to a small space in his own apartment, abused by red guards who at one point hanged his pet cat, and denied visitors for several months, Grey kept sane by yoga and by writing a concealed diary. When he was eventually allowed to see two visitors from the British mission after 249 days, he could scarcely contain his anger. Finally, in October 1969, Grey was released after 806 days. This is a powerful book, engagingly written. Later Grey incorporated some of his experiences into a long novel about China since the establishment of the

Communist Party: *Peking: a novel of China's revolution 1921-1978* (London: Weidenfeld & Nicholson, 1988. 645p.).

138   In two Chinas.
Kavalam Madhava Panikkar.   London: Allen & Unwin, 1955. 183p.

A memoir of life in Beijing by the Indian ambassador to the People's Republic of China at the time of the outbreak of the Korean War in 1950. Panikkar was used by the Chinese Prime Minister, Zhou Enlai, to pass messages to the United States indicating that China would intervene in Korea if United Nations' forces crossed the 38th parallel. His warnings were ignored. Like other such books, Panikkar's gives an indication of what a strange life most foreigners, including diplomats, led in post-1949 Beijing.

139   Legacies: a Chinese mosaic.
Bette Bao Lord.   New York: Alfred A. Knopf, 1990. 245p.

A rather slight set of reminiscences/reflections, many concerning Beijing, by a Chinese-born novelist, who is also the wife of Winston Lord, the United States ambassador in China in the early stages of the movement that developed into the student demonstrations of May-June 1989. Ms Lord also includes an account of her return to Beijing as an interpreter for the CBS network in the early phases of the student demonstrations.

140   Life in Shanghai and Beijing: a memoir of a Chinese writer.
Liang Xiaosheng, translated by Li-ching C. Mair, Ruth-Ann Rogaski.   Beijing: Foreign Languages Press, 1990. 256p. (Phoenix Books).

Liang Xiaosheng was born in Harbin in Heilongjiang province in 1949. After the beginning of the Cultural Revolution, he was sent to the countryside to work on an army farm. Later he went to Shanghai's Fudan University to study Chinese, and from 1977 he was assigned to work in the Beijing Movie Studio as an editor. In this book, he gives short accounts of his early life, of his experiences as a red guard and as a university student, and then devotes over a third of the text to his time in Beijing. There are some interesting asides on working in a major Chinese institution and on attitudes towards officials and foreigners, but on the whole, the tone is flat and the pace slow, and the capital is merely a backdrop to an ordinary life.

141   Mandarin red: a journey behind the 'bamboo curtain'.
James Cameron.   London: Michael Joseph Ltd, 1955. 287p.

The British journalist James Cameron visited China in the winter of 1954. Cameron travelled on an ordinary visa and made no secret of the fact that he was a journalist. About half the book is devoted to his time in Beijing, with reflections on the diplomats and the small foreign community remaining after 1949, together with accounts of visits to factories, schools, one of Beijing's prisons, and more standard tourist fare such as the Great Wall and several temples. Cameron's prose and his sharp eye for detail make this a book still worth reading.

142   A million truths: a decade in China.
Linda Jakobson.   New York: M. Evans & Co., 1998. 224p.

Jakobson spent ten years in China, first as a teacher, and then as a correspondent for the Finnish news magazine *Suomen Kuvalehti*. She travelled all over the country, looking at various aspects of its development in the past decade; education, which she finds severely wanting, is a particular interest, but she is eclectic in her tastes. Much of the book, inevitably, is concerned with the lives of people she met in Beijing. These include ordinary people with harrowing tales of the Cultural Revolution, and others who suffered in the suppression of the Beijing demonstrations of 1989.

143   Peking 1950-53.
Peter Lum.   London: Robert Hale Ltd, 1958. 190p.

Lum was the daughter of the American print maker, Bertha Lum (see item no. 381), and first visited Beijing as a child in 1922, accompanying her mother. She remained in China until 1940, marrying the British diplomat Colin (later Sir Colin) Crowe in 1938. Meanwhile her sister, who married an Italian, continued to live in Beijing, while her mother returned there in the late 1940s. In 1950, after the establishment of the People's Republic, Peter and Colin Crowe also returned to Beijing, where the latter was now a member of the British diplomatic mission. It was a much changed city, but this straightforward account, written soon after she and her husband left Beijing, brings to life the complex life of the small foreign community that existed in China after 1949. For her family it was a period of tragedy, for her sister's husband, Antonio Riva, was arrested and executed by the Communists as a spy. Much later, she recorded more about Beijing in the 1920s and 1930s, describing with affection many facets of the city, from the courtyard houses to the temples in the hills, as well as her experiences in the United States and Japan, in Peter Lum, *My own pair of wings* (San Francisco: China Materials Centre, 1981. 222p. maps).

144   A Peking diary.
Lois Fisher.   New York: St Martin's Press; also published as *Go gently through Peking: a westerner's life in China*, London: Souvenir Press, 1979. 256p.

This is an account of life in Beijing from 1973 to 1976, by an American married to a journalist. Fisher decided to avoid the usual haunts of foreigners, and to concentrate on making contact with ordinary Chinese in shops, restaurants and public places. China and Beijing has changed so much since the early 1970s that this work has now only an historical interest. Other books of the same type, which similarly reflect a largely bygone age, include Colin McCullogh, *Stranger in China* (New York: Morrow, 1973. 292p.), by a Canadian journalist resident from 1968 to 1970, and *Flowers on an iron tree: five cities of China* (London: Heinemann, 1976. 423p.), by the Australian academic, Ross Terrill, which has one chapter on Beijing. The latter largely reflects his experiences in 1971, but there are echoes of an earlier visit in 1964.

145   Prisoner of Mao.

Bao, Ruo-wang (Jean Pasqualini), Rudolph Chelminski.   New York: Coward, McCann & Geohegan, 1973; London: Andre Deutsch, 1975. 318p. Reprinted, Harmondsworth, England; New York: Penguin Books, 1976. 325p.

The author, half French and half Chinese, describes life in Beijing in the early 1950s, when he worked on the edges of diplomatic life – he hints at various roles for unnamed embassies, but he certainly had some contact with the British mission in Beijing at the time. These foreign connections brought him trouble during the political campaigns of that period, and he was eventually arrested and imprisoned. He was released in 1964 as a gesture to mark the establishment of Sino-French diplomatic relations, and allowed to leave China. His memoirs now have a certain period interest.

146   Prisoners of liberation.

Alleyn Rickett, Adele Rickett.   New York: Cameron Associates, 1957. 288p; new ed. San Francisco: China Books, 1981. 343p.

This is an unusual account, by two American teachers, of life in Beijing on the eve of the Communist take-over, and their subsequent experiences in Chinese prisons. The Ricketts went to Beijing in 1948 to study Chinese at Qinghua University, and unlike most of their compatriots, stayed on after the establishment of the People's Republic on October 1949. At first they had few difficulties, but after China intervened in the Korean War in October 1950, anti-American feeling grew strong, and they were arrested as spies. Although this was perhaps not technically correct, the Chinese had some grounds for their suspicions since Alleyn Rickett had by his own admission reported to the US embassy's military attaché on the fighting around Qinghua in 1948-49. Following the departure of the embassy staff in 1950, he had agreed to watch developments with a view to further reporting. The Ricketts were released in 1955.

147   The private life of Chairman Mao: the inside story of the man who made modern China.

Li Zhisui, translated by Tai Hung-chao, with the editorial assistance of Anna F. Thurston, foreword by Andrew J. Nathan.   London: Chatto & Windus, 1994. 682p.

The title page of this book carries the subtitle 'the memoirs of Mao's personal physician'. Dr Li became one of Mao's medical team in 1955, and subsequently his chief physician. His last act for the Chairman was to embalm his body in 1976. This gossipy and scurrilous account of the Great Leader has enjoyed some popularity, and contains much information about people and places in the People's Republic of China. But Dr Li, at least after Mao's death, sees everything in black – Mao and his immediate associates – and rather murky shades of white – everybody else. For those interested in Beijing, and especially those parts of the city reserved for the Communist Party leadership and thus off limits for ordinary Chinese and foreign visitors alike, there is a wealth of fascinating detail, which is probably more reliable than the personal gossip. More reliable on Mao as a person and a leader is Philip Short, *Mao: a life* (London: Hodder & Stoughton, 1999. 782p. map), which inevitably includes much about Beijing.

148   Red China blues; my long march from Mao to now.
Jan Wong.   Toronto; New York; London; Sydney; Auckland, New
Zealand: Bantam Books, 1997. 405p.

Jan Wong is a Canadian citizen of Chinese origin. She grew up in Montreal, where her
father owned a series of restaurants. In the early 1970s, in the last phase of the Cultural
Revolution, she went to China to study. It was perhaps not the unqualified success that
she expected, and she found herself frequently in trouble with the authorities at Beijing
University. Despite difficulties, she kept returning, and married the only American
Vietnam war draft dodger to settle in China, who worked for the glossy magazine *China
Reconstructs*. Later, she returned to China as a newspaper correspondent for the Toronto
Globe and Mail, and was there during the 1989 Tiananmen incident. She writes with
verve, and provides interesting accounts of major events in Beijing since the early 1970s.
However, the slightly jokey tone of some of the earlier writing, the apparent ability to
recall twenty-year old conversations, and her insistence on translating Chinese names, all
become a bit wearisome.

149   Re-encounters in China: notes of a journey in a time capsule.
Harold R. Isaacs.   Hong Kong: Joint Publishing Co., 1985. 192p.

As a journalist in China in the 1920s-30s, Harold Isaacs produced one major work on the
abortive revolution of the 1920s, and later, a study of the impression made by China and
India on the United States, both of which are still of interest today. In 1980, he and his
wife went back to China, and this short book records their experiences. They met many
old friends and were able to renew contacts from the Beijing of the 1930s. But they also
became aware of the difficulties these former friends faced, and the strains under which
intellectuals lived in post-1949 China. As well as renewing contacts, the Isaacs did many
of the ordinary tourist things in Beijing, including visiting Mao's mausoleum. The result
is an interesting, if at times, sobering, account of China in the early 1980s.

150   Return to China.
James Bertram.   London; Melbourne; Toronto; Cape Town; The
Hague: Heinemann, 1957. 251p.

Before the Second World War, James Bertram, a New Zealander, had been a journalist in
China. During the war, he was briefly the acting press attaché at the British embassy in
China's wartime capital, Chongqing, and then a prisoner of the Japanese for four years.
During his pre-war days, he had spent much time in Beiping, as the former capital had
then become, and provides here interesting descriptions of places and people; he shared a
room, for example, with a Chinese student who later, having changed his name to Huang
Hua, was to become foreign minister of the People's Republic of China, and he knew left-
wing writers such as Agnes Smedley and Edgar Snow. In 1956, he revisited China with a
group of New Zealanders, and wrote this rather starry-eyed account of the people he met,
including fellow New Zealander Rewi Alley (see item no. 126), and the places he visited.
The comparisons of the new developments in the capital with pre-Communist Beijing,
however, are worth reading.

151 Spider eaters: a memoir.

Rae Yang. Berkeley, California; Los Angeles; London: University of California Press, 1997. 285p.

This powerfully written memoir by a Chinese woman relates one person's experiences of growing up in the 'new China'. Although much of her life was spent away from her native Beijing, where she was born in 1950, the city always remained as the focus of her thoughts and family affections. After early years in Switzerland, where her parents worked in the Chinese consulate in Berne, she returned to Beijing for her education, participated in the red guard movement, then in 1968 moved to a state farm in Heilongjiang to receive 're-education' from the peasants. Disillusioned with what she saw as the Communist Party's exploitative position in Chinese society, and scared of remaining stuck indefinitely in the 'Great Northern Wilderness', she manoeuvred her way back to Beijing, but in 1981 left for the United States. Her account reveals the problems of residence and the need for good connections, and the devastating impact of the Cultural Revolution on her own personality and on her own and others' family life.

152 Sweet and sour: one woman's Chinese adventure, one man's Chinese torture.

Brooks Robards, Jim Kaplan, foreword by Andrew J. Nathan. Northampton, Massachusetts: Summerset Press, 1995. 234p.

The authors, a married couple, both journalists, spent five months in Beijing from 1993 to 1994. Robards, on an academic exchange scheme, taught journalism. Kaplan accompanied her as a 'dependent spouse', but got work polishing broadcast news scripts and newspaper copy. Their account is written chapter by chapter by each of them in turn. As the title indicates, Robards enjoyed the experience, whereas Kaplan did not. As many a wife who has accompanied her husband on a foreign posting might testify, his frustration may have been caused by his dependent status. The breezy, informal style deliberately adopted by the two authors keeps their story from sinking into a whine. Their account has interesting insights into such areas of Chinese life as teaching methods, the film industry, feminism, bridge-playing (Kaplan was a bridge-player) and hospital out-patient care, as well as into work in the Chinese foreign-language press.

153 Traveller without a map.

Hsiao Ch'ien. London; Sydney; Auckland, New Zealand; Johannesburg: Hutchinson, 1990. 276p.

Hsiao is a well-known writer and translator, who spent some time in England before the Second World War, and who still retains much affection for the country. He was born in Beijing's slums, and provides a graphic account of growing up there during the warlord period. Later, after the Communist victory, he returned to Beijing, and describes living there under the very changed circumstances of the 1950s. Condemned as a 'rightist' in the 'Hundred Flowers' campaign in 1957, he worked on a farm then and during the Cultural Revolution. Eventually, however, he was allowed back to Beijing, and recommenced his literary work. The book was completed in 1989, when for a time he felt that China might revert to the ways of the 1950s and 1960s. Yet the story is an affecting one, told without histrionics, and the translation reads well.

154 Worlds apart: China 1953-55; Soviet Union 1962-65.
Humphrey Trevelyan. London; Basingstoke, England: Macmillan London Ltd, 1971. 320p. maps.

Humphrey Trevelyan, later Lord Trevelyan, was a distinguished British diplomat, who acquired a reputation for being able to cope with difficult situations, a reputation which began with his time as British chargé d'affaires in China from 1953 to 1955. The Chinese government had refused to accept British diplomatic recognition in 1950, and the British embassy in Beijing occupied a curious half-world. Trevelyan describes the restricted life which he and his colleagues were forced to lead, living in the palatial, if faded, splendour of the British embassy compound, but with only limited contact with their official hosts or with the people of the city. Nevertheless, something of the old city still lingered on into these early days of Communist rule, and Trevelyan conveys a pleasing picture of many aspects of Beijing life before the building campaign of the late 1950s began to destroy it, while also giving an account of the political, economic and social problems faced by the government of the PRC.

155 Visa for Peking.
A. de Segonzac, translation with the co-operation of Marion Barwick. London: William Heinemann Ltd, 1956. 205p.

This account of a two-month visit to China in the autumn of 1954 by a reporter for the French newspaper *France-Soir* follows fairly standard lines. The second part is devoted to Beijing. He describes a city which had generally become off-limits to outsiders, giving accounts of social and economic changes following the establishment of the People's Republic. Of more interest, perhaps, are the asides on some of the lesser known groups in the small foreign community, such as the French Roman Catholic nuns, the Russians and the small band of US and British prisoners-of-war from Korea who had decided not to return home at the end of the fighting in July 1953.

156 Xu Beihong: life of a master painter.
Liao Jingwen, translated by Zhang Peiji. Beijing: Foreign Languages Press, 1987. 365p.

The artist Xu Beihong (1895-1953) is best known for his traditional studies of horses, but he worked in a variety of mediums including oils to depict a wide range of subjects. This biography is written by his second wife, Liao Jingwen, and so takes on something of the characteristics of a joint memoir. Xu was born in Jiangsu province into a poor family but eventually managed to study and work in Europe from 1919 to 1927, where he was much influenced by Western styles of painting and where he acquired a Western form of his name, Peon Xu. Back in China he held a number of teaching posts, continued to travel abroad and became increasingly well known both inside and outside China. Only in 1946 did he settle in Beijing. Xu was sympathetic to the new Communist regime and enjoyed the support of the new Chinese leaders who in 1949 asked him to head the Central Institute of Fine Arts. This did not prevent the Memorial Hall established after his death in 1953 from being demolished during the Cultural Revolution. A new Memorial Hall and museum (see item no. 438) were erected in northwest Beijing.

Flora and Fauna

General

157   China's nature reserves.
Li Wenhua, Zhao Xianying, translated by Penny Edwards.   Beijing: Foreign Languages Press, 1989. 191p. maps.

This well-researched and well-presented volume on the country's nature reserves shows the location of reserves, admittedly few in number, in the vicinity of Beijing and Tianjin, and lists brief details on these in an appendix of facts and figures for reserves throughout China (including Taiwan), valid for 1986.

Fauna

158   Birds in China.
Xu Weishu, translated by Zhou Lifang, Liu Bingwen, illustrations by Wang Binying.   Beijing: Foreign Languages Press, 1989. 72p.

This attractive book, with colour photographs and illustrations and black-and-white photographs and line drawings, covers the whole of China and does not refer specifically to the Beijing area. Indeed, the only discussion of a species associated with the capital is of the white Peking duck (p. 10), which is thought to share a common ancestry with the domestic duck found in the south of the country. References to species and distribution of birds in North China (p. 39) can be taken to cover the region around Beijing.

159 Birds of the Ming valley.
Janus Paludan. In: *The Imperial Ming Tombs.* Ann Paludan.
New Haven, Connecticut; London: Yale University Press; Hong
Kong: Hong Kong University Press, 1981, Appendix B, p. 227-30.
bibliog.

This short appendix by Janus Paludan to his wife's book enumerates the birds they saw
on their trips in the mid-1970s to the valley of the Ming Tombs northwest of Beijing.
English and Latin ornithological names are listed and the season and, in some cases,
frequent location of these birds are named. It has its own short bibliography.

160 Handbook of North China: amphibia and reptiles (herpetology of North China).
Alice M. Boring, Liu Ch'eng-chao, Chou Shu-ch'un. Beijing:
Peking Natural History Bulletin, 1932. 64p. (Handbook No. 3).

This handbook covers a very wide area, extending as far as Mongolia, Siberia and Korea,
and the study by no means focuses on Beijing. However, given the absence of natural
barriers between these northerly regions, it can be assumed that most of the amphibians
and reptiles described here would be, or would have been, found in the Beijing area. The
book is an example of the type of study produced, sometimes jointly, by Chinese and
foreign scholars in Beijing in the 1930s (see item nos. 162 and 163). The text is in
English, with zoological, English and Chinese (character) names given for each species.
It is illustrated with line drawings.

161 Pekingese.
Ian Harman. London: Williams & Norgate Ltd, 1949. 95p.

Most of this book is taken up with the Pekinese as a pet or as a show dog, with details of
diet, illnesses, breeding and all the other subjects which are likely to interest dog lovers,
together with many good black-and-white photographs of these ever popular dogs.
However, there is also a brief history of the breed, tracing its origins in the court dogs of
imperial China, and recounting how it first reached Europe after the Franco-British
military expedition of 1860. A similar account can be found in Anne Coath Dixey, *The
lion dog of Peking: a history of the Pekingese dog* (London: Davies, rev. ed., 1967.
155p.).

Flora

162 The familiar trees of Hopei.
Chow Hang-fan. Beijing: Peking Natural History Bulletin, 1934.
370p. (Handbook No. 4).

The *Peking Natural History Bulletin* was a quarterly journal available on subscription
during the 1920s and 1930s. It published a number of handbooks on the fauna and flora
of North China (see item nos. 160 and 163) and other works on Chinese materia medica,
botany, mineralogy and zoology, including a *Manual of the dragonflies of China: a*

monographic study of Chinese odonata, by J. G. Needham (Beijing: Peking Natural History Bulletin, 1930. 355p.). This study of trees in the northeastern and northwestern parts of Hebei province surrounding Beijing has a text in English and many fine line drawings. Species are identified by their botanical and English names and in Chinese characters and transliteration. A typical entry gives a botanical description and notes on the tree's distribution and uses.

163 Wild flowers of North China and South Manchuria.
H. S. D. Garven. Beijing: Peking Natural History Bulletin, 1937.
117p. (Handbook No. 5).

Fifth in the series of handbooks published in the 1920s and 1930s by the *Peking Natural History Bulletin* (see item nos. 160 and 162). Though intended as a 'first book' on wild flowers, the text (in English) is arranged in an orderly fashion, with botanical descriptions, lists of flowers by families and indexes of scientific and common names. The Chinese names are given in characters and romanization. The text is followed by 102 plates of line drawings of flowers found at Beidaihe and elsewhere, annotated in English and Chinese. The book has no bibliography, but refers to several other works on the plants of North China.

Shells of Peitaiho.
See item no. 477.

Prehistory and Archaeology

164 The cave home of Peking man.
Chia Lan-po (Jia Lanpo).   Beijing: Foreign Languages Press, 1975.
52p.

This short illustrated account of Zhoukoudian (Peking Man) by a well-known palaeoanthropologist has now little more than curiosity value, though at the time of its publication it was one of the few texts available in China to foreigners on its subject. It provides a description of how Peking Man may have lived, together with an account of what happened to the original archaeological findings, which disappeared during the Sino-Japanese War (1937-45). It is illustrated with some poor-quality photographs. More satisfactory is the same author's *Early man in China* (Beijing: Foreign Languages Press, 1980. 60p., plus approx. 40 unnumbered pages of plates). By 1980, some of the requirements of the Maoist era on scholars were beginning to be relaxed, and this is altogether a more scholarly account of its subject. It includes a substantial amount on Zhoukoudian and Peking Man, and places the findings at Zhoukoudian in the wider context of archaeological findings in China.

165 Mysteries of ancient China: new discoveries from the early dynasties.
Edited by Jessica Rawson.   London: British Museum Press, 1996.
303p. maps. bibliog.

Beijing assumed its position of eminence only from the 12th century, and earlier dynasties located their capitals to the west or south. The area around Beijing nonetheless has several ancient sites, the best known of which is that at Zhoukoudian southwest of Beijing, where during the 1920s and 1930s the remains of human burials were discovered in a cave. The fossils unearthed, dated to around 16,000 BC, were named as Upper Cave Man or, more commonly, Beijing or Peking Man (*Sinanthropus pekinensis*). Lei Congyun and Chen Lie, two of the illustrious contributors to this magnificent catalogue prepared for the British Museum exhibition of the same name, briefly discuss the significance of the Zhoukoudian burial site (p. 219 and p. 269) in their essays. The bibliography is extremely full.

166 Peking man.
Harry Lionel Shapiro.   London: Allen & Unwin, 1976. 190p.

Tells the story of the discovery of Peking Man at the Zhoukoudian cave complex, how the bones came to be lost, and the continuing search for them in China and Japan.

167 The story of Peking man: from archaeology to mystery.
Jia Lanpo, Huang Weiwen, translated by Yin Zhiqi.   Beijing: Foreign Languages Press; Hong Kong; Oxford; New York: Oxford University Press, 1990. 270p.

Originally published in Chinese, this book by Jia Lanpo, a veteran Chinese archaeologist (see item no. 164), tells the story of the discovery of a major archaeological site at a small town near Beijing in 1921, and of the subsequent fate of the bones. The town, Zhoukoudian, has been famous ever since as the home of the ancestors of the Chinese, Peking (usually thus in English, even in China) Man. The discoveries made in 1921 and in the years leading up to the Second World War advanced knowledge of early man not only in China but in the wider world. That was not the end of the story, however, for not only was this an exciting scientific discovery in its own right, but the subsequent history of the fossils, which disappeared during the war and have never been found, provides an interesting additional story. There is also an informative analysis of the relevant literature, together with numerous photographs. For some of the problems that faced scholars such as Jia and the general debate about Zhoukoudian, as well as much more on the development of anthropology as a science in China, see Gregory Eliyu Guldin, *The saga of anthropology in China: from Malinowski to Mao* (Armonk, New York; London: M. E. Sharpe, 1994. 298p. bibliog. [Studies on Modern China]).

History

General

168 Ancient China.
C. Patrick FitzGerald. Oxford: Elsevier-Phaidon, 1978. 151p. maps. bibliog. (The Making of the Past).

The object of this series is to reveal through archaeology and related disciplines the early history of a civilization on which was based its subsequent flowering. When this volume on China was published, Western viewers had only recently seen the evidence (in overseas exhibitions) of archaeological excavations carried out in China in earlier decades. Many of the most splendid finds were from sites in western and central China and, apart from the discovery of Peking Man at Zhoukoudian, FitzGerald does not report anything of antiquity in the Beijing area. He does, however, discuss the Forbidden City and the Ming Tombs, relating their design to much older models and practices, and links the present Great Wall with its ancient prototypes. The book is attractively illustrated with photographs and drawings and has a helpful glossary. The author, writing as C. P. FitzGerald (by which name he is more commonly known), had already developed similar arguments in his *China: a short cultural history* (London: The Cresset Press, 1961. 3rd ed. 624p. maps). This work was first published in 1935, when archaeology in China was in its early stages. He discusses Beijing largely in the context of its unsuitable location as a capital city for the Ming and Qing, and suggests again that it was constructed following ancient models. His scant treatment of Beijing puts a different perspective on the city's place within the long history of Chinese civilization.

169 Beijing relics.
Wang Jinlu, general editor, translated by Wang Minyuan, Lu
Shaochen, Chen Ruilan, Wen Jie, Shen Lixin, prefaces by Chen
Xitong (mayor of Beijing) and Wang Jinlu, photographs by Luo
Zhewen and twenty-five others. Beijing: Beijing Yanshan
Publishing House, 1990. 181p. maps.

Offers a rapid journey through the history of Beijing through the medium of its relics from
the Palaeolithic age to the present. The story is told through photographs, maps and
captions. It opens with the site of Peking Man at Zhoukoudian, where bones and stone
artefacts of Homo erectus were discovered in 1929, and closes with the Monument to the
People's Heroes in Tiananmen Square. The captions are in Chinese and English, but the
maps are lettered in Chinese. An appendix lists useful and hard-to-find information:
details of the various organizations under the Beijing Administrative Bureau of Cultural
Relics; UNESCO World Historical and Cultural Heritage Sites in and near Beijing; the
main state-protected historical sites in the Beijing area, together with Beijing
Municipality protected historical sites; museums in Beijing; and a brief chronology.

170 Beijing: the treasures of an ancient capital.
Yan Chongnian, edited by Wang Yanrong, Ma Yue, translated by
Arnold Chao, Tan Aiqing, Wang Xingzheng, Fang Zhenya, English
text edited by Arnold Chao, photographs by Yan Zhongyi, Hu Chui,
Liu Zhigang, Sun Guiqi. Beijing: Morning Glory Press, 1987.
285p. maps.

A cultural history of Beijing and of the earlier sites in the region that highlights four
characteristics: the length of the area's history; the city's incorporation of a feudalistic
concept of monarchical and religious authority; its wealth of art treasures; and its people.
From Peking Man through Neolithic settlements and evidence of ancient Shang culture,
the account moves to later dynasties when the city of Ji, in the region of modern Beijing,
was the capital of a prefecture. From being a Liao and Jurchen capital, the city became
Dadu of the Yuan, then achieved eminence as the Ming and Qing capital. The text,
accompanied by many fine photographs, details the layout and construction of Beijing
and surrounding sites, the life of the imperial court and the flourishing of art and culture
under these two dynasties, then describes the life of the people. A chronology and a very
full index are attached, though the naming of sites in their English translations rather than
with their Chinese names could lead to confusion.

171 The British in the Far East.
George Woodcock. London: George Weidenfeld & Nicholson Ltd,
1969. 259p. bibliog. (Social History of the British Overseas).

Beijing flits in and out of this entertaining narrative, as one might expect. From 1860 to
1900, few foreigners apart from diplomats lived in the city, and even thereafter, although
numbers increased, Beijing was never one of the chief areas of foreign residence in the
Far East. Woodcock's book, however, provides useful background on the way of life of
the British communities in China generally, and from time to time, the Beijing foreign
community and its social circle briefly occupies the centre stage. There is one splendid
photographic section, between p. 124-25, relating to the Boxer incident of 1900.

172 Cambridge history of China.
Edited by Denis Crispin Twitchett, John King Fairbank, and others.
Cambridge, England; New York: Cambridge University Press, 1978- .
15 vols. planned. maps. bibliog.

This major historical undertaking has more than doubled in expected size since its commencement in 1978, and had not been completed as of mid-1999. For the history of Beijing, the reader needs to consult volumes 6 onwards, all of which contain much information about the city and its development from the time of the Mongols until the 1980s. Each chapter has been written by an international expert and generally provides an up-to-date account of scholarship at the time it was written. From volume 10, dealing with the later Qing, there is also information about Tianjin. The extensive bibliographies in each volume are a further important aid to scholarship. Most volumes are available in Chinese translation.

173 The Cambridge illustrated history of China.
Patricia Buckley Ebrey.   Cambridge, England; New York;
Melbourne, Australia: Cambridge University Press, 1996. 352p.
maps. bibliog.

This excellent introduction to Chinese history, aimed at the general reader with no specialist knowledge, inevitably contains much about Beijing and its people. The text is clear and authoritative, and there is a good selection of illustrations, many of which relate to Beijing, together with clear maps. The bibliography is extensive.

174 China and the West: society and culture 1815-1937.
Jerome Ch'en.   Bloomington, Indiana; London: Indiana University
Press, 1979. 488p. maps. bibliog.

An excellent introduction to the history of the relationship between China and the West from the early 19th century to the outbreak of the Sino-Japanese War in 1937. Ch'en does not deal with Beijing as such, but there is much about the various foreign communities in the capital, and on schools, colleges and churches. The bibliography is particularly useful.

175 China: a cultural history.
Stephen G. Haw.   London: B. T. Batsford Ltd, 1990. 224p. maps.
bibliog.

This short and very readable history of China is a 'cultural' history in the sense of describing the development of Chinese society and institutions, as well as providing a chronological account of the country's history. Beijing receives no special treatment, but reappears constantly in the account. Even more detail will be found in Jacques Gernet, translated by J. R. Foster, *A history of Chinese civilization* (Cambridge, England; New York; London; Melbourne, Australia; Sydney: Cambridge University Press, 1982. Reprinted, 1987. 772p. maps. bibliog.). Again Beijing and its predecessors appear regularly in the text.

176 A Chinese biographical dictionary.

Herbert A. Giles.   London: Bernard Quaritch; Shanghai: Kelly & Walsh Ltd, 1898. Reprinted, Taipei: Ch'eng-wen, 1966; Boston, Massachusetts: Cheng & Tsui, 1998. 1,022p.

This huge dictionary, by the then Professor of Chinese at Cambridge and one of the devisors of the Wade-Giles system of transliteration of Chinese, lists some 2,579 officials from ancient times to the late 19th century, including some who are known to be fictitious. Each person's entry includes the characters and pen names, and gives details of the place of birth, family history and similar information. Many of the officials listed lived or worked in Beijing, and this makes the dictionary a valuable tool for the study of the capital's history. Additional biographical information for the Ming era (1368-1644) and the Qing era (1644-1911) can be found in *Dictionary of Ming biography, 1368-1644*, edited by Luther Carrington Goodrich, Fang Chao-ying (New York: Columbia University Press, 1976. 2 vols.), and Arthur William Hummel, *Eminent Chinese of the Ch'ing period (1644-1911)* (Washington, DC: United States Government Printing Office, 1943, 1944. Reprinted, New York: Paragon, 1964; Taipei: Ch'eng-wen, 1967. 2 vols.). These list Chinese, Manchu and Mongol men and women, many of whom were connected with the court or the capital. For the Republican period (1912-49), there is Howard L. Boorman, Richard C. Howard, *Biographical dictionary of Republican China* (London; New York: Columbia University Press, 1967-71. 4 vols.). For more recent biographies, there are Donald W. Klein, Anne B. Clark, *Biographic dictionary of Chinese communism, 1921-65* (Cambridge, Massachusetts: Harvard University Press, 1971. 2 vols. [Harvard East Asia Monographs, no. 57]); and *Who's who in China* (Beijing: Foreign Languages Press, 1989, revised regularly).

177 Chinese imperial city planning.

Nancy Shatzman Steinhardt.   Honolulu, Hawaii: University of Hawaii Press, 1990. 228p. maps. bibliog.

Beijing's development forms only one part of this wide-ranging book, which traces the origins and development of China's capital cities from the earliest times to the present. The author shows that, despite the belief among Chinese and foreigners that China's capitals have followed a standard unvarying pattern, which can be traced to the distant past, in reality each dynasty made significant changes in order to take account of contemporary requirements. The brutal changes introduced since 1949 therefore have historical precedents.

178 Chronicle of the Chinese emperors: the reign-by-reign record of the rulers of imperial China.

Ann Paludan.   London: Thames & Hudson, 1998. 224p. map. bibliog.

The present capital of China, Beijing, is not the first on the site. Earlier cities each occupied slightly different terrain and had other names. While the focus of imperial authority lay further south or west, the city's location in the north made it of secondary importance. Successive northern invaders who seized power over the empire, however, favoured the site; Ann Paludan's chronicle shows how closely Beijing came to be identified with imperial might, from the Khitan (dynastic title Liao), who in 1153 moved their seat of government there, to the Mongols (dynastic name Yuan), who created their capital Dadu in the same spot. In turn they were ousted by the Ming dynasty which eventually re-established Beijing as the capital in 1421, an arrangement accepted by the succeeding Qing. This beautifully illustrated account has sections devoted to the Great Wall, the Grand Canal, the Forbidden City, the Temple of Heaven, the Ming Tombs, and the Jesuits and the Summer Palace.

179 The Forbidden City: the great within.
May Holdsworth, Caroline Courtauld, photography by Hu Chui, introduction by Jonathan D. Spence. London; New York: I. B. Tauris Publishers, 1995. 140p. map. bibliog.

Published as a companion volume to a documentary film of the same title made by Totem Film Productions, which marked the seventieth anniversary of the Palace Museum established in 1925 within the Forbidden City. Text, illustrations and photographs follow the succession of Ming and Qing emperors from the Yongle emperor (reigned 1403-24) to the last Qing ruler, Pu Yi (abdicated 1911). A section entitled the 'Outer Court' discusses the relationship between the ruler and the ruled, the administration of the empire and its dealings with the world beyond China. The following section describes daily life in the imperial household, in the 'Inner Court'. The final part charts the heyday and decline of the Qing dynasty. The book is perhaps over-elaborately produced and does not break new ground, but it is a most attractive volume.

180 The Forbidden City: heart of imperial China.
Gilles Béguin, Dominique Morel, translated from French by Ruth Taylor. London: Thames & Hudson; published as *The Forbidden City: centre of imperial China*, New York: Harry N. Abrams Inc., 1997. 143p. maps. bibliog. (New Horizons Series in Britain; Discoveries Series in the United States).

Originally published in Paris by Gallimard/Paris-Musées in 1996, this lavishly illustrated pocket-format book provides a good introduction to the Forbidden City, the heart of imperial Beijing. The text is by two distinguished French museum curators, and takes the reader through the origins and development of the Forbidden City from the Ming dynasty (1392-1644) to the fall of the last dynasty in 1910-11, together with an account of its gradual transformation into China's greatest museum. In addition, there is a selection of texts about the city, chosen from a range of Western sources.

181 Imperial Peking: seven centuries of China.
Lin Yutang, with an essay on the art of Peking by Peter C. Swann. London: Elek Books Limited, 1961. 227p. maps. bibliog.

Lin Yutang focuses on three elements: nature, art, and the life and character of the people of Beijing. He writes about the seasons, the city itself and its citizens, whom he greatly admires, and the activities of those who ruled China from Beijing, and contributes two essays on 'Studies in form'. In an appendix he assesses earlier attempts to calculate the location and size of former city sites in the Beijing area. In a contributory essay (p. 176-99) the art historian Peter Swann discusses the art to be viewed in Beijing, principally in the Palace Museum. The book is well illustrated with maps, line drawings and colour and black-and-white reproductions and photographs. Lin Yutang's style is discursive, at times anecdotal, and his approach is often subjective, but his work is always easy to read. He uses his own romanization, which can be irritating. His attachment to Beijing led him to choose it as the location for some of his novels, such as *Moment in Peking: a novel of contemporary life* (New York: The John Day Company, 1939. 815p.), and *The red peony*, which first appeared in 1961 (Taipei; New York: Mei Ya Publications, Inc., 1975. 400p.).

182 Péking: histoire et description. (Beijing: history and description.)
Alphonse Favier.   Beijing: Imprimerie des Lazaristes au Pé-t'ang,
1897. 562p. maps. Reprinted, Paris; Lille, France: Desclée, de
Brouwer et Cie., 1902. 416p. maps.

The two editions of this history are identical in text and illustrations (photographs and line-drawings). The larger first edition, however, has more illustrations and they are of better quality than in the later edition. Favier, a priest of the French Lazarist order, served as Apostolic Missionary and Vicar of the Catholic Church in Beijing. (In 1900 he survived the Boxer siege of his cathedral.) His history is a work of piety, since he recounts in detail the arrival, alleged or actual, of Christian missionaries in the city from early times. His own order was admitted in 1783. As an account of relations between the Roman Catholic Church and China, his history has interest, and the index lists the names of many missionaries; but it is otherwise hardly reliable. His description of the city, of the life and customs of its people, its climate, flora and fauna and economy is of greater value. He concludes with essays on ancient bronzes and ceramics. There is no bibliography, but a list of authors and works consulted.

183 Peking: the old imperial city.
Otto Constantini, introduction by Tilemann Grimm, translated by
G. A. Colville.   Munich: Wilhelm Andermann Verlag, distributed
by Doubleday & Co. Inc., Garden City, New York, 1958. 62p.
(Panorama-Books).

This is a collection of colour plates of views of the imperial city in Beijing, with a short introduction. So much has changed since the 1950s that its main interest now is as a historical record of what has gone.

184 Peking: a tale of three cities.
Nigel Cameron, Brian Brake, foreword by Luther Carrington
Goodrich.   New York; Evanston, Illinois: Harper & Row; Tokyo: J.
Weatherhill, 1965. 263p. maps. bibliog.

A general history of the city from the Mongols to the early years of Communist rule. The story is well-told, with plentiful illustrations, many in colour; the photographs include several by Brake, a professional photographer. It concludes just as the authorities of the People's Republic of China were in the process of destroying much of the old city so praised by foreigners, in a drive to turn Beijing into a modern, industrial city.

185 The search for modern China.
Jonathan D. Spence.   London; New York: W. W. Norton, 1990.
876p. maps. bibliog.

A detailed history of China from the fall of the Ming in 1644 and the coming of the Manchu Qing empire, excellently told, full of fascinating detail, and eminently readable. Spence's canvas is the whole of China but Beijing features prominently both in the text and in the large collection of illustrations. There is also a detailed bibliography of English-language works, arranged by topic.

186   The sextants of Beijing: global currents in Chinese history.
Joanna Waley-Cohen.   New York; London: W. W. Norton &
Company, 1999. 322p. maps. bibliog.

The sextants in the old Beijing observatory, placed there in the 17th century by Jesuit
missionaries, are taken as symbols of Chinese interest in foreign inventions and recurring
willingness to maintain contact with the outside world. The author's purpose in this book
is to develop that argument, and she is concerned with Beijing only insofar as it is the
setting for encounters with foreigners and with external influences. She thus discusses the
toleration of Christian Catholic missionaries in the 17th-18th centuries, Macartney's
embassy of 1793 to the Qianlong emperor, the 1860 looting of the Yuanmingyuan and
consequent Convention of Beijing which led to the establishment of foreign legations in
the capital, the Boxer movement of 1900, Chinese use of foreign experts and technology,
and the role of foreigners in establishing Beijing University. Even the new China is not
immune, and the slogans of Democracy Wall (1978), the 'Beijing Spring' of 1979 and the
Tiananmen protests of 1989 all showed the imprint of foreign ideas.

The monuments of civilisation: China.
See item no. 414.

Yuan (1260-1368)

**187   Archaeological and historical researches on Peking and its
environs.**
E. Bretschneider.   Shanghai: American Presbyterian Mission Press;
London: Trübner & Co., 1876. 63p. maps.

Bretschneider was physician to the Russian legation in Beijing when he wrote this study
of the history of the city before the Ming reconstruction in the early 15th century. He
based his observations on Chinese textual evidence and on the visual evidence of remains
of pre-Ming walls around Beijing. A discussion of the various names by which the capital
was known leads to an analysis of these remains which confirms the pattern of shifting
sites of successive cities in the Beijing area. He compares the descriptions of the capital
given by Marco Polo and others with the statements of contemporary Chinese authors in
an attempt to arrive at the veracity of the Westerners' accounts. He discusses further the
network of canals connecting Beijing with the river system of China, the irrigation of the
Beijing area, the Lugouqiao ('Marco Polo' bridge) and the roads leading to the Mongol
(i.e. Yuan) summer residence at Shangdu north of Beijing. The four maps are annotated
in Chinese only. There is no bibliography, but the author notes a number of Chinese works
and several in European languages and in Russian.

188 Did Marco Polo go to China?

Frances Wood. London: Secker & Warburg, 1995. 182p. map. bibliog.

Whether or not the Venetian merchant Marco Polo ever did reach the court of the great khan at modern Beijing is an intriguing question, prompted by some apparently surprising omissions from the traveller's account. Tea is not mentioned, yet the Chinese were by the 13th century long-established consumers. Although the Great Wall would not reach its most complete form until the Ming dynasty, there were already by 1260 many sections of the wall in existence; Polo does not mention them. So, despite his descriptions of the city of 'Cambaluc', the common Turkish-derived name for the Mongol city of Dadu, or 'great capital', there has grown up much doubt about the veracity of his claims to have visited China at all. Frances Wood, head of the Chinese Department of the British Library, examines some of the evidence in this nicely written and light-hearted book, concluding that, wherever else he went, Marco Polo did not go to China.

189 Marco Polo: Venetian adventurer.

Henry H. Hart. Norman, Oklahoma: University of Oklahoma Press, 1967. 306p. maps. bibliog.

This is a complete revision of the same author's *Venetian adventurer* (Stanford, California: Stanford University Press, 1942), which provides a long, well-written account of the life of Marco Polo, with much detail about those whom he is supposed to have met such as Genghis Khan, the emperor of China, and the Mongols generally. Hart clearly has no doubts about whether Marco Polo went to China, and accepts fully his account of 'Cambaluc', the capital of the great khan and the precursor of Beijing. He explains away Polo's omissions by saying that he wrote about what he thought would interest his readers and thus convince them of the truth of his account, rather than of everything he saw. The wise reader might also like to consult other works such as that by Frances Wood (see no. 188), in order to consider possible alternative explanations. For a wide-ranging study of the influence of Marco Polo's writings, including his description of the Mongol capital, which would eventually become Beijing, see John Larner, *Marco Polo and the discovery of the world* (New Haven, Connecticut; London: Yale University Press, 1999. 250p. maps. bibliog.). Both the maps, in full colour, and the bibliography in this well-written work are excellent.

190 Tatu, the Yuan capital.

Ku Yen-wen. In: *New archaeological finds in China: discoveries during the cultural revolution.* Beijing: Foreign Languages Press, 1972, p. 20-29. map.

China's Cultural Revolution, which is usually dated from 1966 to 1976, is more noted for its destruction of ancient sites than for its contribution to archaeology. However, some work was done on finds made during the period, and this short essay describes some of those made relating to the Yuan (Mongol) capital of Dadu (Tatu is the older, Wade-Giles transliteration), which partly overlaps modern Beijing. The essay is a curious mix of archaeological report and polemic on the exploitation of the working class (sic) in Mongol times.

Ming (1368-1644)

191   Early Ming government: the evolution of dual capitals.
Edward L. Farmer.   Cambridge, Massachusetts: Harvard University
Press, 1976. 271p. bibliog. (Harvard East Asian Monographs, no.
66).

This is an examination of the reasons that prompted the third Ming emperor to move the
capital from Nanjing to Beijing. Drawing on the official records, Farmer shows how
defence considerations led the emperor to move the capital north, in order to meet the
threat posed to China from Central Asia, and explains how Dadu, the capital of the
despised Mongols, renamed Beijing, or Northern Capital, came to be chosen.

192   Voices from the Ming-Qing cataclysm: China in tigers' jaws.
Edited and translated by Lynn A. Struve.   New Haven, Connecticut;
London: Yale University Press, 1993. 303p.

A collection of eye-witness accounts of the end of the Ming dynasty in 1644 and its
replacement by the Manchu Qing. The canvas covers the whole country, but there are
some accounts of what happened in and around Beijing, including Liu Shangyou's
descriptive piece on how 'A survivor of Beijing "settles his thoughts" ', a vivid picture of
the final events in the Imperial Palace.

193   The wise man from the west.
Vincent Cronin.   London: Rupert Hart-Davis, 1955. Reprinted,
London; Glasgow: Fontana Books, 1961. New ed., London: Harvill
Press, 1999. 300p. maps. bibliog.

One of the world's great adventure stories is that of the Jesuit, Matteo Ricci, who died in
Beijing in May 1610. Born in the Papal States in 1522, Ricci joined the Society of Jesus
and in 1578 reached Macau. From there he began visiting China and learning Chinese,
but it would be many years before he reached Beijing, which would remain his home until
his death. Cronin's account of Ricci and of his life in Beijing has enjoyed great popularity
since its first publication. Although his prime interest is in Ricci as a missionary who
adapted himself to Chinese ways, there is much about Beijing and the imperial court,
derived from the Jesuit archives and other contemporary sources. Also of interest, though
more scholarly, is Jonathan D. Spence, *The memory palace of Matteo Ricci* (New York:
Viking; Harmondsworth, England: Penguin, 1984. 350p. map. bibliog.), which examines
Ricci's use of mnemonics to illustrate his career and beliefs.

Qing (1644-1911)

194 The Arrow war: an Anglo-Chinese confusion 1856-60.
Douglas Hurd. London: Collins; New York: Macmillan, 1967.
254p. maps. bibliog.

The 'Arrow' War, named after a small Chinese-rigged but theoretically British-registered ship, and sometimes known as the 'Second Anglo-Chinese War' or the 'Second Opium War', continued the process of opening China to the West that began with the 'First Opium War' of 1839-42. The French, although more concerned with the privileges of Roman Catholic missionaries than with trade, also had their grievances with the Chinese, and the military force deployed against the Chinese quickly became a Franco-British one. The war went through several phases, culminating in an attack on Beijing in 1860, the burning of the Summer Palace, and the formal opening of China's capital to residence by Western diplomats. Between 1856 and 1858, most of the action was in South China. Thereafter it shifted north, first to Tianjin, where treaties were signed in 1858, and then to the capital. Douglas Hurd, a former diplomat who was later British Foreign Secretary, tells the story with verve, quoting from the British and French archives and a wide range of published sources, but does not pay much attention to the Chinese side of the story.

195 Barbarian lens: western photographers of the Qianlong emperor's European palaces.
Régine Thiriez. Amsterdam, the Netherlands: Gordon & Breach Publishers, 1998. 191p. maps. bibliog. (Documenting the Image, vol. 6).

The author's main interest is 19th- and early 20th-century photographers of Beijing and the extent to which their work has survived. At the same time, she throws light on the foreign community in Beijing from c. 1861 to c. 1925, and also provides some splendid photographs of the remains of the various Western-style palaces around the city, which were destroyed by Western forces in 1860 and 1900 in order to punish the imperial court. The ten-page bibliography is a useful guide to works on Beijing and on photography in China.

196 Behind the scenes in Peking.
Mary Hooker (Polly Condit Smith). London: John Murray, 1910. Reprinted, with an introduction by H. J. Lethbridge, Hong Kong; Oxford; New York: Oxford University Press, 1987. 209p. map. bibliog.

This is an account of the siege of the legations in 1900, reconstructed some years later from letters and a diary, by a visiting American, Polly Condit Smith, who took the pen-name Mary Hooker. Arriving from Japan, she found herself caught up in the violent events of that summer, and ten years later published an account which remains fresh, and in places amusing, in spite of adversity. She was not privy to the discussions going on at the higher level during the siege, but she seems to have watched and listened carefully, picking up much of the atmosphere of international tension and bickering that marked the siege. H. J. Lethbridge's introduction provides the context, and there are good photographs both of people and of the city.

197 Beleaguered in Peking. UL : Rare books : P.30.7
Robert Coltman, Jr. Philadelphia, Pennsylvania: F. A. Davis Co.,
1901. 248p.

An American missionary account of the siege of the legations in 1900. Coltman was
highly critical of most of those trapped in the legations, and was particularly scathing
about the British, in whose compound he spent the siege. He concluded that only the
missionaries had emerged from the ordeal with their reputation enhanced.

198 Besieged in Peking: the story of the 1900 Boxer rising.
Diana Preston. London: Constable, 1999. 322p. maps. bibliog.

Diana Preston retells the story of the 1900 siege of the Beijing legations with verve and
enthusiasm. She draws on some unpublished material, mainly diaries and letters from
those caught in the siege, or from members of the foreign relieving forces, but most of the
book derives from the considerable number of published accounts of what happened in
North China in 1900. There are numerous interesting anecdotes about people such as Sir
Claude MacDonald, the British minister, and the slightly shady Sir Edmund Backhouse
(see item no. 261). The Empress Dowager is perhaps the main Chinese character, as much
for her fearsome reputation among foreigners as anything else. Otherwise, the Chinese are
generally in the background.

**199 Bluejackets and Boxers: Australia's naval expedition to the
Boxer uprising.**
Bob Nicholls. Sydney; London; Boston, Massachusetts: Allen &
Unwin, 1986. 164p. maps. bibliog.

An account of the Australian forces from New South Wales, Victoria and South Australia
who took part in the Western expeditionary force which went to North China in 1900 to
suppress the Boxer rebellion. After a short account of events in China from 1860 to the
eve of the Boxer outbreak in the late 1890s, the author concentrates on the rather limited
role of the Australian forces. They arrived well after the end of the siege of the legations,
and found themselves largely confined to police and public order duties, including
sanitation work and anti-looting activities, in Beijing and Tianjin. It was not very heroic
work, and they were quite pleased to give it up. This account is based on contemporary
publications, including newspapers, and while perhaps not very profound history, it is
entertaining and informative about a little-known aspect of the events of 1900.

200 The Boxer uprising: a background study. New Hall 951.
Victor Purcell. Cambridge, England: Cambridge University Press, PuR
1963. 349p. maps. bibliog.

This is less a study of the Boxer incident or of the Boxers themselves, but more a general
introduction to the subject. In elegant prose, Purcell explains how China was governed in
the late 19th century, and how the traditional order of society was in the process of being
changed – and ultimately destroyed – by the impact of the West. He examines the
demands of the Western powers for concessions and the impact of the missionaries, and
then links these to the rise of the Boxer movement in North China. He also examines the
connection between the Manchu court and the Boxers, and explains how the latter began
as an anti-dynasty movement but eventually changed. Developments in and around the
capital, including the siege of the legations, figure in the book, which is also of interest

for its examination of the question of the 'Diary of Chin-Shan [Jing Shan]', now generally believed to have been a forgery perpetrated by Sir Edmund Backhouse (see item no. 261).

201 British diplomacy in China 1880-83.
E. V. G. Kiernan.   New York: Octagon Books; Taipei: Rainbow-Bridge Book Co., 1970. 327p. bibliog.

This pioneering study, based on archival research, of Britain's diplomacy in China in the early 1880s originally appeared in 1939, and was reprinted with a new introduction in 1970. Kiernan's prime concern was the interaction of Britain and the other great powers with China and Korea, but there is much incidental information on the trials and tribulations of the Beijing diplomatic community from its beginning in the 1860s through to the 1900 Boxer incident. There are also accounts of Chinese institutions and buildings in the capital which still make interesting reading.

202 British policy in China 1895-1902.
L. K. Young.   Oxford: Clarendon Press, 1970. 356p. maps. bibliog.

This is a major study of British diplomatic relations with China at the end of the 19th century, drawing extensively on archive materials and a wide range of published sources. Inevitably, it is concerned with high policy, but it also gives an account of the Boxer incident, the 1900 siege of the Beijing legations, and of the diplomatic settlement that followed. It thus provides essential background to more descriptive accounts of those events, helping to put them into a wider international context.

203 Cherishing men from afar: Qing guest ritual and the Macartney embassy of 1793.
James L. Hevia.   Durham, North Carolina; London: Duke University Press, 1995. 292p. bibliog.

This important study of the Macartney mission is likely to be of interest mainly to specialists. Hevia is concerned to get behind the traditional 'clash of empires' view of the expedition (see item no. 207) to a deeper understanding of what went wrong with Macartney's embassy. In the process, however, much incidental information emerges about the imperial court and how its affairs were conducted both in Beijing and at the summer retreat at Chengde (Rehe), while a number of the illustrations show buildings in Beijing.

204 China 1890-1938: from the warlords to world war: a history in documentary photographs.
Eric Baschet, introduction by Han Suyin.   Zug, Switzerland: Swan Productions, 1989. 260p. maps.

There is little text in this work; even Han Suyin's introduction is only about four pages long. What matters is the photographs, even though we are told very little about them or the artists who took them. They cover the whole of China, but a good proportion deal with events in Beijing or nearby areas, from the luxurious lives of Europeans to the violent executions of alleged 'Boxers'. The captions, and such linking material as is provided, are very literal translations from the French; when it comes to the maps, the editors appear to have given up, for all the captioning remains in French. Nevertheless, the collection is both interesting and illuminating.

205 The China helpers: western advisers in China 1620-1960.
Jonathan D. Spence. London; Sydney; Toronto: The Bodley Head, 1969. 335p. map.

From the vast array of foreigners who have lived and worked in China since the 17th century, Spence chooses sixteen Western advisers to illustrate who they were and what they did. They range from the Jesuits Adam Schall and Ferdinand Verbiest, who served the Ming and Qing courts, through to the American helpers of Chiang Kai-shek (Jiang Jieshi) and the Soviet advisers to the People's Republic. Inevitably, many of them lived and worked in Beijing, and the city and its people feature frequently. There are sketches of the Jesuits at the imperial court, more on Robert Hart, head of the Chinese customs (see item no. 223), and on other prominent foreigners in Beijing's history such as W. A. P. Martin. Some of the same cast, at least as far as the late 19th and early 20th century are concerned, also appear in Charles Drage, *Servants of the dragon throne, being the lives of Edward and Cecil Bowra* (London: Peter Dawnay Ltd, 1966. 283p. maps. bibliog.).

206 The Ch'ing imperial household: a study of its organization and principal functions, 1662-1791.
Preston M. Torbert. Cambridge, Massachusetts; London: Council on East Asian Studies, Harvard University, 1977. 267p. bibliog. (Harvard East Asian Monographs, no. 71).

A detailed account, primarily for the specialist, of how the Chinese imperial court was organized and how it functioned during the height of Manchu power. Power came from access to the emperor, and such access was very tightly controlled.

207 The collision of two civilisations: the British expedition to China 1792-94.
Alain Peyrefitte, translated by Jon Rothschild. London: Harvill, 1993. 630p. bibliog. Published in the United States as *The immobile empire*, New York: Alfred A. Knopf, 1992.

This work was originally published in French as *L'empire immobile ou Le choc des mondes* (The immovable empire or the clash of the worlds) by Librairie Arthème Fayard, Paris, 1989. Peyrefitte, a well-known French historian, diplomat and politician, who died in 1999, here tells in considerable detail the story of Lord Macartney's expedition to China in 1792-94 on behalf of the East India Company. The mission was a failure, since the Chinese would not agree to trade on terms of equality, but Macartney and his party spent much time in Beijing and at the imperial summer resort of Chengde. Although the book has been criticized for presenting a rather old-fashioned view of the significance of the Macartney mission, its sheer detail, and its descriptions of Beijing and the imperial court, mean that it cannot be ignored. Much the same ground, with similar descriptions of Beijing and Chengde, can be found in Aubrey Singer, *The lion & the dragon: the story of the first British embassy to the court of the emperor Qianlong in Peking 1792-94* (London: Barrie & Jenkins, 1992. 192p. maps. bibliog.).

208 Correspondence de Pékin 1722-59. (Beijing letters 1722-59.)
Antoine Gaubil, edited by Renée Simon, preface by Paul Demiéville, appendices by Joseph Dehergne. Geneva: Librairie Droz, 1970. 1,004p. maps. bibliog. (Etudes de Philologie et d'Histoire, no. 14).

This comprehensive selection from the letters of Father Antoine Gaubil, of the Society of Jesus, make available to the contemporary reader some of the work of the chief Western Sinologist of the 18th century. Most of the letters are in French, but a few, including some to the Royal Society in London, are in Latin. Gaubil was born at Gaillac in the Languedoc region of France in 1689 and died in Beijing, where he had lived from 1723, in 1759. While in China he undertook many studies of all aspects of China, and became a foremost source throughout Europe for information about that country, its capital and its government. There is much more in the letters than the affairs of Beijing, but the city provides the backdrop for many of Gaubil's observations. These include the effects of an earthquake in September 1730, eclipses, reflections on literature and Chinese chronology. The appendices are by Father Joseph Dehergne S. J., himself a former missionary in China, and author of 'La mission de Pékin vers 1700: étude de géographie missionaire' (The Peking mission around 1700: a study in missionary geography) in *Archivam historicum Societatis Jesui*, vol. xxii (1953), p. 314-38. They provide a detailed chronology of Father Gaubil, a bibliography of his works, a lexicon, and unusually, an index. Another prominent Jesuit is the subject of Rachel Attwater, *Adam Schall: a Jesuit at the court of China 1592-1666* (London: Chapman & Hall, 1963. 163p. maps), and the history of the Jesuit mission as a whole can be found in Allan's *Jesuits at the court of Peking* (q.v.).

209 The correspondence of G. E. Morrison.
Edited by Lo Hui-min. Cambridge, England; London; New York; Melbourne, Australia: Cambridge University Press, 1976. 2 vols.

George Morrison was an Australian, who qualified as a doctor in Edinburgh and who arrived in Beijing in 1895 as the correspondent for the London *Times*. He remained the *Times*'s Beijing correspondent until 1912, when he became an adviser to the new republican government of China, a post he held until his death in 1920. He kept an enormous volume of papers, including correspondence, diaries and notes. These two volumes, carefully edited by Lo Hui-min, who provides both linking material and notes, cover his years in China, the first, from 1895 to 1912, as correspondent, the second as an adviser. They are full of incidental information about Beijing and events in the city, including the siege of the legations in 1900 – Morrison was in the British legation – and the revolution that overthrew the Manchu dynasty in 1910-11. They are an essential source for the history of China's foreign relations and offer valuable insights on the Beijing foreign community and its way of life.

210 Cultures in conflict: the Boxer rebellion.
William J. Duicker. San Rafael, California; London: Presidio Press, 1978. 226p. maps. bibliog.

The uprising which swept through North China at the end of the 1890s, which became known as the Boxer rebellion, did not only involve Beijing. But it has become so closely linked with developments in and around the capital, and particularly with the siege of the legations in the summer of 1900, that it cannot be ignored in any account of the capital's history. There are a number of popular accounts concentrating on the siege, which are likely to appeal to the general reader, but Duicker's work will appeal to those who wish to go into the causes of the Boxer movement in somewhat more depth. He argues, as his title suggests, that the cause of the outbreak was the clash between the dynamic self-confident, and somewhat arrogant Westerners, and the more traditionally minded, if equally self-confident and arrogant, Chinese. With each side convinced of the righteousness of its position, a clash was inevitable. There are a number of interesting photographs, but the quality of reproduction is often poor.

211 Daily life in the Forbidden City: the Qing dynasty 1644-1912.
Chief compilers Wan Yi, Wang Shuqing, Lu Yanzhen, translated by Rosemary Scott, Erica Shipley. Harmondsworth, England; New York; Ringwood, Australia; Ontario, Canada; Auckland, New Zealand: Viking/Penguin Press, 1988. 327p. bibliog.
Originally published in Chinese, this is a beautifully illustrated volume covering all aspects of court life under the Qing or Manchu dynasty, which ruled China from 1644 to the revolution of 1911-12. As well as the court in Beijing, there are accounts of life on the imperial hunting and fact-finding exhibitions, and there are sections on other imperial centres such as Chengde, but the main emphasis is on the capital and the Forbidden City. The translation is good and the standard of the pictures uniformly high.

212 Death throes of a dynasty: letters and diaries of Charles and Bessie Ewing, missionaries to China.
Edited by E. G. Ruoff. Kent, Ohio; London: Kent State University Press, 1990. 276p. maps.
Charles Edward and Bessie Smith Ewing went to China in 1894 as missionaries under the auspices of the American Board of Commissioners for Foreign Missions in Boston, Massachusetts, and remained until 1913. Most of their time was spent in either Beijing or Tianjin. They were in the British legation during the Boxer siege, and later Charles witnessed the end of the Manchu dynasty. The letters, some to the Mission Board headquarters, some to family members, especially during the years when Charles was on his own, are principally concerned with missionary affairs, but also provide insights into many aspects of late Qing China, as well as a missionary view of foreigners' life in China. There are a number of photographs.

213 Description de la ville de Peking [sic]: pour servir à l'intelligence du plan de cette ville, gravé par les soins de M. de l'Isle. (A description of the city of Peking, to aid in understanding the layout of that city, engraved at the undertaking of M. de l'Isle.)
Joseph Nicholas de l'Isle, Alexandre Guy Pingré. Paris: J. Th. Herissant, 1765. 45p. maps.
J. N. de l'Isle was a cartographer, geographer and astronomer active in Paris, together with his brother, in the mid-18th century. On the basis of information he acquired through over thirty years' correspondence with the French Jesuit missionaries in China, especially with Antoine Gaubil (see item no. 208), de l'Isle engraved a set of maps of Beijing and of individual sites, to which he subsequently added the written descriptions contained in this book along with the six maps and a map of China. The basic features, such as the walls, gates, lakes and the Imperial City, are clearly recognizable from the maps, which attest to the accuracy of the original information from which he worked. He introduces

his account of the city with a short history of its foundation and concludes his detailed descriptions with observations on the *li* or Chinese mile and on the longitude and latitude of Beijing. This is a rare book, but it is of great interest in establishing the extent of European knowledge about China 250 years ago.

214   Documents in Chinese from the Chinese secretary's office, British legation Peking, 1861-1939.
P. D. Coates.   *Modern Asian Studies*, vol. 17, no. 2 (1983), p. 239-55.

Although the title may sound somewhat dull, this is in fact an interesting and informative account of the functioning of a very important part of the British diplomatic mission in Beijing. The Chinese secretary was a British official, a member of the consular service, who oversaw the work of the office that handled all correspondence with the Chinese government. He and his office were therefore at the heart of Britain's diplomacy in China, and those who worked there often went on to more important things. Coates has also written *The China consuls: British consular officers 1843-1943* (Hong Kong; Oxford; New York: Oxford University Press, 1988. 619p. bibliog. map), which touches on the Beijing legation and the consulate-general in Tianjin.

215   The dragon empress: life and times of Tz'u-hsi, 1835-1908, empress dowager of China.
Marina Warner.   New York: Macmillan; London: Weidenfeld & Nicholson, 1972. Reprinted, London: Cardinal, 1974. 271p. maps.

The Dowager Empress Cixi (Tz'u-hsi is the older Wade-Giles transliteration) is widely credited with bringing down the Manchu empire in China, which collapsed within two years of her death in 1908. Warner's biography, based entirely on Western sources, is a lively account of the life and times of the 'Old Buddha' who dominated, for better or generally for worse, the last years of the Manchus. Most of her life was lived out against the backdrop of Beijing's Forbidden City and the Summer Palace, and, more distantly, the capital city itself. Not the least bizarre of the events involving her life, which included the siege of the legations in 1900 and tea parties with foreign ladies thereafter, was the robbing of her grave by bandits at the Eastern Qing tombs in 1928. There have been many books about Cixi. One similar account, with perhaps more emphasis on the sexual side of Cixi's life, can be found in Sterling Seagrave, *Dragon lady: the life and legend of the last empress of China* (New York: Knopf, 1992. 601p. maps. bibliog.), while Daniele Varè's elegant account, written in the 1930s, is still enjoyable to read: Daniele Varè, *The last of the empresses and the passing of the old China to the new* (London: John Murray, 1936, cheap ed. 1938. 258p.). Cixi and her life and times also feature in two works by the supposed Manchu princess, Der Ling, *Old Buddha* (New York: Dodd, Mead & Co., 1929. 347p.), and *Two years in the Forbidden City* (New York: Moffat Yard, 1912. Reprinted, San Francisco: Chinese Materials Centre, 1977. 383p.), and in many other books.

216   The dragon wakes: China and the West, 1793-1911.
Christopher Hibbert.   New York: Harper & Row; London: Longman, 1970. 427p. map. bibliog.

This very traditional, Western-orientated history of China enjoyed much popularity when it was first published. Hibbert writes well, concentrating on the story rather than on any deep analysis, and portrays an unchanging China, buffeted by Western attacks. Beijing, and the surrounding area, features frequently, whether in his account of Lord Macartney's visit in 1793 or the capture and torture of Sir Harry Parkes in 1860, as the essential backdrop to the narrative. There are numerous entertaining illustrations, including many of Beijing.

217 A dream of Tartary: the origins and misfortunes of Henry P'u Yi.
Henry McAleavy.   London: George Allen & Unwin Ltd, 1963.
292p. map.

Before China's 'last emperor' had written his own account of his life and misfortunes, Henry McAleavy, then a lecturer at the School of Oriental and African Studies of the University of London, had pieced together this account, relaying mainly on Chinese and Japanese sources. It remains an important, if often unacknowledged source, for the life of the boy emperor, who would, in Chinese eyes, attract enmity as the Japanese puppet emperor of 'Manzhouguo'. Much of the focus of McAleavy's book is on Pu Yi's ancestry and his time in Beijing from his birth in 1905 to his expulsion from the Forbidden City in 1924. This book, therefore, is an ideal way to learn of the ways of the imperial court in its last manifestation, as well as an account of Pu Yi's life in Manzhouguo. For events after that, the reader is advised to turn to Pu Yi's autobiography (see item no. 136).

218 Embassies in the East: the story of the British and their embassies in China, Japan and Korea from 1859 to the present.
James Edward Hoare, foreword by Lord Hurd of Westwell.
Richmond, England: Curzon Press, 1999. 239p. bibliog. (British Embassy Series, no. 1).

Based on archives, a wide range of published material and many personal reminiscences, this book uses the history of the British embassy buildings to tell the stories of the people who worked and often lived in them, to illustrate Britain's role in East Asia from its days as the mightiest power in the world to its more humble position in the 1990s. About one-third of the book is devoted to the British Legation, later Embassy in Beijing, from its establishment in 1861, through the heady days of the Boxer uprising, its eclipse in the Second World War, and the forced move from the grandeur of a former palace to the more modest buildings of post-1949 China. There are incidental descriptions of the city and its broader history over the same period. Similar ground is covered in the same author's article 'Building politics: the British embassy Peking 1949-1992' (*Pacific Review*, vol. 7, no. 1 [1994], p. 67-78), which concentrates on what happened after the establishment of the PRC. Diplomatic life in Beijing also figures in Beryl Smedley, *Partners in diplomacy* (Ferring, England: The Harley Press, 1990. 214p. bibliog.).

219 The Englishman in China during the Victorian era as illustrated in the career of Sir Rutherford Alcock K.C.B., D.C.L. many years consul and minister in China and Japan.
Alexander Michie.   Edinburgh, Scotland; London: William Blackwood & Sons, 1900. 2 vols. maps.

This very standard Victorian biography is far more concerned with the public than the private life of Sir Rutherford Alcock, the first British minister to Japan (1859-65), and subsequently minister to China. However, it does contain occasional insights on Beijing, including a chapter (vol. 2, p. 130-55) devoted to a description of the life of the foreign community in the capital in the late 1860s. Apart from that chapter, there is much on the difficulties of diplomacy in Beijing, and on government structures in the late Qing, all of which make this a still valuable book today, especially as no other biography of Alcock has yet appeared. There are interesting photographs of Chinese officials and of buildings such as the Roman Catholic cathedral.

220 The foreign establishment in China in the early twentieth century.
Albert Feuerwerker. Ann Arbor, Michigan: Centre for Chinese Studies, University of Michigan, 1976. 120p. (Michigan Papers in Chinese Studies, no. 20).

A useful background note that explains the origins, makeup and functions of the foreign community in China at the height of its power in the years after 1900. Aspects of foreigners' lives in both Beijing and Tianjin are dealt with, including the foreign military garrisons that developed after the Boxer incident. There is no index. A shorter version of the paper, which should be regarded as the more authoritative version, appears in the volume on Republican China in the *Cambridge History of China* (q.v.).

221 Foreigners within the gates: the legations at Peking.
Michael J. Moser, Yeone Wei-Chih Moser. Hong Kong; Oxford: Oxford University Press, 1993. 158p. maps. bibliog.

This fully illustrated book traces the history of the Beijing legation quarter – the site of the foreign diplomatic missions – from its inception in the early 1860s, through the excitement of the 1900 siege, to its subsequent development into a unique foreign enclave in China's capital, with its own laws and regulations, military guards and highly developed, if incestuous, social life. The book concentrates on the years before the Second World War; the last years of the old order (1937-41) are dealt with in three brief paragraphs, while a final chapter looks at what has happened to the quarter since 1949. While some parts of the quarter were still used as diplomatic premises until c. 1959, and thereafter the Chinese Communists made use of the old buildings, they never liked the area. Today, what little remains is under constant threat from the rapid redevelopment that is sweeping the city. The Mosers therefore record a world which is rapidly disappearing, and if there is no great depth to their study, it is nevertheless an interesting tribute to the past.

222 Guide to Peking: with maps of Peking and country round Peking.
Mrs Archibald Little (Alicia Bewicke). Tianjin, China: Tientsin Press Ltd, 1904. 91p. maps.

The British novelist Alicia Bewicke (1845-1926) was married to a British businessman trading in China, whose name she took in authoring a series of books on life and conditions in China as well as novels with a Chinese setting and children's stories. She was an early campaigner against the practice of footbinding. Her *Guide to Peking* was published against the backdrop of the then recent siege of the legation quarter in the capital (1900), but is not unduly coloured by this event. She acknowledges her recourse to earlier foreign works on Beijing in preparing her guide, which lists the customary sights, not all open to visitors, in and around the capital and which extends as far as Beidaihe, Qinhuangdao and Shanhaiguan. Two appendices name the six government and other boards and official and rank distinctions. The same author's *Round about my Peking garden* (London: T. Fisher Unwin, 1905. 284p.), probably inspired by the same visit to Beijing, is more discursive and random, but is very pleasingly written and has an interesting selection of photographic plates.

223 Hart and the Chinese Customs.
Stanley F. Wright.   Belfast, Northern Ireland: Wm. Mullan & Son (Publishers) Ltd, for the Queen's University Belfast, 1950. 949p. bibliog.

Sir Robert Hart (1835-1911) originally joined the British consular service in China, but he is most associated with the Chinese Imperial Maritime Customs Service, of which he was Inspector-General from 1863 to 1906. During that time, he lived in Beijing, only making visits home to Europe in 1866 and 1878. Hart was a major figure on the Beijing foreign scene, not only as head of the customs organization, but also as a knowledgeable student of things Chinese. In addition, he organized a band of Chinese musicians, who often provided music – of a sort – at diplomatic functions, and he was present in the British legation during the 1900 siege. This biography by Wright, a former member of the customs' staff, relies heavily on official customs' records and British Foreign Office records. It is less concerned with Hart the man than with Hart the public official, but occasional glimpses of Beijing and the Beijing foreign community do come through, and there is much on subjects like the Boxers. Hart's letters as Inspector-General are available in *The I. G. in Peking: letters of Robert Hart, Chinese Maritime Customs, 1868-1907,* edited by John King Fairbank, Katherine Frost Bruner, Elizabeth Macleod Matheson, introduction by Lester Knox Little (Cambridge, Massachusetts: Harvard University Press, 1975. 2 vols.), and *Archives of China's Imperial Maritime Customs: confidential correspondence between Robert Hart and James Duncan Campbell 1874-1907*, compiled by the Historical Archives of China Institute of Modern History, Chinese Academy of Social Science, chief editors Chen Xiafei, Han Rongfang (Beijing: Foreign Languages Press, 1990. 4 vols.). Hart's early journals have been published as *Entering China's service: Robert Hart's journals 1854-63*, edited with narratives by Katherine Frost Bruner, John King Fairbank, Richard J. Smith (Cambridge, Massachusetts: Council on East Asian Studies, Harvard University, distributed by Harvard University Press, 1986. 427p. bibliog. [Harvard East Asia Monographs, no. 125]), and *Robert Hart and China's early modernization: his journals 1863-66*, edited with narratives by Richard J. Smith, John King Fairbank, Katherine Frost Bruner (Cambridge, Massachusetts: Council on East Asian Studies, Harvard University, distributed by Harvard University Press, 1991. 583p. maps. bibliog. [Harvard East Asia Monographs, no. 155]). All are full of incidental information about Beijing and its foreign community. Hart's own account of the siege and the events surrounding it can be found in Robert Hart, *These from the land of Sinim: essays on the Chinese question* (London: Chapman & Hall, 1901. 254p. maps). An older work, by his niece, has now mainly curiosity value, although there are a few good stories about Hart and his position in Beijing, and some interesting photographs of the city: Juliet Bredon, *Sir Robert Hart: the romance of a great career* (London: Hutchinson & Co., 1909. 252p.).

224 History in three keys: the Boxers as event, experience, and myth.
Paul A. Cohen.   New York; Chichester, England: Columbia University Press, 1997. 429p. maps. bibliog.

Paul Cohen is a distinguished historian of modern China. In this book on the Boxer movement, he first outlines the 'events', the course of the movement from its beginnings in Shandong province to its culmination in the anti-foreigner riots in Tianjin and Beijing in the summer of 1900. He then probes the conflicting and distorted 'experiences' that Chinese and foreigners often had of each other and shows how natural and economic disasters in northern China at the end of the 19th century came to be linked by many Chinese with the foreign presence in the country. He then examines the ways in which 'myths' were constructed by both Chinese and Westerners around the Boxer movement, the Chinese responses varying to reflect the agendas of reform, nationalism and communism. The Western response to the Boxers is well known. Much of the value of Cohen's book lies in its elucidation of Chinese attitudes.

225 History of the Peking summer palaces under the Ch'ing dynasty.
Carroll Brown Malone. Urbana, Illinois: University of Illinois, 1934. 247p. maps. bibliog.

This attractive book uses Chinese and Western sources to chart the development, flourishing and decline from the late 17th to the late 19th century of the parks laid out to the northwest of Beijing by rulers of the Qing dynasty. The Qing emperor, Kangxi, drawn to this area, set about the systematic construction of a park, the Changchunyuan, which has since been demolished. His son, Yongzheng, started work on the Yuanmingyuan, which his own son, Qianlong, consolidated. Though intended primarily as private retreats, these palaces were nonetheless the setting for various state events, and the Yuanmingyuan (known in English as the Old Summer Palace) was looted and burnt in the ferocious Anglo-French revenge for the maltreatment of British and French prisoners in 1860. The Empress Dowager Cixi spent much time and funds from the 1880s onwards on creating the Yiheyuan (the New Summer Palace). The text is complemented by reproductions of contemporary prints, drawings, engravings and photographs particularly of the Yuanmingyuan and by a very full bibliography.

226 Indiscreet letters from Peking, being the notes of an eye-witness, which set forth in some detail, from day to day, the real story of the siege and sack of a distressed capital in 1900 – the year of great tribulation.
'Edited by B. L. Putnam Weale' [Bertram Lennox Simpson]. New York: Dodd, Mead & Co., 1907. Reprinted, 1922. 447p. map.

Since this book's first appearance, there have been debates about its value and authenticity. It is certainly full of scandal about those taking part in the 1900 siege of the legations, with allegations of cowardice and incompetence levelled against several important participants, and the author, B. Lennox Simpson, was certainly there. But if it was a genuine account, why did he write under a pseudonym, and why was his version so at variance with others? Probably nobody will now ever know, but the *Indiscreet letters* remain a source of entertainment, even if not the truth about what happened in the legations.

227 The international relations of the Chinese empire.
Hosea Ballou Morse. London; New York: Longmans, Green & Co., 1910-18. Reprinted, Taipei: Ch'eng-wen, 1965. 3 vols. maps. bibliog.

While there has been much historical research produced since Morse first wrote his survey history, it remains a principal source for the history of China under the late Qing dynasty. It is also of great importance for the history of Beijing. For many of the events that Morse describes, such as the forced opening of the capital in 1860-61, the background to the Tianjin massacre of 1870, or the siege of the legations in 1900 and the subsequent settlement, this remains a primary source, for Morse was an assiduous reader of contemporary published material and occasionally had access to private archives.

228   The last stand of Chinese conservatism: the T'ung-Chih restoration, 1862-74.
Mary Clambaugh Wright.   Stanford, California: Stanford University Press, 1957. 426p. bibliog. (Stanford Studies, in History, Economics and Political Science, no. 13).

This major political study of the Chinese reaction to the changes imposed on China by the 1858 and 1860s treaties contains much incidental information about Beijing and its development as a diplomatic centre after 1861. Wright covers the establishment and development of China's first modern Foreign Office in some detail, and the court and its intrigues is never far away.

229   Lettres édifiantes et curieuses de Chine par des missionnaires jésuites 1702-76. (Letters, edifying and curious, relating to China, by the Jesuit missionaries 1702-76.)
Chronology, introduction, notes and references by Isabelle Vissière, Jean-Louis Vissière.   Paris: Garnier-Flammarion, 1979. 502p. maps. bibliog.

The Jesuit mission in Beijing, which began with the visit of Matteo Ricci at the end of the Ming dynasty, and which lasted until the suppression of the order in the 1770s, was a prime source of information about China throughout Europe. One of the most important sources of this information was the collection of letters published from 1702 onwards relating to the mission's work. What was originally confined to China alone soon expanded to cover other areas where the Jesuits operated, and the series became known as *Lettres édifiantes et curieuses des missions étrangères par quelques missionnaires de la Compagnie de Jésus.* By the 1780-81 edition, edited by P. de Querbeuf, there were twenty-six parts, in twelve volumes. As well as information about the Jesuits' mission and its buildings in Beijing, there is information on the life of the city's inhabitants, the court and the emperors. This selection, which gives a good indication of the overall contents, is accompanied by an introduction which explains how the letters came to be written, why they made such an impact, and on whom they made it. A useful bibliographical note covers the various editions, and lists some of the works that derived from the collection, as well as other related works. There are also notes on some of the principal missionaries and a chronology from the founding of the Jesuits in 1540 to the Macartney embassy of 1792-94, whose participants were able to verify many of the stories told by the Jesuits.

230 Life of the emperors and empresses in the forbidden city.
Edited by Lu Yanzhen, Li Wenshan, Wan Yi, translated by Wang
Dianming, Yang Qihua, photographs by Meng Zi, Yang Yin, Zhang
Guanrong, E Yi, Ou Zhipei, Chen Shubo, Liu Yingjie, Li Miao.
Beijing: China Travel and Tourism Press, 1983. 2nd ed. 121p. map.

This album, with texts and captions in English, Japanese and Chinese, fills in some of the
details on the daily routine of imperial life of the Qing emperors and their consorts in the
Forbidden City in Beijing. Information on ceremonies, meals, attire, furnishings,
entertainment, cultural and religious life is illustrated by fine full-colour photographs.

**231 Morrison of Peking: explorer, foreign correspondent, political
adviser and one of the makers of the Chinese republic.**
Cyril Pearl. Sydney: Angus & Robertson, 1967. Reprinted,
Harmondsworth, England; Ringwood, Australia: Penguin Books,
1970. 431p. bibliog.

George Morrison, for many years the London *Times*' correspondent in Beijing, was a
towering figure among the foreign community of the capital city in the last years of the
Manchu emperors and the early years of the republic. He gave his name to what became
the principal shopping street of the city (now again known by its Chinese name,
Wangfujing), collected a massive library that was eventually purchased by the Toyo
Bunko in Tokyo, and, though he seems to have known little or no Chinese, established a
reputation as the foreigner best informed about Chinese politics. He was present at the
siege in 1900 and at most of the other major developments in China between 1895 and
his death in 1920, though it was widely felt that he failed to see the faults of the new
republic. Pearl tells the story of this somewhat larger than life figure with great verve,
making much use of Morrison's correspondence (see item no. 209), and including much
information about Beijing.

232 Notes on Peking and its neighbourhood.
W. Lockhart. London: Royal Geographical Society, 1866. 29p.
map.

Lockhart (1811-96) was an early British medical missionary to China. He established a
hospital in Beijing in 1861 after the city was opened up the year before to foreign
residents. His lecture to the Royal Geographical Society ranges fairly widely from the
tributary system which brought Mongolian and Korean emissaries to Beijing, through
observations on the decay of the Qing dynasty to a description of the appearance and
administration of the city, including the Muslim community, beggars and executions. He
visited the ruins of Yuanmingyuan, which was destroyed in 1860, and describes their
condition.

233 Palikao (1860): le sac du palais d'été et la prise de Pékin.
(Palikao [1860]: the sack of the summer palace and the taking of
Peking.)
Raymond Bourgerie, Pierre Lesouef. Paris: Economica, 1995.
158p. maps. bibliog. (Collection Campagnes et Stratégies).

In this military history the pillage of the Summer Palace in October 1860 is presented as
one episode, if the most destructive, in the joint Anglo-French military campaign of that

year to oblige the Chinese to ratify the Treaty of Tianjin (1858) and to allow permanent diplomatic missions in Beijing. The Chinese had successfully repulsed an earlier expedition in 1859 to enforce the treaty. The 1860 expedition, under Generals Montauban and Hope Grant, seized the forts at Dagu, captured Tianjin and then routed the Chinese at the bridge of Baliqiao (Montauban was later named Count of Palikao). The authors do not excuse the looting of the Palace, although they claim that Chinese also participated and refer to the British practice of seizing and auctioning enemy valuables, and they make it clear that the palace was fired on the orders of the British diplomat Lord Elgin. They are primarily interested in analysing the military and strategic aspects of the expedition as experienced by the French side. The book has a short bibliography of works in French and will appeal to military historians.

234 A particular account of the emperor of China's gardens near Pekin: in a letter from F[ather] Attiret, a French missionary, now employ'd by that emperor to paint the apartments in those gardens, to his friend at Paris.
Translated by Sir Harry Beaumont.   London: R. Dodsley, 1752. 50p.

The letter in question, dated 1 November 1743, was translated from volume 27, published in 1749, of correspondence from French Jesuit missionaries that appeared in a total of thirty-four volumes spread over more than seventy years, under the title of *Lettres édifiantes et curieuses* (see item no. 229). In this translation, Attiret (1702-68) describes his journey to Beijing, confined in a boat and a litter, then breaks into a vivid and detailed account of the gardens and pavilions at Yuanmingyuan. He describes the miniature 'town' erected within the park where the emperor and his family attended 'fairs' served by the eunuchs, notes the rich decoration and furnishing of the buildings and praises the variety and inventiveness of Chinese crafts. He notes both the symmetry in building layout and the Chinese 'natural and wild' approach to landscape design. His description is invaluable as among the few firsthand Western accounts of the monuments in Qianlong's capital. The Yuanmingyuan continued to fascinate Western writers and has given rise to a great deal of literature. Two examples, from very different periods, are: John Barrow, *Travels in China: containing descriptions, observations and comparisons collected in the course of a short residence at the imperial palace of Yuen-min-yuan, and on a subsequent journey through the country from Peking to Canton* (London: T. Cadwell & W. Davies, 1804. 2nd ed. 1806. Reprinted, Taipei: Ch'eng-wen, 1972. 632p.), a work deriving from the Macartney mission; and Hope Danby, *The garden of perfect brightness: the history of the Yuan Ming Yuan and of the emperors who lived there* (Chicago, Illinois: H. Regenery Company, 1950. 239p. map).

235 Peking and the Pekingese during the first year of the British embassy in Peking.
David F. Rennie.   London: John Murray, 1865. 2 vols.

Rennie was a doctor with the British expeditionary force to China in 1860, who stayed on as a member of the British legation after its establishment in 1861. He provides good descriptions of the former palace which became the legation building, and the problems that the British and other foreigners faced in establishing themselves in China's capital. There are also accounts of travels in and around Beijing, including expeditions to the Great Wall and beyond, and to the hills. The book has numerous illustrations, engraved from early photographs.

236 Peking in the early seventeenth century.
Keith Pratt. London; Oxford: Oxford University Press, 1971. 51p.
maps. (Cities and Societies).

Clearly intended for high-school and first-year university students. It would nonetheless
serve as a comprehensive and illuminating introduction to the historical city for the
general reader. The 17th century was marked by the change of dynasty from the Ming to
the Qing, and both eras are touched on in the book. Its ten chapters examine the city itself,
the emperor, the people of Beijing, houses and gardens, work, dress and food, transport,
temples and festivals, religion and funerals, and the region beyond Beijing. The
availability of sources doubtless accounts for the greater emphasis on the life of the rich,
but all classes are covered. The illustrations are taken from contemporary prints or are
photographs of contemporary objects. This is overall an attractive volume.

237 Public service and private fortune: the life of Lord Macartney 1737-1806.
Edited by Patrick Roebuck. Belfast, Northern Ireland: Ulster
Historical Foundation, 1983. 376p. maps. bibliog.

While all the essays in this book provide useful background on the life and times of Lord
Macartney, chapter 7 (p. 216-43), by J. L. Cranmer-Byng of the University of Toronto,
describes the major mission that Macartney led to China in the 1790s. Although
Macartney's mission failed in its main objective, the formal establishment of trade
between China and Britain, it succeeded in other ways. Macartney reached Beijing and
then followed the emperor to his summer retreat at Chengde. From the point of view of
the capital, the main interest is in the account that Macartney provided of the city and its
palaces. Cranmer-Byng includes some of this material here, but the reader should also
consult his edition of Macartney's diary and journal: see George Macartney, *An embassy
to China: being the journal kept by Lord Macartney during his embassy to the Emperor
Ch'ien-lung, 1793-94*, edited, with an introduction and notes by J. L. Cranmer-Byng
(London: Longmans, 1962; Hamden, Connecticut: Archon Books, 1963. Reprinted, St
Clair Shores, Michigan: Scholarly Press, 1972. 421p. maps).

238 Le quartier diplomatique de Pékin: étude historique et juridique. (The diplomatic quarter of Peking: historical and juridical study.)
Marcel Trouche. Paris: Librairie Technique et Economique, [n.d.],
after 1935. 208p. maps. bibliog.

The experience of the siege of the foreign legations in 1900 in Beijing left the diplomatic
community determined to strengthen its position against the possibility of renewed
Chinese aggression. Protocols established first the status and limits of the quarter (1901),
then the distribution of sites and the management of its defences (1904). The quarter was
to control its own policing, and no Chinese could live within its boundaries. The
diplomatic quarter was, in fact, a unique institution and could not really be compared with
the foreign concessions in China. The protocols and the administration that represented it
had no clear foundation in international law. The author examines in detail the principles
and practice of its functioning, even challenging the foundations on which the diplomatic
corps proceeded. He throws light on the uneasy relationship between the foreign powers
and China and on relations between the legations within the quarter. The maps and
bibliography are invaluable for those interested in its status and history. An English-

language study, covering much the same ground, is Robert Moore Duncan, *Peiping municipality and the diplomatic quarter* (Beijing: Department of Political Science, Yenching University, 1933. 153p. maps).

239 Ritual & diplomacy: the Macartney mission to China 1792-94: papers presented at the 1992 conference of the British association for Chinese studies, marking the bicentenary of the Macartney mission to China.
Edited by Robert A. Bickers.   London: Wellsweep Press/British Association for Chinese Studies, 1993. 93p.

A selection of essays from a symposium to mark the bicentenary of the Macartney mission to China. There is a generally revisionist air about the essays, which strive to show that the Macartney mission, in both its Beijing and Chengde stages, was more successful than recent historians have allowed. Although there is no general bibliography, some of the individual essays have their own bibliographies, hinting at a much wider debate.

240 The Russian ecclesiastical mission in Peking during the 18th century.
Eric Widmer.   Cambridge, Massachusetts; London: East Asian Research Centre, Harvard University, 1976. 262p. map. bibliog. (Harvard East Asian Monographs, no. 69).

Few visiting Beijing today realize that the vast Russian (formerly Soviet) embassy situated in the north east of the old city was until the 1950s one of several sites occupied by a Russian ecclesiastical mission that began in the 18th century. The Russian mission, dogged by scandals and shortages of funds, never matched the importance of the Jesuits, and yet its presence in Beijing, and Russian political interest in China, make an interesting story. Widmer's book, although primarily intended for the specialist, will appeal to those who are interested in the lesser by-ways of history as well. The appendices list all the Russian priests and students who made up the seven groups sent to China between 1716 and 1794, as well as the rulers of China and Russia during the same period.

241 The siege at Peking.
Peter Fleming.   London: Rupert Hart-Davies, 1959. Reprinted, with an introduction by David Bonavia, Hong Kong; Oxford; New York: Oxford University Press, 1983. (Oxford in Asia Series); 1986. 273p. maps. bibliog. (Oxford Paperbacks).

The siege of the Beijing diplomatic missions in 1900 marked the culmination of the movement known to Westerners as the 'Boxer rebellion'. For fifty-five days, rebel forces and Imperial troops surrounded the legation quarter in the heart of the city, subjecting it to regular bombardments. Inside the area, several hundred foreigners and thousands of Chinese Christians existed behind makeshift barriers, with steadily diminishing food supplies, and fought off the various attacks launched against them. The raising of the siege on 14 August 1900 was followed by looting and by summary executions of Chinese, which has left a residue of bitterness in China. Peter Fleming, an explorer and writer, provides a well-written and exciting account of these events, using Western sources. While there are more profound studies of the Boxer movement, this book will still appeal to the general reader. David Bonavia's introduction provides more background on the events leading to the siege and to its consequences, as well as drawing attention to some of Fleming's blind spots.

242   Le siège de Pe-t'ang dans Pekin en 1900, le commandant Paul Henry et ses trente marins. (The siege of Beitang in Peking in 1900, Commander Henry and his thirty marines.) Leon Henry.   Beijing: Imprimerie des lazaristes de Pe-t'ang, 1921. 366p. maps.

When covering the events of summer 1900 in Beijing, most accounts concentrate on the siege of the legation quarter. In the north of the city, however, a group of French marines, together with the clergy of the Beitang Cathedral and large numbers of Chinese Roman Catholics, went through an even more horrific siege, with far fewer supplies or military resources. This somewhat pious work records their experiences. More information on this aspect of 1900 can be found in Jean Marie Planchet, *Documents sur les martyrs de Pékin pendant la persécution des Boxeurs* (Documents about the Peking martyrs during the Boxer persecution) (Beijing: Imprimerie des lazaristes de Pe-t'ang, 2 vols. 1922-23. map).

243   The siege in Peking: China against the world, by an eye witness. William Alexander Parsons Martin.   New York; Chicago, Illinois; Toronto: Fleming H. Revell Company, 1900. Reprinted, Wilmington, Delaware: Scholarly Resources, 1972. 190p. map.

In 1900, W. A. P. Martin, by then a long-term resident of China and the translator of Wheaton's *International Law* into Chinese, was the president of the Imperial University in Beijing (now Beijing University). As the Boxer movement increasingly threatened the capital in that year, he and his foreign colleagues abandoned their exposed position in the city and moved into the legation quarter. There they experienced the siege and Martin's account, written soon after the end of the affair, has an immediacy which still remains fresh, and is still of value, though perhaps his view of how the Boxer movement had developed and its relationship with the court was rather simplistic. There are many interesting illustrations including several contemporary photographs. Martin also wrote *A cycle of Cathay, or China, south and north. With personal reminiscences* (New York; Chicago, Illinois; Toronto: F. H. Revell Co., 1896. 464p. map), which includes some material on Beijing.

244   The siege of the Peking legations: a diary. Lancelot Giles, edited with an introduction, *Chinese anti-foreignism and the Boxer uprising*, by Leslie R. Marchant, foreword by Robert Scott.   Nedlands, Australia: University of Western Australia, 1970. 212p. map. bibliog.

Lancelot Giles was the youngest son of Herbert Giles (see item nos. 21 and 176), the well-known British Sinologist, from whom he later became estranged. Like his father, Lancelot joined the British China consular service, and in 1899 was posted to the Beijing legation as a student interpreter. His diary, sent home to his father and published in an abbreviated form in the *Christ College Magazine*, survived and eventually surfaced in Australia. Like that of his fellow student, W. H. Hewlett (see item no. 245), it is an artless but lively account of the siege and the lives of the foreign community during that event. The foreword by Sir Robert Scott, himself a later member of the China consular service, gives much detail about the service and about Giles, who ended his career as consul-general in Tianjin. The detailed introduction, which takes up more than half the book, gives the wider context of the Boxer movement and the siege, and much information about Beijing during the crisis. There are excellent photographs.

245 The siege of the Peking legations June to August 1900.
W. Meyrick Hewlett. Harrow-on-the Hill, England: F. W. Provost for the editors of the 'Harrovian', 1900. 75p.

This little book, part letter and part diary, is a fascinating eye-witness account of events in Beijing in the summer of 1900, as seen by a twenty-year old. Meyrick Hewlett was a student interpreter at the British legation in Beijing at the time of the Boxer rebellion in 1900. Taken from his studies when the Boxers began their attack on the legations in June 1900, he found himself appointed secretary to the British minister, Sir Claude MacDonald, and therefore right at the heart of events, for Sir Claude, a former soldier, was designated commander-in-chief of the garrison resisting the Boxer attacks. The tone is somewhat *Boy's Own Paper*, as might be expected, although from time to time Hewlett realizes that he ought to be more serious. A briefer account of the same events appears in his autobiography, *Forty years in China* (London: Macmillan & Co., 1944. 262p. maps). He never served again in Beijing.

246 Sir Harry Parkes in China.
Stanley Lane-Poole. London: Methuen & Co., 1901. 386p.

Sir Harry Parkes (1828-85), a major figure in 19th-century Sino-British relations, went out to China as a boy of fourteen. He spent much of his career as a British consular and later diplomatic officer in China, although from 1865 to 1883, he was the second British minister to Japan. In 1860, he was a member of Lord Elgin's expedition to Beijing to force the Chinese government to accept the treaties ending the Second Opium War, which led to his capture and imprisonment. It was in consequence of this action, and the execution of others captured at the same time as Parkes, that Lord Elgin ordered the burning of part of the Summer Palace. In 1883, Parkes returned to Beijing as minister, and letters from him and from his daughters describe the city and the British legation as it was in those years. This account, written by a long-standing admirer of Parkes, is drawn from the China sections of Frederick Victor Dickins, Stanley Lane-Poole, *Life of Sir Harry Parkes* (London: Macmillan, 1894, 2 vols.).

247 Spatial order and police in imperial Beijing.
Alison Dray-Novey. *The Journal of Asian Studies*, vol. 52, no. 4 (November 1993), p. 885-922. maps. bibliog.

This substantial article, derived from the author's 1981 Harvard PhD on the policing of imperial Beijing, deals with the emergence of a uniformed, armed and bureaucratically controlled police force in the Qing period. She argues that this development casts doubt on the generally held belief that such modern police forces are associated with industrialization, and that instead they are the product of the growth in size of a city, and the consequent emergence of different groups whose interests may conflict, and therefore need control. To illustrate this theme, she draws on a variety of accounts of Beijing from Western and Chinese sources, casting much light on the city and its people generally, as well as on the specific area of policing.

248 Through Peking's sewer gate: relief of the Boxer siege, 1900-01.
Richard A. Steel, edited and introduced by George W. Carrington,
foreword by Sir Colin Crowe. New York; Washington, DC;
Atlanta, Georgia; Los Angeles; Chicago: Vantage Press, 1985. 101p.
maps.

Lieutenant Steel was a member of the British contingent in the multinational relief force
sent from Tianjin to Beijing in 1900 to break the Boxer siege of the legation quarter. The
British group was mobilized in India and contained a number of Indian troops, some of
whom appear in photographs in this book. Indeed, Sikh soldiers were said to have been
the first to enter the quarter by the 'sewer gate'. Steel remained in Beijing from 1900 to
1901. The book is an edited collection of letters to his family. They do not add much to
the history of the siege but they do offer a lively account of the action as seen by a junior
officer. The book has some interesting photographs of members of the international force
and of old Beijing.

**249 Der verboden stad/The Forbidden City: Hofcultuur von der
Chinese keizers (1644-1911)/Court culture of the Chinese
emperors (1644-1911).**
Introductory essay by Shan Guoqiang, foreword by Wim Crouel.
Rotterdam, the Netherlands: Museum Baymans-van Beunigan, 1990.
245p. maps.

An impressive catalogue, with text and captions in Dutch and English, of an exhibition
on life in the Forbidden City during the Qing dynasty, showing court dress, furniture and
the interiors of the buildings. The introductory essay provides the historical context, and
the quality of the illustrations is very good.

**250 *Wayfoong*: the Hongkong and Shanghai Banking Corporation: a
study of East Asia's transformation, political, financial and
economic, during the last hundred years.**
Morris Collis, art editor Charles Rosner. London: Faber & Faber
Ltd, 1965. 269p.

Morris Collis has produced a lavishly illustrated, popular and uncritical account of the
Hong Kong and Shanghai Bank's operations in Asia from its foundation in 1865 to its
centenary year. As with all his works, the text flows smoothly, and he has a good eye for
an anecdote. Beijing and Tianjin both feature, the former mainly because of the work of
Guy Hillier, the bank's manager there around 1900. Collis also includes an account of the
siege of the legations, although in little depth. A more detailed account of the bank and
its China operations can be found in Frank H. H. King, *The history of the Hong Kong and
Shanghai Banking Corporation* (Cambridge, England; New York: Cambridge University
Press, 1987-88. 3 vols. bibliog.).

251 The Yi He Tuan movement of 1900.
Compilation group of the 'History of Modern China' series.
Beijing: Foreign Languages Press, 1976. 133p. maps.

This translation of part of a standard Chinese textbook on modern Chinese history gives
a Chinese account of the events of 1898-1900 usually known as the 'Boxer rebellion'. The

Boxers are here given their more prosaic name of the 'Society for Righteousness and Harmony' and the story is told from a Marxist perspective. For the authors, the Boxers are revolutionary heroes who succeeded in smashing imperialist advances at various stages. In this version, the siege of the Beijing legations becomes less a tale of foreign bravery than one of foreign intrigue designed to dismember China. Similarly, the Boxer attack on the foreign concessions (residence areas) at Tianjin is seen as having been provoked by the foreigners. Most of the anti-foreign comments, especially about the behaviour of the foreign troops who relieved the legations, are based on Western sources, and while the book's quotations from Chairman Mao would probably not appear in a 1990s textbook, the story would be told in broadly the same way.

A research guide to China-coast newspapers 1822-1911.
See item no. 507.

Republic of China (1912-49)

252 Baedeker's Russia 1914.
Karl Baedeker.   Newton Abbot, England: David & Charles Newton; London: George Allen & Unwin, 1971. Originally published as *Russia with Teheran, Port Arthur, and Peking: handbook for travellers*, Leipzig, Germany: Karl Baedeker, Publishers; London: George Allen & Unwin Ltd; New York: Charles Scribner's Sons, 1914. 590p. maps.

This facsimile edition of one of the great pre-First World War travel guides contains some forty pages on China, mostly devoted to Beijing, as one of the termini of the Trans-Siberian railway. Other places around the capital are included, but in much less detail. Although much has changed since 1914, it would still be possible to tour Beijing using this guide, for the main sights are still very much as they were in 1914, when some areas of the Forbidden City, hitherto closed off to all but the imperial family, had just been opened to the public. Other sights regarded as important in 1914, such as Legation Street, have scarcely survived the rapid development which has taken place since the late 1970s.

253 The China yearbook.
London: Routledge, 1912-28; Tianjin, China: Tientsin Press, 1912-30; Shanghai: North China Daily News and Herald, 1931-39. Reprinted, New York: Gordon Press, 1977. 20 vols.

This yearbook, produced under the auspices of China's most important treaty-port newspaper, is a major original source for information on all aspects of China from the revolution which overthrew the Qing (Manchu) dynasty to the Sino-Japanese War. Political and economic developments in both Beijing and Tianjin receive detailed coverage, and the volumes also contain much biographical information about Chinese personalities. From the mid-1950s, the title was revived by the Chinese Nationalist government on Taiwan, but the two productions should not be confused.

85

254 City of lingering splendour: a frank account of old Peking's exotic pleasures.
John Blofeld. London: Hutchinson, 1961. Reprinted, Boston, Massachusetts; Shaftesbury, England: Shambhala Publications Inc., 1989. 255p.

A book that perhaps promises more than it delivers, if one takes the subtitle too seriously. In fact, Blofeld, who taught English for three years in Beiping, as it then was, in the 1930s, provides an entertaining account of the life and contacts of a young foreigner with plenty of time and some money in what was officially a political backwater, but in reality still an imperial capital. Opium smokers, hermaphrodites, courtesans and warlords flit in and out in this entertaining, and perhaps sometimes fanciful, account of ways of life that have long disappeared.

255 Cook's guide to Peking, North China, South Manchuria and Korea.
Thomas Cook & Son. Beijing: Thomas Cook & Son, 1924. 5th ed. 143p. maps.

Two-thirds (p. 1-95) of the text of this guidebook is devoted to Beijing. Notes on the history of the city, its people, the 1900 siege of the legation quarter, and the 'four cities' of the capital are followed by practical information and a description of sites and monuments within and around Beijing. Chinese customs and practices are explained as part of the account of the site being visited. Of the places listed in the sightseeing programme of 1924, the majority still exist and, with some exceptions, can still be visited. Notes on Tianjin (Tientsin) and Beidaihe (Peitaiho) follow the section on Beijing. The third edition, entitled *Peking and the overland route: with maps, plans, and illustrations* (London: Thomas Cook & Son, 1917. 181p. maps), had already set the pattern. It also carried twenty-three pages of advertising, which throw a fascinating light on the amenities of the Western communities in Beijing and northeast Asia at the time.

256 Elegant flower: recollections of a cadet in Cathay.
Desmond Neill. London: John Murray, 1956. Reprinted, with a new introduction by the author, Hong Kong; Oxford; New York: Oxford University Press, 1987. 202p. map. (Oxford Paperbacks).

Desmond Neill, a cadet (i.e. a trainee administration officer) in the British colonial administration in Malaya, went to Xiamen (Amoy) for Chinese-language training in 1948. While there, he managed to visit Beijing, flying via Shanghai, and one chapter of this delightful book is devoted to what he found and what he saw in the last days of Nationalist Beijing. This was Beijing before the Communists began its transformation – still a place of camel trains and thieves' markets, and of the impressive, if decayed, Forbidden City. There are no great insights and no profound opinions, but Neill's simple account still has much charm.

257 Foreign devils in the flowery kingdom. *UL Nfr A.6*
Carl Crow. London: Hamish Hamilton, 1941. 340p. *625.22. c.9*

This rambling – by the author's own admission – account of foreigners' lives in China is a mixture of anecdotal history and contemporary account, written by a veteran American journalist. It is full of interesting information, some accurate, some less so, generally provided in the form of little stories. Shanghai and the other major treaty ports occupy the prime position, but there is also much about Beijing, and the lordly diplomats who lived there, away from the hurly-burly of the treaty ports. It is now all very dated, yet there are still insights to be gleaned both about the distant past and the world that came to an end in 1941.

258   Goodbye to old Peking: the wartime letters of U. S. marine captain John Seymour Letcher, 1937-1939.
John Seymour Letcher, edited by Roger B. Jeans and Katie Letcher Lyle.   Athens, Ohio: Ohio University Press, 1998. 242p. maps. bibliog.

From 1937 to 1939 Letcher commanded one of the six companies of marines guarding the US legation in Beijing. In July 1937, following the 'Marco Polo bridge incident', China and Japan went to war, and the ensuing hostilities provide the 'wartime' background of Letcher's letters to his parents. They report on early engagements in the Sino-Japanese war and on the Japanese occupation of Beijing. Once Japanese control had been asserted, Letcher was permitted to travel north of the city to Chengde, Manzhouguo and Kalgan for hunting and sightseeing. He writes much about expatriate social life in Beijing, which was not greatly inconvenienced by the war, but less about the Chinese population. He expresses strong views on the relative fighting qualities of the Japanese and Chinese and on the conduct of the European war. His letters, though personal in tone, nonetheless provide a vivid snapshot of Beijing at a difficult moment. Notes, maps and bibliography are all useful additions.

259   Guide to 'Peking'.
'The Leader'.   Beijing: 'The Leader', 1931. 88p. map.

By 1931 Beijing was being described as the 'old' capital of China; hence the inverted commas around 'Peking', when the city was officially known as Peiping (Beiping in the pinyin system). This guide is an introduction to the social amenities of the foreign community resident in the city at the time, as well as to the local monuments. It also contains a historical introduction, an account of theatres and theatre-going, information on museums, handicrafts, festivals and industries, an introduction to the *hutongs* of Beijing, and advice on shopping and food. The advertisements confirm that the modern shopping attractions of Beijing have simply carried on long-established traditions.

260   Guide to Peking and its environs near and far.
Fei-Shi.   Tianjin, China; Beijing: The Tientsin Press, 1924. fully revised ed. 237p. maps.

This guide, clearly by a Chinese writer, follows the conventions of the time in dividing Beijing into the Chinese and Manchu cities, the former Imperial City, the Forbidden City, and the legation quarter and other foreign institutions, which are presented as tourist attractions in their own right. It gives a detailed list of temples. Its wide coverage of the environs of Beijing takes in the Western and Eastern Qing tombs, Chengde (Jehol), Beidaihe, Qinhuangdao and Shanhaiguan, and extends as far as the Mongolian border and further afield. A section of advice on preparations for travel and on the hazards of touring is illuminating on conditions away from the capital. Information on Chinese religions and the workings of government, together with an essay on the early history of Beijing up to the Ming, round out the guide. The indexes are very full.

261 Hermit of Peking: the hidden life of Sir Edmund Backhouse.
Hugh Trevor-Roper. London: Eland, 1993. 405p.

Backhouse was co-author with J. O. P. Bland of *China under the empress dowager: being the history of the life and times of Tzu Hsi, compiled from state papers and the private diary of the comptroller of her household* (London: William Heinemann, 1910. 525p. map) and *Annals and memoirs of the court of Peking* (London: Heinemann; Boston, Massachusetts: Houghton Mifflin, 1914. Reprinted, New York: AMS Press, 1970. 531p.). He arrived in China in 1898, and died in Japanese-occupied Beijing in 1944. Backhouse was a Sinologist, claiming access to Chinese circles, of which he made much in his dealings with the foreign community in China. He was a man whose activities – both in business and in scholarship – engendered much confusion and irritation. Charges of gullibility at the hands of Chinese dealers and of the forgery of documents soon arose, in particular over the alleged diary of Jing Shan, comptroller of the Dowager Empress's household, which formed part of the 1910 work. Backhouse lived for many years as a recluse. His memoirs were passed to Trevor-Roper by a Swiss physician who knew Backhouse in his last years in Beijing. Trevor-Roper's unravelling of some of the complicated strands in Backhouse's life and his revelation of Backhouse as a fraud and fantasist have the excitement of a good detective story. His account was first published as *A hidden life: the enigma of Sir Edmund Backhouse* (London: Macmillan London Ltd, 1976. 316p.).

262 Journey to the beginning.
Edgar Snow. London: Victor Gollancz Ltd, 1959. 434p.

Edgar Snow, who died in 1971, was probably the most famous American journalist of his generation. His greatest scoop was the interviews he conducted with the little-known Mao Zedong in the revolutionary base of Yan'an (Yenan) in 1936, which later appeared in *Red star over China* (q.v.). In *Journey to the beginning*, he gives an account of how he came to be in China, and describes the life of a foreign correspondent in the war-torn 1930s. Although Beijing does not feature greatly, there are short vignettes of Beiping, as it had then become, and of some of the foreign characters living there, together with accounts of anti-Japanese demonstrations by the city's students and of the Snows' own experiences learning Chinese in the little village of Haidian, now the capital's computer centre. Other books by Snow, dealing with post-1949 China in a generally uncritical way, include *The other side of the river: red China today* (New York: Random House, 1962; London: Victor Gollancz, 1963. 810p. maps. bibliog. Reprinted, with a new preface, 'China in the 1970s', Harmondsworth, England; Ringwood, Victoria, Australia: Penguin Books, 1970, 1971. 749p. maps. bibliog.), and *The long revolution* (London: Hutchinson, 1973. 269p. map), published after his death. Both include accounts of Beijing as it was transformed after 1949, and both are generally uncritical of Mao and his revolution. There is also a recent biography of Snow, which includes much information on his life in Beijing: S. Bernard Thomas, *Season of high adventure: Edgar Snow in China* (Berkeley, California; Los Angeles; London: University of California Press, 1996. 416p. map. bibliog.).

263 The lion and the dragon: British voices from the China coast.
Christopher Cook. London: Elm Tree Books, 1985. 184p. map.

Based on the style and content of Charles Allen's *Plain tales from the Raj*, this is a collection of reminiscences by former employees of Butterfield and Swire (now John Swire and Sons Limited), one of the great British trading companies that dominated the China trade in the 19th century. It deals with the 1920s and 1930s, by which time the British predominance was coming to an end, although superior attitudes lingered on. The emphasis, for a variety of reasons, is on the social and personal lives of those interviewed, and the result is a fascinating insight into the semi-colonial world of the treaty port, a world that has long since vanished. Both Beijing and Tianjin feature, but this is really a book about the mental world of the foreigner rather than about any particular place. This is how foreigners lived in China, whether they were in Beijing or the remoter river ports. There are many good, and little-known, photographs. For a book dealing more with the business side of foreign life in China, see Patrick Brodie, *Crescent over Cathay: China and ICI, 1898 to 1956* (Hong Kong; Oxford; New York: Oxford University Press, 1990. 294p. map), which has many references to Beijing and Tianjin. An important study of Swires' shipping operation is Sheila Mariner, Francis E. Hyde, *The senior: John Samuel Swire 1825-98: management in Far Eastern shipping trades* (Liverpool, England: Liverpool University Press, 1967. 224p. map), which includes a little about the company's Tianjin operations.

264 **Making urban revolution in China: the CCP-GMD struggle for Beijing-Tianjin 1945-49.**
Joseph K. S. Yick. Armonk, New York; London: M. E. Sharpe, 1995. 233p. maps. bibliog.

A pioneering study of the struggle between the Chinese Communist Party (CCP) and the Guomindang (GMD or Chinese Nationalist Party, usually known as the KMT from the Wade-Giles' reading of its initials) in North China from the end of the Second World War to the Communist victory in 1949. Yick shows that, contrary to the widely held view that the Communist success was a rural-based one, the ability to control the cities also mattered. The CCP's successes in urban areas not only helped to win the Civil War, but also made the post-1949 task of changing Beijing and Tianjin much easier, since a lot of the ground work had already been done.

265 **The May fourth movement: intellectual revolution in modern China.**
Chow Tse-tsung. Boston, Massachusetts: Harvard University Press, 1960. Reprinted, Stanford, California: Stanford University Press, 1967. 486p.

On 4 May 1919, students in Beijing took to the streets in protest at the Versailles Peace Treaty and the Chinese government's weakness towards Japan. Ever since, 'May Fourth' has been a symbol of the role of Chinese students as critics of bad government, and of the modern Chinese revolution. Chow's study goes far beyond the events of that day, to consider the intellectual movement that had brought the students to a willingness to protest, and the more long-term consequences. But much of the earlier part of the work includes an account of the development of university education in Beijing, together with a detailed description of the Beijing students' actions on and after 4 May. It is thus an important contribution to the history of modern Beijing, as well as to the study of China's intellectual history.

266 On a Chinese screen.

William Somerset Maugham. London: William Heinemann Ltd, 1922. Reprinted, with an introduction by H. J. Lethbridge, Oxford: Oxford University Press, 1985. 237p. (Oxford Paperbacks).

The novelist Somerset Maugham visited China in 1919 and 1921; this book was the product of the second visit. While Maugham knew no Chinese, he seems to have had some sympathy for the Chinese people and rather less for his fellow Europeans. How long he spent in Beijing and Tianjin is not clear, but he produced several short sketches that reflect the society and the people that he found in each place. None is very profound, but each helps to explain the way life was in the 1920s for rich foreigners and less wealthy Chinese. Lethbridge's short introduction helps to set Maugham's stories in the context both of their times and of Maugham's life.

267 Pékin: ses palais, ses temples, & ses environs: guide touristique illustré. (Peking: its palaces, temples and surroundings: an illustrated tourist guide.)

Maurice Fabre, illustrated by Y. Darcy, original layout by J. Malval. Tianjin, China: Librairie Française, 1937. 347p. maps.

This comprehensive guidebook must have been very useful in its day, even if the outbreak of the Sino-Japanese War in 1937 and the subsequent disruption of North China, including Beijing, quickly reduced the numbers of those likely to use it. There are detailed and well-illustrated sections on the major sights of the capital, with Chinese characters given for all the places mentioned, something still of use today, and there is much information on subjects such as religion, the Chinese geological survey and tramways. Sections on 'Peking today' and on the French in China are now mainly of historical interest, but are still worth consulting. The same is true of the maps and plans, which are models of clarity.

268 Peking politics 1918-23: factionalism and the failure of constitutionalism.

Andrew J. Nathan. Berkeley, California; Los Angeles; London: University of California Press, 1976. 299p. map. bibliog. (Michigan Studies on China).

This detailed analysis of the emergence of warlord politics in China will mainly interest specialists. Nathan provides much information on the various army groupings and their leaders in and around Beijing, who eventually became semi-independent warlords, even while paying lip service to the idea of a unified, republican China.

269 Recent events and present policies in China.

John Otway Percy Bland. London: William Heinemann, 1912. 482p. maps.

Treaty port newspaper editor and later secretary to the Shanghai (foreign) Municipal Council, J. O. P. Bland was already well-known as a commentator on developments in China when he wrote this account of the fledgling revolution which brought down the Qing (Manchu) dynasty and set China on its modern course. Although much has been written about these events since Bland wrote, and much new material is available, this remains of interest. Bland describes and interprets events in the capital surrounding the fall of the dynasty, and provides vivid pen-portraits of the principal actors, such as Yuan Shikai, and a devastating account of the misery that accompanied the collapse of the social order in North China. There are also interesting asides on issues such as the opium trade, Japanese expansionism and the trade rivalry between Britain and Germany, together with some fascinating photographs. A new edition was planned by the Curzon Press (Richmond, England), for January 2000. For a less positive account, see 'A resident in Peking', *China as it really is* (London: Eveleigh Nash, 1912. 201p.), whose author is described as born in China and as having spent two-thirds of his life there. Familiarity with Chinese and foreigners in Beijing appears to have bred contempt in this instance, and the author perhaps did well to choose anonymity, for he is most dismissive of the old pre-1912 regime and of Chinese institutions in general. His hope is that the republican future would bring better administration; he must therefore have experienced further disappointment.

270 Red star over China.
Edgar Snow, introduction by John King Fairbank.   London: Victor Gollancz, 1937; New York; Random House, 1938, reprinted 1944. First revised and enlarged edition, Harmondsworth, England; Ringwood, Australia: Penguin Books, 1972. 621p. maps. bibliog.

The main interest in this book lies in Snow's interviews with the Communist leader, Mao Zedong in 1936, and in his accounts of the Chinese Communist Party's revolutionary areas. But it also contains material about Beijing, a city which Snow lived in from 1932, including Mao's own memories of his life there when he worked in the university library. There is also information about the Communist movement in Tianjin, some of which was derived from conversations with Zhou Enlai.

271 Rickshaw Beijing: people and politics in the 1920s.
David Strand.   Berkeley, California; Los Angeles; London: University of California Press, 1989. 364p. map. bibliog.

Taking the newly established trade of rickshaw-puller as his central theme, Strand looks at all aspects of Republican Beijing, or Beiping, as the city became after the Nationalist decision to move the capital to Nanjing in 1928. The result is a fascinating account of how the once proud imperial city coped with the political changes which left it as a museum-like backwater, while at the same time, economic modernization unleashed new tensions. The result was frequent demonstrations inspired by a whole range of political, economic and social grievances, which periodically burst into more savage violence, often centred around the fraught relationship between the rickshaw-pullers and the streetcar companies and their employees. The book works at various levels, providing not only solid academic analysis, but also much fascinating detail about the lives of the city's lower classes. There is an imaginative set of illustrations, drawn from the Library of Congress and contemporary publications.

272 Sagittarius rising.
Cecil Lewis.   London: Peter Davies, 1936. Reprinted, London: Corgi Books, 1969. 224p.

Most of this book is taken up with Lewis's experiences as a fighter pilot in the First World War. The last chapter, however, entitled 'Teaching the Chinese to fly', recounts the author's experiences in trying to set up an air force for the somewhat ramshackle 'Central

Government' in Beijing. It tells of the chaotic situation of China in the grip of warlords, the problems of communicating a wholly new technology to people who had barely learnt to cope with the steam engine, and the somewhat unusual life of expatriates in Beijing at the beginning of the 1920s.

273 Sidelights on Peking life.
Robert W. Swallow, introduction by Hardy Jowett. Beijing: China Booksellers, 1927. 135p. map.

This is a delightful book, full of information about life in Beijing in the 1920s. Swallow was not concerned to provide a guide to the city, but to describe the way of life of a whole variety of its inhabitants. Here are details of lanes and alleyways, of itinerant peddlers and blind musicians, of courtesans and actors. He records the ceremonies that marked marriages and births. There are tales of water ghosts, wall building ghosts, and hanging ghosts, but also of means of combating them. Like George Kates (see item no. 123), Swallow clearly loved the city and its people, and the result is a most entertaining compilation, which certainly deserves to be better known. A series of black-and-white photographs add to the book's interest.

274 Social life of the Chinese in Peking.
Jermyn Chi-Hung Lynn. Beijing; Tianjin, China: China Booksellers Limited, 1928. 182p.

Written in English by a Chinese primarily for the enlightenment of Western visitors. It is basically a guide to the social customs of educated Chinese circles in Republican Beijing and thus a manual of good manners. It is charmingly and wittily written. At the same time the author records changes he has noticed on his return to China after a long stay in the United States, such as public access to the formerly forbidden imperial parks, the effects of new styles of education and the new freedoms for women. There is an index in Chinese and English.

275 Sous le ciel de Pékin. (Under the Peking sky.)
André Duboscq. Paris: Editions Georges Crès & Cie., 1919. 161p.

Duboscq, a novelist and travel writer, recorded his reactions to and impressions of Beijing, which was one stop in a much longer tour of China, Korea, Japan and Hawaii. The Chinese capital clearly excited his imagination, and his descriptions of some of the great monuments and of the arts and crafts, natural sights and people and customs of Beijing are delicately rendered, even if impregnated with a certain exoticism. The book is beautifully printed and bound on fine stiff paper.

276 Stilwell and the American experience in China, 1911-45.
Barbara W. Tuchman. New York: The Macmillan Company, 1971. Reprinted, New York: Bantam Books, 1972. 794p. maps. bibliog.

General 'Vinegar Joe' Stilwell is remembered as the American general who fell out with the Chinese President, Chiang Kai-shek, during the Pacific War and was recalled to Washington at the latter's request. Stilwell first visited China in 1911 as the anti-Manchu revolution got under way, and he returned in 1920 as the army's first Chinese-language officer. Later he commanded the American garrison in Tianjin, and in the 1930s, he was appointed American military attaché, remaining in Beijing (then Beiping) until August 1939. About one third of this book deals with Stilwell's time in Beijing and Tianjin. Much of it is concerned with Stilwell's travels to other parts of China, but there is a fair amount of information about foreign life in both cities, and the politics of the region during a time of great turbulence.

277 The unknown war: north China 1937-45.
Text and photographs by Michael Lindsay. London: Bergström & Boyle Books Limited, 1975. 112p. maps. bibliog.

The British academic Michael Lindsay lived in China from 1937 to 1945, during which time he first taught at Yanjing (Yenching) University in Beijing, then, after Pearl Harbour (December 1941), joined up with the Chinese Communist forces. He had already travelled into parts of northwest China and was supporting the Communist underground resistance to Japanese occupation through purchases of medicine, wireless parts and books. These activities obliged him and his Chinese wife to leave Beijing once Yanjing, an American-supported university, lost its protected status. Lindsay helped the Communists considerably with their wireless and receiving equipment and at their headquarters in Yan'an was active in setting up a radio transmitter. Most of this book deals with his and his family's experiences with the Communist forces in rural northwestern China, but it also contains some interesting passages on teaching at Yanjing during unsettled conditions.

278 When tigers fight: the story of the Sino-Japanese war, 1937-45.
Dick Wilson. New York: Viking Press, 1982; Harmondsworth, England; New York; Ringwood, Australia; Markham, Canada; Auckland, New Zealand: Penguin Books, 1983. 269p. maps. bibliog.

Although for most of the period of the Sino-Japanese war (1937-45), Beijing was out of the action and under Japanese occupation, the conflict began just outside the city (then Beiping). On 7 July 1937, during a Japanese exercise, Japanese and Chinese troops clashed at the Lugouqiao, an ancient bridge known to foreigners as the Marco Polo Bridge, for the Venetian traveller describes it in his work. The first chapter of the veteran journalist Dick Wilson's popular account of the Sino-Japanese war describes this incident and the subsequent move of the Japanese to occupy Beijing. With the occupation completed on 7 August, the war moved on from Beijing, which remained under Japanese control until the surrender in 1945.

279 Yuan Shih-k'ai. UL: 624:52.c. 95.38 /N.Fr H.6
Jerome Ch'en. Stanford, California: Stanford University Press, 1972. 2nd ed. 258p. bibliog.

This biography first appeared as *Yuan Shih-k'ai (1859-1916): Brutus among the purple* (London: George Allen & Unwin; Stanford, California: University of Stanford Press). It tells the story of one of the most intriguing officials to emerge in late Qing China, whose career marks the change from imperial to republican China. Yuan Shikai served the Qing well, in a variety of capacities, including the suppression of the Boxer rebellion of 1900. By 1908 he was out of favour and was thus on the sidelines when the revolution that would overthrow the Manchu (Qing) dynasty began in 1911. He was quickly called back to office by the ailing Qing and became prime minister, only to find that the rebels were equally keen to court him. Despite some opposition, he eventually became president of the new republic. Then, in a bizarre turn of events, he decided to make himself emperor at the end of 1915. This provoked widespread opposition, but before the issue could be resolved, Yuan died in June 1916. While Ch'en's biography is not directly concerned with Beijing, the capital featured much in Yuan's later years, both in his period as president and then as emperor, and this is reflected in the book.

China 1890-1938: from the warlords to world war: a history in documentary photographs.
See item no. 204.

A dream of Tartary: the origins and misfortunes of Henry P'u Yi.
See item no. 217.

Embassies in the East: the story of the British and their embassies in China, Japan and Korea from 1859 to the present.
See item no. 218.

An American transplant: the Rockefeller Foundation and Peking Union Medical College.
See item no. 350.

Britain in China: community, culture and colonialism 1900-49.
See item no. 480.

Little foreign devil.
See item no. 488.

People's Republic of China (1949-)

280   The Beijing diplomatic community and the US-North Korea talks, 1988-94.
Geoffrey R. Berridge, Nadia Gallo.   Leicester, England: Centre for the Study of Diplomacy, University of Leicester, 1995. 21p. bibliog. (Discussion Papers in Diplomacy, no. 8).
From 1988 to 1994, a series of talks between United States and Democratic Republic of Korea (North Korea) officials took place in Beijing. The talks led nowhere, since relations were moved to a new, and ultimately more productive level, following concerns about a possible North Korean nuclear weapons' programme, but the authors use these events to construct an ingenious argument that the place where diplomatic exchanges occur may have an influence on the outcome of the negotiations. There is much information about the Beijing diplomatic community and the physical arrangements made by the Chinese for them, which makes the paper an interesting addition to the long line of books and essays on the subject; however, the basic premise scarcely stands up. A revised version of

the paper, entitled 'The role of the diplomatic corps: the US-North Korean talks in Beijing, 1988-94', appears as Chapter 12 in *Innovation in diplomatic practice*, edited by Jan Melissen (London: Macmillan, 1999. 267p.).

281 Beijing spring.
Photographs by David Turnley, Peter Turnley, text by Melinda Liu, introduction by Orville Schell, foreword by Howard Chapnick, captions by Li Ming.   Hong Kong: Asia 2000 Ltd, 1989. 176p.

Provides a brief account of the events leading up to the clearing of Tiananmen Square by the Chinese People's Liberation Army on 4 June 1989, written by Melinda Liu of *Newsweek*, and reflecting some of her reporting during April-June 1989. What really makes the book stand out, however, are the stunning photographs, taken over the same period by two American professional photojournalists. They capture the early hope and enthusiasm of the student demonstrators, chart the growth of the protest movement as it began to include workers and intellectuals, and conclude with sombre pictures of the night of 3-4 June, and of the uncertain days immediately afterwards, as gun-toting troops patrolled the streets of Beijing.

282 Beijing spring, 1989: confrontation and conflict: the basic documents.
Edited by Michel Oksenberg, Lawrence R. Sullivan, Marc Lambert, introduction by Melanie Manion, featuring 'Death or rebirth?: Tiananmen: the soul of China', by Li Qiao et al., translated by H. R. Lan, Jerry Dennerline.   Armonk, New York; London: M. E. Sharpe, Inc., 1990. 403p. map. (An East Gate Book).

The events leading up to the action by China's People's Liberation Army against the remaining demonstrators in and around Tiananmen Square on 4-5 June 1989 led to a spate of books on the subject. Some dealt specifically with events in Beijing; others looked at the wider context, and were perhaps more concerned with the broad sweep of Chinese social, economic and political developments that underlay the specific events of June 1989. This collection falls more into the latter category, though the introduction does describe those aspects which are specific to Beijing. The documents themselves, selected from a wide range of sources, provide useful background, and there is a helpful glossary of names, organizations and acronyms. The lack of a bibliography is perhaps understandable, but not the absence of an index.

283 Beijing turmoil: more than meets the eye.
Che Muqi.   Beijing: Foreign Languages Press, 1990. 232p. maps.

Che Muqi is a veteran Chinese journalist, a former editor-in-chief of the People's China Press, which produces a Japanese-language monthly called *People's China*. By 1989, he had retired, but was brought out of retirement to produce this official defence of the Chinese government's actions against the student and workers' demonstrations in Beijing's Tiananmen Square of May-June 1989. If one accepts the basic premise of the book, that the government acted in reasonable fashion against a dangerous conspiracy organized by radical students, then this is a plausible case. If not, and few are likely to do so outside China, it is a cleverly constructed, but ultimately mendacious polemic. There are some useful documents, but even those can be obtained elsewhere.

284 Black hands of Beijing: lives of defiance in China's democracy movement.

George Black, Robin Munro. New York; Chichester, England; Brisbane, Australia; Toronto; Singapore: John Wiley & Sons, Inc., 1993. 390p. (A Robert L. Bernstein Book).

The Chinese authorities claimed that the events leading up to the crackdown of 4 June 1989 were masterminded by a group of 'black hands'. This book describes what led three of those so described to the protests of 1989. It includes a detailed and comprehensive account of the events of the final days in Tiananmen Square, including what happened on the night of 3-4 June based on eye-witness accounts; they conclude that official claims that there was no massacre in the Square – narrowly defined – are correct, although there were clearly killings elsewhere. There is an account of some of the subsequent trials and the horrific conditions that those convicted had to face in Beijing's prisons. Overall, the authors provide an important account of one of the least attractive events in Beijing's recent history.

285 The broken mirror: China after Tiananmen.

Edited, with an introduction by George Hicks, foreword by Chalmers Johnson. Harlow, England: Longman Group UK Ltd; Chicago, Illinois: St James Press, 1990. 526p.

This series of essays by a group of well-known Western scholars of China reflects the pain and anger many felt in 1989 at the way the Chinese Communist Party and the Chinese state behaved towards its own people. Inevitably studies such as this are concerned with issues far beyond the effect of April-June 1989 on Beijing, but since the capital was the backdrop against which that drama was played out, it and its citizens feature in several of the papers. Many of the essays are perhaps too close to their subject in time to be regarded as in any sense impartial assessments of what happened in 1989. However, the chronology of selected documents and speeches, and the short biographical section on 'Who was who during Beijing Spring', both by Joseph Y. S. Cheng, retain value because they are less emotional.

286 China: alive in the bitter sea.

Fox Butterfield. New York: Times Books; London; Sydney; Auckland, New Zealand; Toronto: Hodder & Stoughton, 1982. 468p. map.

In 1979, Fox Butterfield became the first *New York Times* correspondent in Beijing since 1949. Like the British diplomat, Roger Garside (see item no. 290), he has written a work combining contemporary history with eye-witness reporting. Taking advantage of the opening up that began in 1978, Butterfield's account is not only concerned with the capital, but also reflects his travels over large areas of China. However, much of his writing is about Beijing and the struggles of its citizens. His account, as its title indicates, is more downbeat than Garside's, which is partly a reflection of the realization that while Mao had gone, as had his widow and her supporters, and there was a new atmosphere under Deng Xiaoping, little had changed. For most Chinese, life remained a hard struggle. There are sixteen pages of black-and-white photographs, many by the author.

287 China observed: a current first hand report of the Chinese power struggle by two Australian teachers.
Colin Mackerras, Neale Hunter. London: Sphere Books, 1968. 185p.

An account by two Australian teachers of living and working in China during the period leading up to the Cultural Revolution and its earliest days. Mackerras was in Beijing, teaching English at the Foreign Language Institute, while Hunter was in Shanghai. Both were, by this account, remarkably naive in their assessment of China and of the events through which they were living. This is now a work of curiosity, as both authors might acknowledge, rather than one of scholarship. It contains a few charming misprints; 'rotten eggs', a standard Chinese insult, comes out as 'rolling eggs' at one point, which must have puzzled many readers. There is no index.

288 China's last emperor as an ordinary citizen.
Wang Qingxiang. Beijing: China Reconstructs, 1986. 85p. (Great Wall Books).

A short account of the life of Aisin-Gioro Pu Yi, China's last emperor, sometimes known as Henry Pu Yi, in the years after his release from prison until his death in October 1967 during the Cultural Revolution. In effect, it takes up Pu Yi's life story from the end of his autobiography *From emperor to citizen* (q.v.), filling in the details of his life in Beijing from 1959 until his death, and specifically refuting the charges of crimes against the people made against him during the Cultural Revolution. There are also details of other members of Pu Yi's family, including his brother, Pu Jie. While it lacks the personal touch of Pu Yi's own account, it is nevertheless useful in filling in some of the background of his later years as an ordinary worker in Beijing.

289 The Chinese people's movement: perspectives on spring 1989.
Edited by Tony Saich. Armonk, New York; London: M. E. Sharpe, Inc., 1990. 207p. bibliog. (An East Gate Book).

This collection of eight essays, largely from European scholars, suffers from being too close to the events with which it is concerned. It is thus less an academic study, despite the use of 'perspectives' in its title, and more a series of instant impressions, some of which may prove to be of more long-term interest. The first essay, by Jeffrey N. Wasserstrom, on 'Student protests and the Chinese tradition, 1919-89' (p. 3-24), draws on the author's PhD thesis about student protest in Shanghai, to provide the historical background against which the 1989 students were demonstrating. Frank Niming's 'Learning how to protest' (p. 83-105) shows how the movement spread from the students to the capital's workers, a development that really began to alarm Chinese leaders. There is a useful chronology, tracing events from the death of the former Communist Party secretary-general, Hu Yaobang on 15 April 1989 to 1 July 1989, by which time the government and party were once again firmly in control.

290 Coming alive! China after Mao.
Roger Garside. London: Andre Deutsch, 1981. 458p. maps. bibliog.

Roger Garside was a British diplomat in Beijing from 1976 to 1979, and thus occupied a ringside seat during the momentous change from the era of Mao Zedong to that of Deng Xiaoping. Much of his account is based on personal observation in the capital during those years, or is derived from the observations of fellow diplomats and other foreigners living and working in Beijing. As a Chinese speaker, Garside was also able to interview and hold discussions with many Chinese, which are reflected in his text. He provides a dramatic description of the suppression of the April 1976 demonstrations in Tiananmen Square, which foreshadowed the more bloody suppression of June 1989; a great deal of information on the fall of Mao's widow and the other members of the 'Gang of Four' in autumn 1976; and a detailed account of 'Democracy Wall', which flourished briefly in Beijing in 1978-79. Although much has happened since 1979, Garside's contemporary history remains a readable and enlightening introduction to an important period in modern Chinese history.

291 Comrade Chiang Ch'ing.
Roxane Witke.   Boston, Massachusetts; Toronto: Little, Brown & Co., 1977. 549p. maps.

This is a biography of Mao Zedong's last wife, Jiang Qing, based largely on discussions the author had with her in 1972. Much of it is concerned with the politics of China from the 1930s onwards, but there are occasional insights into the lives of the leaders in Beijing, into cultural developments, especially the adaptation, now abandoned, of traditional Peking opera forms to 'revolutionary models', and into the Cultural Revolution in the capital. The work has perhaps dated rather more than many others from this period.

292 Crime and punishment in post-liberation China: the prisoners of a Beijing gaol in the 1950s.
Frank Dikötter.   *China Quarterly*, no. 149 (March 1997), p. 147-59.

A relatively rare account of a Chinese prison in the early years after 1949, based on a prison register. Dikötter uses this to provide a picture of the types of criminals and crimes to be found in one Beijing jail in the 1950s. From the point of view of Beijing, the interest lies in that fact that many of those held in the jail were from the capital or its environs, although it is not clear which of Beijing's prisons it is. Dikötter notes that the prison inhabitants in the 1950s were a clear mix of political (mainly former Nationalists) and ordinary criminals.

293 The cultural revolution at Peking university.
Victor Nee, with Don Layman.   New York; London: Monthly Review Press, 1969. 91p.

Despite its title, over half this little book is an essay on Beijing University's relationship with the Communist regime from 1949 to 1966 rather than an account of what happened there during the Cultural Revolution. Beijing University, generally known as Beida, began as the Imperial University in 1898. After the 1911 revolution that overthrew the monarchy, Beida became a centre of student political activism, and the venue of major protests against the Versailles Peace Treaty in 1919 (the May Fourth Movement) and against the Japanese in 1935. At the same time, it also acquired a reputation as a centre of privilege. In 1952 it was moved from the middle of the city to the site of the Yanjing University campus, an American missionary institution then just outside the city proper, and continued to develop as an elite institution until the Cultural Revolution. About a third of the text deals with the launching of the Cultural Revolution at the university in May-June 1966, which is presented in a positive light. There is no index.

294 Die demokratiebewegung in China 1989: die mobilisierung durch studentenorganisationen in Beijing. (The democracy movement in China 1989: mobilization through student organizations in Beijing.)
Thomas Reichenbach. Hamburg, Germany: Institut für Asienkunde, 1994. 360p. bibliog. (Mitteilungen des Instituts für Asienkunde Hamburg, no. 228).

This monograph, in the impressive series of reports published by one of the foremost centres for Asian studies in Europe, offers an analytical review of the organization and development of the 1989 protest movement in Beijing. Its aim, indeed, is to provide 'analytical material for the political discussions on the future of democratization in China'. The author examines the movement in the light of Western sociological studies on social movements, then proceeds to a reconstruction of the circumstances of mobilization before the movement of spring 1989. A case-study of the 1989 mobilization campaign follows, together with an examination of the protesters' moves and of the reactions of Chinese Party leaders. The author concludes that the experiences of 1989 formed a process of political enlightenment for the participants. This detailed study is accessible to non-German readers through a summary in English. There is a very full bibliography of works in Chinese and Western languages.

295 The dragon's brood: conversations with young Chinese.
David Rice. London: HarperCollins, 1992. 294p. maps. bibliog.

David Rice is a former Dominican friar turned journalist, who went to China to train young journalists for the New China News Agency. After June 1989, he returned again to China to conduct a series of semi-clandestine interviews with young people, in order to try to assess what 1989 meant in retrospect and what they thought about the future. Clearly not all the interviews took place in Beijing, but a significant number seem to have done so. Rice includes a number of eye-witness accounts of what happened in Beijing on 4-5 June 1989, together with more general interviews on sex, love and politics. The picture that emerges is of a generation scarred but not cowed by 1989. There are many excellent photographs, mostly of the events of 1989.

296 Historical dictionary of the People's Republic of China.
Lawrence R. Sullivan, with the assistance of Nancy Hearst.
Lanham, Maryland; London: The Scarecrow Press, 1997. 279p. map. bibliog. (Asian/Oceanian Historical Dictionaries, no. 28).

A useful, straightforward compendium of information about China since 1949, which includes numerous charts and a detailed chronology. Beijing features prominently, including entries on individuals connected with the city, Beijing University and Peking opera.

297 History of the Chinese Communist Party: a chronology of events (1919-90).

Compiled by the Party History Research Centre of the Central Committee of the Chinese Communist Party. Beijing: Foreign Languages Press, 1991. 524p.

After the defeat of the Chinese Nationalists in 1949, and the re-establishment of Beijing as China's capital, much of the action in the Chinese Communist Party switched to Beijing, which is thus a constant backdrop in this chronological account. It is, of course, party history seen through party eyes, but the discerning reader should be able to read between the lines.

298 Hundred day war: the cultural revolution at Tsinghua university.

William Hinton. New York; London: Monthly Review Press, 1972. 288p.

Qinghua (Tsinghua in Wade-Giles) University is situated on the edge of Beijing's university district, in the north of the city. It was established in 1911, with American Boxer indemnity funds, and is renowned as China's premier university institute devoted to science and technology. Like other Beijing university institutions, its students were heavily involved in the most violent stage (1966-71) of the Cultural Revolution (1966-76, in official Chinese terms). William Hinton is firmly on the side of Mao Zedong and his followers, seeing in the events at Qinghua, which included pitched battles involving homemade bombs and machine guns, a vindication of Mao's call to 'bombard the headquarters', or attack those in authority. While nobody would now read it as an authentic account of what happened at Qinghua from 1966 to 1971, it has considerable period interest. There is no index.

299 Inside Peking: a personal report.

Beverley Hooper, foreword by Stephen FitzGerald. London: Macdonald & Jane's, 1979. 178p. map.

Beverley Hooper is a former Australian diplomat, who studied in China from 1975 to 1977. She was thus present for the last act of the Cultural Revolution (1966-76), but in many ways this is peripheral to her experience of being a foreign student in China. It was clearly not an easy time. She was not as idealistic as some other students, and describes the conditions under which she lived and the petty humiliations suffered in a generally detached way. Sometimes, however, the tensions break through the surface, and the sheer difficulties of trying to live in a Chinese environment in the mid-1970s come through. The final chapter, recording a brief 1979 return visit, seems to offer more hope, as her former contacts relax in a more benevolent atmosphere. A somewhat more light-hearted account, written well after the event by another student from that period, but which makes many of the same points, is Frances Wood, *Hand-grenade practice in Peking: my part in the cultural revolution* (London: John Murray, 2000. 256p.).

300   June four: a chronicle of the Chinese democratic uprising.
Photographers and reporters of the *Ming Pao News*, translated by Zi
Jin, Qin Zhou.   Fayetteville, Arkansas; London: University of
Arkansas Press, 1989. 171p.

This detailed chronological account of the events leading up to the military suppression
of the students in Beijing on 4 June 1989 was originally published in Chinese in Hong
Kong, and is based on the experiences of staff of the Hong Kong *Ming Pao* newspaper. It
is full of eye-witness accounts and dramatic pictures. There is little real analysis of either
the student movement or the government's reaction, but the immediacy of the writing, the
inclusion of several important statements and other documents, and the intensity of many
of the pictures, make it a useful addition to the material available on the events of April-
June 1989 in Beijing. There is no index.

**301   Die kulturrevolution an der universität Beijing: vorgeschichte,
ablauf und bewältigung.** (The Cultural Revolution at Beijing
University: early history, course and termination.)
Uwe Richter.   Hamburg, Germany: Institut für Asienkunde, 1988.
274p. map. bibliog. (Mitteilungen des Instituts für Asienkunde
Hamburg, no. 169).

From 1976 to 1980, Richter, as a young German scholar, studied Chinese language and
history at Beijing Language Institute and Beijing University (Beida). He thus arrived at
the very end of the Cultural Revolution (generally described by the Chinese as having
lasted from 1966 to 1976) and was able to witness the reckoning that followed the death
of Mao in 1976 and the downfall of Mao's wife and her followers. Beida had been a focal
point in the political struggles of the late 1950s and mid-1960s by means of which Mao
hoped to fight off those trends threatening his concept of a revolutionary society. In this
detailed and minutely documented study, Richter traces the progress of the Cultural
Revolution at Beida through the rise of the red guard movement, the dispatch of soldiers
and workers into the university in 1968, the renewal of political strife in the early 1970s,
and the final restoration of order. An exhaustive bibliography provides leads to further
sources in Chinese, English and German. This is primarily a book for specialists.

302   The legacy of Tiananmen: China in disarray.
James A. R. Miles.   Ann Arbor, Michigan: University of Michigan
Press, 1996, paperback edition 1997. 379p. map. bibliog.

James Miles was for several years the BBC correspondent in Beijing and Hong Kong.
This work, the product of a year spent away from the microphone at an American
university, draws on that experience, to paint a picture of a China that has lost its way.
Despite the impressive economic gains of the last twenty years, Miles argues that there is
no sign that the political issues facing China are being tackled, or that the leadership is
even ready to admit that there are such problems. Although he gets away from the capital
and the limited perspectives it brings, his work is nevertheless informed by the time he
spent in Beijing, and the discerning reader will learn much about the city and its role in
China from this book.

303 Mandate of heaven: a new generation of entrepreneurs, dissidents, bohemians and technocrats lays claim to China's future.
Orville Schell. New York: Simon & Schuster, 1994; London: Little, Brown & Co., 1995. 464p. bibliog.

Orville Schell has been writing about China since the late 1960s, and has visited the country many times since 1975. While the main thrust of this book is the way in which China has been transformed from a monolithic one-party state into something far more diverse, over a third of it deals with the significance of Tiananmen Square in modern Chinese history and with the events of April-June 1989. While Schell left China in late May, his account of the build-up to the army's attack on the square on 4 June 1989 is based on his own interviews and observations in the early period, and many eye-witness accounts from both Chinese and Western sources, providing a well-written and clear account of the tragedy.

304 The May seventh cadre school of eastern Peking.
James C. F. Wang. *China Quarterly*, no. 63 (September 1975), p. 522-27.

May Seventh (the name came from a directive of Mao Zedong issued on 7 May 1966) cadre schools were a device to remind officials of the back-breaking work carried out by China's rural population, and during the Maoist years, they featured prominently in the lives of government officials. This brief account, based on a visit in January 1973, of one school situated on a commune in the Beijing municipal area provides a rare outsider's view of what it was like to attend such an institution. The school's 350 members were drawn from the central government, the capital's administration, factory management, and ordinary schools. They spent on average about six months learning what it was like to be a peasant. The system still continues, though the name has changed, but it is now confined to civil servants.

305 The ordinary and the extraordinary: an anthropological study of Chinese reform and the 1989 people's movement in Beijing.
Frank N. Pieke. London: Kegan Paul International, 1996. 287p. bibliog.

Conducting fieldwork for his planned anthropology PhD thesis in Beijing in 1988-89, Pieke found himself involved in something much wider than an academic study of how Beijing people think about work, marriage and life in general. The result is an illuminating insight into what at least some of those caught up in the events of 1989 thought about the process and how it changed them, which is likely to appeal to a wider audience than might have looked at Pieke's original study.

306 Origines et développement de la révolution culturelle. (Origins and development of the Cultural Revolution.)
Marianne Bastid. *Politique étrangère*, vol. 32, no. 1 (1967), p. 68-86.

An eye-witness account of the outbreak of the 'Great Proletarian Cultural Revolution' at Beijing University (Beida) in the summer of 1966. Marianne Bastid was a history student who was able to witness some of the mass rallies and struggles which marked the early stages of the Cultural Revolution. The article stops in August 1966. Together with a later interview by Mlle Bastid, the article was an important source for *The cultural revolution at Peking university* (see item no. 293).

307 The origins of the cultural revolution.
Roderick MacFarquhar. London: Oxford University Press; New York: Columbia University Press, 1974, 1983, 1999. 3 vols. bibliog.
This massive study of the origins of Mao Zedong's attempt to transform China, some thirty years in the making, obviously covers all of China. But the central role of Beijing means that it is an important work for an understanding of the movements and campaigns that affected the capital at regular intervals during the Maoist era. As the work has progressed, MacFarquhar has increasingly drawn on new and unpublished material, especially to explain the machinations that lay behind the various campaigns. It is an indispensable tool for understanding China after 1949.

308 Peking: eindrücke und begegnungen. (Peking: impressions and meetings.)
Photographs by Eva Siao, introduction by Uhse von Bodo. Dresden, Germany: Sachsenverlag, 1956. 35p.
Eva Siao was a German photographer married to the Chinese poet Emi Siao (Xiao Emi). Her preference lay in the performing arts, as evidenced in the many studies here of dancers, Peking opera singers, puppet theatre and scenes from the opera. Other subjects are writers and children, views of the Forbidden City and other scenic spots, and scenes from daily life. The historical interest of this book lies in the circumstances of its creation: a visit by the East German Uhse von Bodo to China in April-May 1954 to meet Chinese and foreign writers settled in Beijing. In his introduction von Bodo deplores foreigners' past obsession with the art and architecture of China, and their indifference to poverty, corruption and the West's depredations. His text is in praise of the new China, a theme borne out implicitly in many of Siao's photographs. The book is a reminder of how the new People's Republic of China cultivated its 'foreign friends' in its early days and how they in turn saw it as their duty to counteract Western hostility towards China.

309 Peking: today and yesterday.
Hu Chia. Beijing: Foreign Languages Press, 1956. 123p. maps.
This book is both a guide to Beijing, with sections on the geography, history and monuments of the city together with practical information, and a record of the achievements of the new Communist government and municipal administration. Improvements in the capital's infrastructure, living conditions and economy are emphasized, and its role as a revolutionary city and cultural and educational centre is highlighted. For the Western historian, the most interesting information may be that on places of worship. Christian churches are listed by denomination (Catholic, Anglican, Methodist, Congregational) and some are even illustrated. Such detail is absent four years later from *Peking: a tourist guide* (Beijing: Foreign Languages Press, 1960. 192p. maps). In 1957 the Christian churches were reorganized into the Patriotic Catholic and Patriotic Protestant churches. The 1960 guide continues the theme of the city's amelioration under Communist rule and development into an industrial centre, as well as providing detailed information on tourist attractions and amenities.

310 Political participation in Beijing.
Shi Tianjian.   Cambridge, Massachusetts: Harvard University Press, 1997. 322p. bibliog.

This book moves away from the entrenched idea that there is little point in trying to study public opinion in a dictatorial state, and that political techniques that derive from the experience of Western democracies are of little use in trying to understand how Chinese politics function. Shi argues, however, that since the Chinese political system allows for a degree of input at the grassroots level, the political process in China is well worth examining. This he has done through interviews conducted in the Chinese capital in 1988 and 1989, when the political process was relatively open and liberal. The results show a population that is surprisingly active at the political level. The citizens of Beijing are not passive, but engage in strikes, demonstrations and various other political acts. While problems of interpretation and overall significance remain, Shi's study is a welcome advance from stereotypes to the examination of real people and how they operate in a political context.

311 Quelling the people: the military suppression of the Beijing democracy movement.
Timothy Brook.   New York; Oxford: Oxford University Press, 1992. 265p. bibliog. Reprinted, with an afterword, Stanford, California: Stanford University Press, 1998. 269p. bibliog.

Timothy Brook, of the University of Toronto, had actually left China a month before the demonstrators of April and May 1989 were violently dispersed by the People's Liberation Army in June 1989. But he had a long exposure to China, beginning in the 1970s, and he decided to try to establish how events had led to the night of 3-4 June. The result is a detailed reconstruction, which attempts to give all sides of the story, of what happened in the weeks following the death of the senior Chinese Communist Party leader, Hu Yaobang, on 15 April. Brook draws on published accounts, as well as on television and other media sources, but the bulk of the book is based on interviews. Inevitably, therefore, it tends to give the students' and other demonstrators' side of the story in more detail than it does the official account, although that too is well represented. The 1998 edition adds little to the earlier version.

312 Report from Peking: a Western diplomat observes the cultural revolution.
D. W. Fokkema.   London: C. Hurst & Company, 1970. 185p. bibliog.

The author was a diplomat, posted to the Netherlands mission in Beijing from 1966 to 1968, when he left the Netherlands diplomatic service to become an academic. The book was first published in the Netherlands by Uitgeverij de Arbeiderspers as *Standplaats Peking*, and was translated into English by the author. It covers not only the period of Fokkema's direct experience but goes beyond that to include the period up to the Ninth Party Congress in early 1969. This, by general agreement, marked the end of the most extreme phase of the Cultural Revolution, and the beginning of a return to a more settled period. Since Fokkema wrote his account, much more work has appeared on the turmoil of 1966-69, but the book remains of value for its careful observation and sensible interpretations.

313 Spring winds of Beijing.
Gail Copeland.   Lakewood, Colorado: Glenbridge Publishing Ltd, 1993. 329p.

Gail Copeland first visited China in 1982, and has made many visits, some extended, since then. In the spring of 1989, she went out into the streets of the city, mingling among the crowds of demonstrators, both students and workers, and recording their views; this book is the result. In it she explains the social and economic background to the demonstrations in a clear and readable manner, likely to appeal to those who will find many of the academic studies too heavy going for everyday reading.

314 The struggle for Tiananmen: anatomy of the 1989 mass movements.
Lin Nan.   Westport, Connecticut; London: Praeger, 1992. 199p. map. bibliog.

The first chapter of this straightforward account of what happened in China's capital in 1989 begins with a chronology that runs from the death of Hu Yaobang on 15 April 1989 through to the end of martial law in Beijing on 10 January 1990. Succeeding chapters are a good example of well-written contemporary history. Only towards the end, in a chapter that attempts to explain some of the deeper reasons behind the student demonstrations, does the author demonstrate his qualifications as a sociologist. His thesis on the reasons for the failure of the movement to achieve its aims falls into two parts. Once the government realized that the Beijing workers were becoming heavily involved, its members felt that they had to act. But their decision to act was hampered by the divisions within the command structure. The result was that quite inappropriate levels of force were used on 4 June and thereafter, by troops who had little understanding of the issue and the likely effects of their heavy-handed behaviour.

315 Tiananmen: a cartoon series depicting the June 4 massacre.
Morgan Chua.   Hong Kong: Chinatown Publications, 1989. 112p.

Chua, who was born in Singapore, was for fifteen years a cartoonist on the *Far Eastern Economic Review* (q.v.), using the pen name 'Morgan'. He left the *Review* in 1988, but these cartoons are very much in the style of those he had published previously. The main difference, as he points out, is that until 1988 his drawings were often in praise of Deng Xiaoping and his reforms; after the suppression of the demonstrations in June 1989, the tone is bitter and hostile. In addition to the cartoons, there is a brief chronology covering events from the death of Hu Yaobang on 15 April to 29 June 1989, the day on which one of the prominent student leaders, Wu'er Kaixi, was reported to have safely left China.

316 Tiananmen diary: thirteen days in June.
Harrison E. Salisbury.   Boston, Massachusetts; Toronto; London: Little, Brown & Company, 1989. 176p. maps.

Salisbury is a veteran American reporter, with a great reputation and a string of books to his name. Sadly, this is hardly his best. There is too much trivia and too little of what really happened in Beijing in the lead-up to the army crackdown of 4 June 1989; indeed, Salisbury admits to getting much of his picture of what was happening from the BBC World Service. It is hard to believe that such a slight work would have appeared if it had been written by somebody with a less well-known name.

317 Tiananmen: the rape of Peking.
Michael Fathers, Andrew Higgins, edited by Robert Cottrell.
London; New York; Sydney; Auckland, New Zealand: The
Independent, in association with Doubleday, 1989. 148p. map.

An account prepared almost immediately after the event by two British journalists describing the developments in and around Beijing from the death of the veteran party leader Hu Yaobang on 15 April 1989 to the events of 4-6 June 1989. The style is racy and the work as a whole is a good journalistic account, but the analysis of both the causes and the consequences of 4 June lacks real depth. While still of interest, it needs to be read with other more reflective accounts of what happened.

318 The unforgettable days.
Edited by the Photographic Department of Xinhua News Agency,
Jilin Education Publishing House, inscription by Deng Xiaoping.
Jilin, China: Jilin Education Publishing House, 1989. 232p.

A photographic record of the years 1949-88, compiled to mark the fortieth anniversary of the People's Republic of China. Many of the pictures feature events in Beijing. The book appeared in June 1989, and some of the photographs, such as those showing the then premier, Zhao Ziyang, would not appear again. A similar collection, covering much the same period, can be found in *As the dragon stirs: a photographic record of social changes on the Chinese mainland*, edited by Duan Liancheng, Gu Jin, Zhang Yunlei, text by Duan Liancheng, English translation by Zhang Qingnian, preface by Hsiao Ch'ien (Hong Kong: New Horizon Press, 1990. 352p. map). Again, while the work is concerned with developments in the whole country, Beijing features prominently, right up to the events of June 1989, which are, however, quickly glossed over.

The private life of Chairman Mao: the inside story of the man who made modern China.
See item no. 147.

A dream of Tartary: the origins and misfortunes of Henry P'u Yi.
See item no. 217.

Embassies in the East: the story of the British and their embassies in China, Japan and Korea from 1859 to the present.
See item no. 218.

***Wayfoong*: the Hongkong and Shanghai Banking Corporation: a study of East Asia's transformation, political, financial and economic, during the last hundred years.**
See item no. 250.

History of the Chinese Communist Party: a chronology of events (1919-90).
See item no. 297.

Beijing street voices: the poetry and politics of China's democracy movement.
See item no. 360.

Language

319 About Chinese.
Richard Newnham. Harmondsworth, England; Baltimore,
Maryland; Ringwood, Australia: Penguin Books, 1971. 188p.
bibliog.
This is essentially a book for those who wish to learn something about the Chinese
language, without necessarily wanting to learn Chinese. The main emphasis is on the
Beijing dialect, known as 'Mandarin' to many in the West, and now used throughout
mainland China as the national language or *putonghua*. The annotated bibliography is
excellent, describing forty-eight textbooks and dictionaries.

320 L'accentuation en Pékinois. (Accentuation in Beijing Chinese.)
Monique Hoa. Hong Kong: Editions Langages Croisés, 1983.
259p. bibliog.
There is a considerable literature in Chinese on the form of Chinese spoken in the capital
and the Beijing region, but not so much in Western languages. Monique Hoa, a native
speaker of Beijing Chinese, provides here an analysis of the accentuation patterns in that
dialect. Her study is guided by Liberman and Prince's models (1977) for English of the
accentual relationships between strong and weak elements in a syntactic phrase. Her
methods in determining a system governing patterns of accentuation in Beijing Chinese
are complicated and diagrammatic. The chief conclusion arising out of what Hoa sees as
an intermediate study is that context is very important in determining the nature of
accentuation in a phrase. There is a fairly full bibliography, and the literature on the
specific issue of accentuation in Beijing Chinese is listed on p. 16.

**321 The Chinese language and how to learn it: a manual for
beginners.**
Walter Caine Hillier. London: Kegan Paul, Trench, Trübner & Co.
Ltd, 1910. 2nd ed. 297p.
Walter Hillier was a member of the British China consular service, consul-general in
Seoul, later Chinese secretary at the British legation in Beijing, and eventually professor

of Chinese at King's College London. While nobody today would use this book to learn Chinese, it does contain much useful information about the Beijing dialect and how it came to be considered the standard language, which is still worth reading.

322 The Chinese language today: features of an emerging standard.
Paul Kratochvil. London: Hutchinson & Co. (Publishers) Ltd, 1968. 199p. map. bibliog. (Hutchinson University Library).

The 'common speech' or *putonghua* officially encouraged in China is based on the form of the language spoken by educated people in the Beijing region. This has long been judged to be more 'correct', and speakers of other dialects adjust their speech behaviour in favour of it. At the same time Beijing has its own recognizable dialect, a subdivision of the Hebei dialect, itself one of the Northern dialects of Chinese. Kratochvil does not dwell much on the singularities of the Beijing dialect, being more concerned with the processes encouraging the development of a standard form of spoken Chinese. He does, however, single out the widespread use of 'erisation' – the adding of the 'er' suffix to words – in certain styles of the Beijing dialect, and a particular use of the marker 'ba'. Linguistic studies are inevitably largely written in terms not always readily accessible to the general reader. Even Kratochvil's work, although intended as a fairly simple discussion, demands a knowledge of basic linguistic terminology. The reader is helped by a glossary of terms used.

323 Diversity and frequency of usage as a reflection of social factors: the application of variable rules to the analysis of disposal in the Beijing speech community.
Robert Martin Sanders. Ann Arbor, Michigan: University Microfilms International, Dissertation Information Service, 1986. unnumbered. bibliog.

This doctoral dissertation, for which the fieldwork dates from late 1984, has a useful introductory chapter distinguishing between four different concepts of 'Mandarin' Chinese: 'idealized' Mandarin (*putonghua* as the 'ideal' form of the language); 'imperial' Mandarin (the form spoken by imperial officials); 'geographical' Mandarin, spoken over a defined area of China; and 'local' Mandarin as spoken around Beijing, with a subvariety or 'dialect point' within the inner city. Sanders then turns to a detailed examination of the relationship between linguistic and social variables in lexicon, syntax and the use of 'ba' and 'gei' in Beijing speech. He notes that the use of Beijing Chinese as a standard for the national language emerged during the 1920s.

324 A Mandarin phonetic reader in the Pekinese dialect: with an introductory essay on the pronunciation.
Bernhard Karlgren. Stockholm: Kungl. Boktryckerit P. A. Norstedt & Sons, 1918. 187p.

The Swedish Sinologist Bernhard Karlgren made a particular study of Chinese phonetics. In the essay accompanying his selection of texts rendered in characters and in a phonetic script conveying the Beijing dialect, he describes Beijing Chinese as 'one of the many closely related dialects' spoken in North China and notes that the 'fashionable' Beijing pronunciation had been adopted by educated Chinese. Before him, several linguisticians had already recorded the special status of Beijing Chinese: they included Robert Thom, *The Chinese speaker: or, extracts from works written in the Mandarin languages, as*

Language

spoken at Peking: compiled for the use of students (Ningpo, China: Presbyterian Mission Press, 1846. 102p.); Thomas Francis Wade, *The Peking syllabary, being a collection of the characters representing the dialect of Peking* (Hongkong: no publisher indicated, 1859. 83p.); Joseph Edkins, *Progressive lessons in the Chinese spoken language: with lists of common words and phrases, and an appendix continuing the laws of tones in the Peking dialect* (Shanghai: American Presbyterian Mission Press, 1886. 2nd ed. 104p.); Thomas Francis Wade, Walter Caine Hillier, *A progressive course designed to assist the student of colloquial Chinese as spoken in the capital and the metropolitan department* (Shanghai: Inspectorate General of Customs; London: W. H. Allen & Co., 1886. 2nd ed. 3 vols.); and George Carter Stent, *A Chinese and English vocabulary in the Pekinese dialect* (Shanghai: American Presbyterian Mission Press, 1898. 3rd ed. 795p.).

Religion

325 Buddhism in Beijing.
Editorial Board of *Buddhism in Beijing*.   Beijing: Chinese
Nationalities Photographic Art Publishing Company, 1990. 58p.
This booklet is one of several, with Chinese and English texts, devoted to religious life in
Beijing. As with the other two listed here, on Christianity and Islam (see item nos. 327
and 332), the editorial board includes at least one practitioner of the religion in question.
The tone of the text in this booklet on Buddhism is respectful, if a little strained, and
emphasizes the historic and artistic value of surviving temples as much as their role as
centres of devotion. State support for Buddhism and the strength of international links
receive recognition. Representative temples and their ceremonies are illustrated in detail
in full colour. There are brief notes on the Lay Buddhist Association of Beijing and on
Buddhist music. As with the other two works listed, the English text is shaky in places.

326 Buddhism under Mao.
Holmes Welch.   Cambridge, Massachusetts: Harvard University
Press, 1972. 666p. bibliog. (Harvard East Asia Series, no. 69).
This is the third in Welch's series of studies of Buddhism in modern China, following on
from *The practice of Chinese Buddhism 1900-50* (Cambridge, Massachusetts: Harvard
University Press, 1967. 568p. bibliog. [Harvard East Asia Series, no. 26]), and *The
Buddhist revival in China* (Cambridge, Massachusetts, 1968. 385p. bibliog. [Harvard East
Asia Series, no. 33]). However, given the politicization of religion under the People's
Republic of China, and the major role that Beijing played in all aspects of Chinese life
from 1949 onwards, this volume is the one that has most relating to the capital and to the
central government. Reconstructing what happened to Buddhism from interviews and
published Chinese sources, Holmes paints a dismal picture of its condition even before
the Cultural Revolution led to the wholesale suppression of religious practices. He
describes the great Beijing temples, including the Fayuansi and the Lama temple, and
their fate, and the dilemmas the monks faced over issues such as killing in wartime.

327   Catholic church in Beijing.

Editorial Board of *Catholic Church in Beijing*.   Beijing: Chinese
Nationalities Photographic Art Publishing Company, 1990. 60p.

A companion publication to *Buddhism in Beijing* (q.v.) and *Islamic in Beijing* (q.v.), also
with Chinese and English texts. The Catholic Church has had a long, chequered history
in Beijing from an early flourishing in the 14th century and its re-establishment with the
arrival of the Jesuit Father Matteo Ricci in 1601 (whose tomb is here shown). Generally
led by foreign missionaries in the past, the Chinese Catholic Church now has a wholly
Chinese hierarchy and, as reiterated in the preface to this booklet, is self-governing. Its
relations with the Vatican have yet to be regularized, but exchanges with Catholic
communities elsewhere in the world take place and are illustrated here. The booklet
contains photographs of the principal Catholic churches in Beijing and illustrates aspects
of diocesan life. The English text is regrettably poor and full of errors.

328   China.

Frank. L. Norris, edited by T. H. Dodson, G. R. Bullock-Webster.
London; Oxford: A. R. Mowbray & Co., Ltd; New York: Thomas
Whittaker, 2 & 3 Bible House, 1908. 217p. map. bibliog.
(Handbooks of English Church Expansion).

This standard missionary-published account of Anglican Church activities in 19th-
century China is full of the self-confidence and certainty of such works. Its main interest
for students of the history of Beijing is a chapter on 'The English Church enters Peking'
(p. 56-64), but several other chapters touch on the Anglican Church's activities in the
capital. More information on the subject up to 1950 can be found in H. P. Thompson,
foreword by the Archbishop of Canterbury, *Into all lands: the history of the Society for
the Propagation of the Gospel in Foreign Parts 1701-1950* (London: SPCK, 1951. 760p.
bibliog.).

329   China and the Christian colleges 1850-1950.

Jessie Gregory Lutz.   Ithaca, New York; London: Cornell
University Press, 1971. 575p. maps. bibliog.

As well as being a study of the tertiary-level institutions of education established by
foreigners during the century of the 'unequal treaties', this is also a good guide to the
strengths and weaknesses of Christian missionary activity during the same period. While
educating Chinese, the missionaries were also implanting, or attempting to implant,
Western values. When those so trained came up against a strongly nationalistic regime
after 1949, they found that they and the institutions that had produced them were viewed
with intense suspicion. Lutz's canvas is the whole of China, but Beijing and the colleges
there are well covered. The bibliography is very extensive, covering works in Chinese and
English.

330   The dragons of Tiananmen: Beijing as a sacred city.

Jeffrey F. Meyer.   Columbia, South Carolina: University of South
Carolina Press, 1991. 208p. map. bibliog. (Studies in Comparative
Religion).

In this study of the relationship between a cosmic system of symbols and the design of a
place, Meyer examines Beijing as an 'idea become visible in physical, architectural

forms'. The concept of Beijing as embodying cosmological principles has long been familiar at the levels of myth and of intellectual discussion among Chinese, but this may be the first Western study of the city as both a cosmic sacred city laid out along ancient principles of design and a place of local sacral significance. Meyer traces most of the symbolism used in the architecture and planning of Beijing to the *Yijing* (Book of Changes) and the philosophy of *yin-yang* and the five essences (*wuxing*). He examines the influence of astronomical patterns and of principles of axiality, concentricity and geomancy in the layout of the central palace and altars and the suburban altars. Such patterns are now buried under the modern growth of Beijing, but Meyer's study encourages a more penetrating look at its origins.

331 Hudson Taylor & China's open century.

A. J. Broomhall, foreword by Donald Coggan. London: Hodder & Stoughton, The Overseas Missionary Fellowship, 1981-89. 7 vols. maps. bibliog.

The story of the Reverend Hudson Taylor and the China Inland Mission (now the Overseas Missionary Fellowship), from its founding in the 1860s to the Boxer rebellion, told at great length. The books draw heavily on the mission's archives, but also take account of many other sources. They also cover more than just Hudson Taylor's work, including information, for example, on the Roman Catholic missions in Beijing from the 17th century, as well as the activities of the China Inland Mission in North China, including both Beijing and Tianjin. The final volume, subtitled 'It is not death to die!', includes coverage of the Boxer rebellion. The bibliographies attached to each volume provide a very comprehensive survey of works in English, and each volume also includes notes on most of the prominent people mentioned.

332 Islamic in Beijing.

Editorial Department of Picture Album *Islamic in Beijing*. Beijing: Chinese Nationalities Photographic Art Publishing Company, 1990. 48p.

More than Buddhism or Christianity, Islam in China is bound up with the role of national minorities. The largest group of Muslims in China is known as the Hui nationality and in Beijing, which has a fairly strong Islamic community, this group far outnumbers representatives of other nationalities, such as Uighurs and Kazakhs. Small pockets of Muslim believers are scattered throughout Beijing municipality, and this booklet illustrates some of the fair number of small mosques that serve them, in addition to two large and historic ones in the centre of Beijing. Islamic religious activity and training and Muslim living conventions are also depicted. The authenticity of the information given in this booklet seems impeccable, given the large number of Muslims listed on the editorial committee, but the standard of the English text is atrocious, even in the translation of the opening invocation to Allah.

333 Jesuits at the court of Peking.

Charles Wilfrid Allan. Shanghai; Hong Kong; Singapore: Kelly & Walsh, 1935. Reprinted, Arlington, Virginia: University Publications of America, 1975. 300p. bibliog.

A good popular history of the Jesuits in Beijing, from the earliest days of Matteo Ricci to the suppression of the order in the 1780s. Allan writes well, and the work perhaps deserves to be better known, even if the specialist will prefer to go back to the original sources.

334 The missionary enterprise in China and America.
Edited, with an introduction, by John King Fairbank. Cambridge, Massachusetts: Harvard University Press, 1974. Reprinted, Taipei, Taiwan: Rainbow-Bridge Book Co., 1977. 442p. (Harvard Studies in American-East Asian Relations, no. 6).

A series of essays providing a preliminary exploration of the missionary relationship between the United States and China. None of the essays are concerned with missionary activities in Beijing in any great detail, yet the importance of institutions in the city such as Yanjing (Yenching) University, and the equally important role for the missionary community of events such as the 1870 Tianjin massacre and the 1900 Boxer uprising means that Beijing features in many of the papers.

335 Peking paper gods: a look at home worship.
Anne Swann Goodrich. Nettetal, Germany: Steyler Press, 1991. 501p. bibliog. (Monumenta Serica Monograph Series, no. 23).

Visitors to Beijing who stroll away from the main streets into the *hutongs* or lanes, especially around New Year, may come across brightly coloured figures painted on doorways. These are guardians, and they are part of a tradition of paper gods that goes back a long way in China. Frowned upon during the Cultural Revolution, the paper gods of Beijing have been making a steady comeback since the late 1970s. This detailed study describes their history and their importance in Chinese folklore.

336 Yung-ho-kung: an iconography of the lamaist cathedral in Peking, with notes on lamaist mythology and cult.
Ferdinand Diederich Lessing, in collaboration with Gösta Montell, preface by Sven Hedin. Göteborg, Sweden; Stockholm: Elanders Boktryckeri Aktiebolao, 1942, reprinted 1993. 179p. map. bibliog. (Reports from the scientific expedition to the north-western provinces of China under the leadership of Dr Sven Hedin – the Sino-Swedish expedition – publication 18; VIII. Ethnography, 1).

This detailed work, the outcome of nearly two decades of research and collaboration between German and Swedish scholars, is probably the most thorough introduction in English to the Yonghegong, the 'Lama temple' in the northeast corner of the old city of Beijing. It covers, however, only a few of the temple's courts and halls. Three other volumes were intended that would have completed the study of the temple's iconography and lamaist cults. The disruption of the Second World War (and probably the advent of a new regime in China in 1949) clearly prevented further work on the project. This sole volume describes minutely the entrance courts, the fourth court and the first and second halls of the temple and adds a note on four rites: those for conjuring up prosperity; the alms-begging rite; the kiosk of threads; and the rite of burnt offering. Copious notes, a bibliography of pre-war studies, diagrams, line drawings and thirty-two black-and-white plates augment the value of this book.

Péking: histoire et description.
See item no. 182.

The wise man from the west.
See item no. 193.

Correspondence de Pékin 1722-59.
See item no. 208.

Lettres édifiantes et curieuses de Chine par des missionnaires jésuites 1702-76.
See item no. 229.

Peking: today and yesterday.
See item no. 309.

Social Conditions

337 Accepting population control: urban Chinese women and the one-child family policy.
Cecilia Nathansen Milwertz. Richmond, England: Curzon Press, 1997. 249p. bibliog. (Nordic Institute of Asian Studies, Monograph Series, no. 74).

Data for this study of women's attitudes towards China's one-child family policy were collected in one Beijing city district and two districts in the northeastern city of Shenyang. None of the districts was further identified. Milwertz examined three aspects of the policy: the extent to which it was at variance with traditional norms and values; whether it was perceived as interfering with reproductive self-determinism; and whether it was welcomed as a positive break with tradition. She found that since the inception of the campaign in 1978-79, Beijing municipality had achieved a one-child family rate of over eighty per cent. Beijing moreover typified the structure of the urban planned birth programme through propaganda, planning and liaison. Milwertz concluded that although they might state a preference for two children, the majority of urban women appeared to accept population control as exercised through the one-child policy and did not see the policy as a violation of human rights and compliance with it as necessarily a negative issue. A full bibliography lists works in English, Chinese and Danish.

338 Beijing children's hospital.
Beijing: Beijing Children's Hospital, 1985. 12p.

More of a publicity handout than a publication proper, this presents a rare account in English and Chinese of the Beijing Children's Hospital. It was founded in 1952 and completed in 1955, replacing a private foundation, the Beiping (later Beijing) Private Children's Hospital, and is linked with the Second Beijing Medical College. Today, it is one of the chief paediatric centres in China. As well as a brief sketch of the hospital's history, there is an account of the range of services that it offers.

339 China's urban villagers: changing life in a Beijing suburb.
Norman A. Chance, Fred Engst.   Fort Worth, Texas: Holt, Rinehart
& Winston, Inc., 1991. 2nd ed. 200p. map. bibliog. (Case Studies in
Cultural Anthropology).

Chance, an American sociologist, carried out his initial fieldwork in Half Moon village in
the former Red Flag Commune twenty-five miles south of Beijing over three periods
between April 1972 and December 1979. His findings were incorporated in a first edition
of this book, *China's urban villagers: life in a Beijing commune* (Fort Worth, Texas: Holt,
Rinehart & Winston, Inc., 1984). They were augmented by four periods of research
undertaken between spring 1984 and summer 1989 by Fred Engst, an American raised
and educated in China, who is co-author of a chapter examining the villagers' reactions
to the Tiananmen incident of June 1989. Chance discusses first the collective life of the
village in its commune days and issues of work, village life, the life-cycle, education,
marriage and family relations. The second part of the book looks at post-1978 changes,
when the issues of modernization and increased productivity in the agricultural sector
received priority. Villagers were obliged to examine the question of new relations
between the individual, the collective and the state, the role of incentives and problems of
corruption and bureaucracy. The result is a stimulating and thoughtful work.

340 The guilds of Peking.
John Stewart Burgess.   New York: Columbia University Press,
1928. 270p. bibliog.

The guild system was a long-established means of regulating craft, commercial and
professional activities in Beijing and China as a whole. A guild's principal functions were
to maintain a monopoly for its members, prevent competition among them and determine
prices and wages. It disciplined members, controlled apprenticeships, undertook
charitable work, especially in organizing funerals, and arranged religious ceremonies in
honour of those deities regarded as its patrons or 'founders'. Guilds had no legal status,
but protected their members by presenting a united front to officials. Burgess combines
observations based on a study of forty-two guilds with case-studies of three of them. He
hints at changes to the system which came about through the advent of new categories of
workers, such as railway workers, unsuited to the guild structure. (The guild system has
long gone; only provincial associations remain in the capital.) Burgess's study is a product
of the sociology department of Yanjing (Yenching) University in Beijing. The
bibliography indicates a healthy literature from the late 19th century of research and field
studies on social conditions in China.

341 Life at the grassroots.
Luo Fu, Jin Hua, Xiang Rong, Zhou Zheng, editor Su Wenming.
Beijing: Beijing Review, 1981. 87p. map. (China Today, no. 2,
Beijing Review Special Feature Series).

This booklet presents profiles of everyday life in four different settings in China. The first
chapter, entitled 'City dwellers', focuses on Weikeng *hutong* ('Reed Bed Lane'), a
'precinct of Beijing', in the spring of 1981. The emphasis is on the administrative
structure of the precinct, in particular the neighbourhood committee, which functions
under one of the eighty-five neighbourhood agencies of Beijing, in accordance with
regulations first promulgated in 1954. The Weikeng *hutong* neighbourhood committee
involves itself in such areas as health, welfare, job-seeking for the young and housing.
Sub-committees handle security and mediation. Salaries among the residents are low, but

when this profile was prepared (1980-81) subsidies were generous. The situation may have changed since. While it is clear on how this basic organ of social administration operates, the booklet, despite including several case histories, gives no indication of how residents actually feel about their neighbourhood committee.

342 Peking: a social survey.
Sidney D. Gamble, assisted by John Stewart Burgess, forewords by G. Sherwood Eddy, Robert A. Woods. London: Humphrey Milford Oxford University Press, 1921. 538p.

Carried out under the auspices of Princeton University Centre in China and the Beijing YMCA, this exhaustive survey, with thirteen appendices, provides detailed and systematic information on social conditions among the Chinese population of Beijing at the beginning of the 1920s, drawing in part on government and police statistics. Beijing suffered great poverty, with twelve per cent of the population existing below the subsistence level and the 'social evil' of prostitution rife. Gamble approached his task from two angles: the need to base definite social programmes on the findings of scientific studies of facts and situations; and the desire to implement a 'more comprehensive application of Christian principles to the social life of the people'. In a later, more rigorous, study, Gamble detailed the finances of a number of Chinese families between July 1926 and November 1927: Sidney D. Gamble, fieldwork in charge of Wang Ho-ch'ien, Liang Jen-ho, *How Chinese families live in Peiping: a study of the income and expenditure of 283 Chinese families receiving from $8 to $550 silver per month* (New York; London: Funk & Wagnalls Company, 1933. 348p. map. bibliog.) and did further work on the wages and incomes of Chinese families in Beijing in the 1920s and 1930s. Similar studies were undertaken by C. C. Chu, Thomas Charles Blaisdell, *Peking rugs and Peking boys: a study of the rug industry in Peking* (Beijing: Peking Express Press, 1924. 47p.), and T'ao Meng-ho in his *Livelihood in Peking: an analysis of the budgets of sixty families* (Beijing: Social Research Department, China Foundation for the Promotion of Education and Culture, 1928. 180p. [Social Research Publications, Monograph no. 1]).

343 Towards a Chinese conception of social support: a study on the social support networks of Chinese working mothers in Beijing.
Angelina W. K. Yuen-Tsang. Aldershot, England; Brookfield, Vermont; Singapore; Sydney: Ashgate Publishing Ltd, 1997. 265p. bibliog.

This study by a Hong Kong researcher on Chinese women's concepts of social support was carried out from September 1993 to September 1994 in a residential neighbourhood in Beijing. The author had established good contacts in Beijing, but also chose the area because she supposed that the ways of thinking and mode of life of its inhabitants would reflect the cultural orientation of urban Chinese in general. Some characteristics of Beijing life intrude: the four-sided courtyard style of accommodation; the employment of household maids from the provinces; the renewal of old neighbourhoods; and the capital's loss of economic edge to competition from southern China. It is, however, difficult to know if the choice of a Beijing neighbourhood as the subject for this research has affected its conclusions or whether its findings can be taken as typical of widespread attitudes. There is nonetheless much good material here on recent practice and on apprehensions over the effects of social change.

Marriage and fertility in Tianjin, China: fifty years of transition.
See item no. 489.

Statistics

344 Beijing statistical yearbook 1991.
Compiled by Beijing Municipal Statistical Bureau, edited by Zhou
Yan, Hou Xiaowei.   Beijing: China Statistical Publishing House,
1991. 120p.

The dates for the major indicators in this collection of statistics are 1952, 1957, 1965,
1978, 1980, 1985 and 1990. It lists the national economic planning periods for China for
the years 1950-90. An earlier summary, *Beijing Statistics in Brief 1988*, compiled by
Beijing Municipal Statistical Bureau (Beijing: China Statistical Publishing House, 1988),
provides a profile of the capital for the years 1986-87. Neither set of statistics compares
Beijing's needs and performance with those of the rest of China. However, standard
formulae and categories that appear to be applied to Beijing are also used in a study such
as *Changes and development in China (1949-89)* (q.v.) and those experienced in the
interpretation of statistics might be able to work out the relevant comparisons from the
two books, at least for the later period.

345 Changes and development in China (1949-89).
China Review Press.   Beijing: China Review Press, 1989. 255p.

Although Beijing is only mentioned occasionally in this volume, produced to mark the
fortieth anniversary of the establishment of the People's Republic of China, there is
nevertheless much useful information in both the text and the figures and charts, some of
which can be linked to the capital.

346 China Facts & Figures Annual.
Edited 1978-98(?) by John L. Scherer, 1999- , by Robert Perrins.
Gulf Breeze, Florida: Academic International Press, 1978- . annual.

The title varies slightly; volumes from 1993 to 1998 have the subtitle *Handbook*. This
publication provides detailed statistical information for all aspects of China from 1976
onwards. It is divided into twenty-eight chapters, covering provinces and special
municipalities, including Beijing, and is an indispensable source of statistical
information.

347 China's provincial statistics, 1949-89.
Hsueh Tien-tung, Li Qiang, Liu Shucheng (et al.).   Boulder,
Colorado; San Francisco; Oxford: Westview Press, 1993. 595p.

Beijing, as one of the municipalities directly under the State Council, and therefore
equivalent to a province, is covered in its own section in this compilation. There are two
parts. The first gives statistical tables for 100 economic and social variables, divided into
fifteen categories, while part two explains how the tables were constructed.

348 Statistical Yearbook of China.
Edited by the State Statistical Bureau of China.   Beijing; Hong
Kong: China Statistical Publishing House, Chinese edition, 1981- .
annual; Hong Kong: Oxford University Press, English edition,
1985- . annual.

The title varies, but this is the most comprehensive collection of statistics about China
available.

Environment

349 Beautiful Beijing.
Edited by the Office of the Capital Afforestation Commission, chief
editor Cong Shi, editor Huang Zu'an, translated by Deng Xin,
photographs by Ding Yuehua and 110 others.   Beijing: China
Photographic Publishing House, 1986. 197p.

This handsome volume of full-colour photographs may at times overstate Beijing's
credentials as a 'green' city, but it does justice to the municipality's great efforts to
improve the city's environment and amenities and at the same time preserve the natural
settings of temples and other ancient sites. In typical Chinese style the book's presentation
combines several skills: calligraphic inscriptions, seal engraving, binding and fine
illustrations. Text and captions are in Chinese and English.

Education

350 An American transplant: the Rockefeller Foundation and Peking Union Medical College.
Mary Brown Bullock. Berkeley, California; Los Angeles; Oxford: University of California Press, 1980. 280p. bibliog.

The Peking Union Medical College – still so called, despite the current use of Beijing – dates from 1921, when the Rockefeller Foundation decided to establish a centre for modern Western medicine in China. The teaching, entirely in English, made no concessions to China's own medical tradition, which was seen as old-fashioned and more akin to superstition than to medicine. Perhaps not surprisingly, given this approach and the general political confusion which reigned in North China during the period 1921-49, the college only produced some 329 qualified doctors before the Communist victory. However, it survived the 1949 take-over and has come to occupy an important place in Chinese medical education. This is a detailed account of its foundation and the way in which it gradually became absorbed into the mainstream of Chinese medical education, which throws light both on foreign attitudes towards China and on Chinese coping methods in the face of a Western onslaught. More information on the college can be found in two other works: Mary E. Ferguson, *China Medical Board and Peking Union Medical College: a chronicle of fruitful collaboration 1914-51* (New York: China Medical Board of New York, 1970. 263p.); and John Z. Bowers, *Western medicine in a Chinese palace: Peking Union Medical College 1917-51* (Philadelphia, Pennsylvania: Josiah Macey Junior Foundation, 1972. 250p.).

351 Beijing daxue/Peking university.
Edited by Hu Wensun, Fen Nansheng, photographs by Sang Yangsen with Li Zhongxin, Fu Qiang, Zhu Chaoping. Beijing: Beijing Art Photographic Publishing Company, 1985. unnumbered.

Presents the history and achievements of 'Beida' – Beijing University, but here called Peking University – from its inauguration in 1912, building on the earlier Metropolitan University founded in 1898, to the 1980s. The university was reconstituted in 1952 with the incorporation of elements from other universities, often with foreign connections, that had existed in Beijing before the establishment of the People's Republic of China in 1949.

The album is well illustrated and lists the various faculties of the university. It comes with a thirty-eight-page bilingual booklet, which to some extent amplifies the main text.

352 Yenching university and Sino-Western relations, 1916-52.
Philip West. Cambridge, Massachusetts; London: Harvard University Press, 1976. 327p. bibliog. (Harvard East Asian Series, no. 85).

Yanjing (Yenching in Wade-Giles) University, founded in 1916, was an attempt by American missionaries to bring the values of modern, Western democracy to young Chinese. Its principles were based on Christianity and Chinese patriotism, at a time when young Chinese were faced with the bewildering world thrown up by the 1911 revolution. Perhaps the height of its success was when its president, John Leighton Stuart, became US ambassador to China in 1946. Unfortunately for Yanjing, and its ideals, Stuart's period as ambassador coincided with the defeat of the Chinese Nationalists by the Chinese Communist Party in the civil war which raged from 1947 to 1949. Stuart's appeals to his former students not to follow the Nationalists into exile but to help build a new China raised suspicions about the university and its links with 'American imperialism'. The Korean War, which saw Americans fighting Chinese, clinched its fate. Yanjing was closed in 1952, and its splendid campus given to Beijing University. Stuart's own account of these events can be found in his autobiography, *Fifty years in China: the memoirs of John Leighton Stuart, missionary and ambassador* (New York: Random House, 1954. 346p. map), while a somewhat critical biography is Shaw Yu-ming, *An American missionary in China: John Leighton Stuart and Chinese-American relations* (Cambridge, Massachusetts: Council of East Asian Studies, Harvard University, 1992. 381p. bibliog. [Harvard East Asian Monographs, no. 158]). Both contain accounts of his time in Beijing.

The May fourth movement: intellectual revolution in modern China.
See item no. 265.

The cultural revolution at Peking university.
See item no. 293.

Hundred day war: the cultural revolution at Tsinghua university.
See item no. 298.

Die kulturrevolution an der universität Beijing: vorgeschichte, ablauf und bewältigung. (The Cultural Revolution at Beijing University: early history, course and termination.)
See item no. 301.

China and the Christian colleges 1850-1950.
See item no. 329.

Economy

General

353 China's economy: a basic guide.
Christopher Howe.   London; Toronto; Sydney; New York: Paul
Elek Granada Publishing, 1978. 248p. maps.

Although written before the major changes introduced by Deng Xiaoping's economic
reforms of 1978, this remains an important textbook covering all aspects of China's
economic development from 1949 to 1978. There are few specific references to Beijing,
but the major role of the central government in economic matters in China, and the
importance of the capital region, ensures that Beijing is never very far away. A
chronology and a note on some of the major players in post-1949 economic development
adds to the book's usefulness. The bibliography appears coyly as Appendix E, p. 223-25,
entitled 'How to find out about and keep up with economic developments in China'.

354 Doing business in China: the last great market.
Geoffrey Murray.   Sandgate, England: China Library, 1994. 350p.
bibliog.

Murray, a journalist with a long exposure to Asia, attempts in this book to describe the
economic reforms that had taken place in China up to the early 1990s, with particular
emphasis on the climate for foreign investment. He also suggests ways of approaching
doing business in China. He touches on joint-venture schemes in Beijing and looks more
closely at the Beijing Jeep venture, which he presents largely as a cautionary tale of what
can go wrong in such situations. Developments in the manufacturing, service and
transport sectors of the port city of Tianjin up to the beginning of the 1990s also receive
brief mention. Murray's book is now outdated, but still offers a useful account of earlier
stages in China's economic reforms.

355 **A history of Chinese currency: 16th century BC-20th century AD.**
Edited by the Editorial Board for *A history of Chinese currency*,
Xinhua (New China) Publishing House, People's Bank of China.
Beijing: Xinhua (New China) Publishing House, N. C. N. Ltd; Hong
Kong: M. A. O. Management Group Ltd, 1983. 220p.

This lavishly illustrated book is obviously concerned with coins and notes issued all over
China, but from the establishment of the Yuan dynasty capital of Dadu near modern
Beijing, Beijing has been an important centre for the issue of currency. Since the
establishment of the People's Republic in 1949, the People's Bank of China, based in
Beijing, is the only source of coins and notes for the whole of China. The book also
includes reproductions of some notes issued by foreign or joint Chinese-foreign banks in
Tianjin.

Manufacturing

356 **Beijing jeep: a case study of western business in China.**
Jim Mann.   New York: Simon & Schuster, 1989. Revised and
reprinted, Boulder, Colorado; Oxford: Westview Press, 1997. 351p.

In 1979, as the post-Mao Chinese leadership began to pursue industrial modernization,
American Motors Corporation (AMC) initiated discussions with the Beijing Automotive
Works (BAW) over establishing a joint venture for the production of new jeeps. The
Beijing Jeep Company (BJC) was eventually launched in 1984 at BAW's southern plant,
in southeast Beijing, on a twenty-year contract. Production was initially slow and was
dogged by differing visions over the goals of the new venture – the Chinese hoped for a
wholly new export model, the Americans for a vast domestic market – by different work
traditions, by a shortage of foreign exchange in 1986, by the take-over of AMC by
Chrysler in 1987 and by the 1989 Tiananmen upheaval. Threats to the company's
progress were sometimes resolved by high-level Chinese intervention. By 1996, however,
about 80,000 jeeps were being produced. The author is a journalist with the *Los Angeles
Times* and he relates BJC's vicissitudes in a fast-moving style though with several detours
into the problems of other Sino-American joint ventures.

357 **China's automobile industry: policies, problems, and prospects.**
Eric Harwitt.   Armonk, New York; London: M. E. Sharpe, 1995.
208p. bibliog. (An East Gate Book; Studies on Contemporary
China).

Harwitt has produced a more analytical study of the problems faced by joint ventures in
automobile manufacturing in China than that offered in *Beijing jeep: a case study of
western business in China* (q.v.). He surveys three other similar ventures in addition to his
chapter (p. 67-91) on 'Beijing jeep's bumpy road'. His conclusions are more summary
than Jim Mann's, but he traces many of the same points. In particular, he suggests that the
proximity of the Beijing plant to the organs of central government in the capital led to a

higher measure of interest by national leaders in the joint venture's problems and to their willingness to intervene on occasion.

Trade

358 Old Beijing shop sign.
Edited by Lin Yan, Huang Yansheng, Xiao Yunru, Ji Lianzhi, Lu Ruizhen, appendix by Wang Shixiang. Beijing: Bo Wen Book Company, 1987. unnumbered.

The English-language synopsis to this collection of signs and signboards formerly displayed by Beijing shops to identify their goods or trade gives just enough information to allow the non-Chinese reader to work out the categories and types of signs introduced here. The rest of the text is in Chinese. The book is nonetheless worth pursuing for those interested in the subject. 23 of its 230 illustrations are in colour; the rest are monochrome reproductions of drawings and photographs of old signs and shop fronts. The appendix (in Chinese only) describes the signs and shop fronts proposed for the 'street of shops' that existed from 1715 to 1885 in the Summer Palace (Yuanmingyuan) for the emperor's entertainment.

Transport

359 CTS in 40 years.
Edited by China Travel Service Head Office.   Beijing: World
Affairs Press, [1989]. 133p. maps.

This glossy publication, prepared for the fortieth anniversary of the company that
eventually became China Travel Service (CTS), covers not just Beijing but the whole of
China. Inevitably, however, given the importance of the capital region for tourism,
Beijing features both in the sections on organization and in the more general sections.
Tianjin also merits a page. Much information is given about CTS offices around China
and overseas, some of which will be out of date.

Literature

Poetry

360 Beijing street voices: the poetry and politics of China's democracy movement.
David S. Goodman.   London; Boston, Massachusetts: Marion
Boyars, 1981. 208p. map. bibliog.

A thoughtful and well-documented account of the protest movement that lasted from mid-November 1978 to early April 1979 and which was centred around 'Democracy Wall' in Xidan in west Beijing. The 'Wall' supported many big-character posters and was the distribution point for a variety of unofficial publications. Much of the protest, which was sparked by a range of general and specific grievances, took the form of poems. Goodman presents a selection of these in translation. He points out the importance of poetry as a vehicle for comment, charts the course of the 'Democracy Movement', assesses its place in a recurring Chinese pattern of dissent and relates it to the protest gatherings of April 1976 to commemorate Zhou Enlai. Photographs, magazine illustrations, the original character texts of some of the poems, appendices gathering together original editorials and statements, checklists of the unofficial press and a glossary of terms, together with a full bibliography and indices, make this an invaluable source of information on the movement of 1978-79.

Fiction

361 Absolute measures.
Humphrey Hawksley.   London: Headline Books, 1999. 312p.

Hawksley draws on his experience as an Asian correspondent for the British Broadcasting Corporation, including a spell in Beijing, as background for this thriller of international

Literature. Fiction

finance and local conflict. Part of the action is set in the Beijing expatriate world of the 1990s, where past discomforts have given way to an abundance of supermarkets and shopping malls. The result is an enjoyable read, from which the reader may learn a little about Beijing and its denizens.

362   The adventures of Wu: the life cycle of a Peking man.
H. Y. Lowe (Luo Xinyao).   Beiping [Beijing]: Henri Vetch, 1940. Reprinted, with an introduction by Derk Bodde, Princeton, New Jersey: Princeton University Press, 1983. 512p.

Based on a series of newspaper articles written in English for the *Peking Chronicle* by a Chinese journalist, *The adventures of Wu* is a fictionalized autobiography, which provides much detail of ordinary life in Beijing from the 1911 revolution to the outbreak of the Sino-Japanese war in 1937. Wu's story is that of a man and his family who were not rich, but who drew satisfaction from simple pleasures such as eating and drinking. The author includes in this account of Wu from birth to marriage descriptions of the fairs and festivals that were such a marked feature of pre-Communist Beijing, and which have begun to reappear since the reforms of 1978. The introduction to the 1983 edition provides additional background on Beijing and its various customs and festivals, and has an index. Wu's adventures have been translated into Japanese, and the author's son, Luo Jinde, was translating it into Chinese when this bibliography went to press.

363   Beijing Odyssey: based on the life and times of Liang Shiyi.
Steven T. Au.   Mahomet, Illinois: Mayhaven Publishing, 1999. 250p.

Liang Shiyi was a real person, who figured prominently in economic and political circles in the early years of the 20th century. He organized Chinese labourers to go to Europe during the First World War, helped found a bank, and was later prime minister for one of the short-lived Beijing governments that succeeded Yuan Shikai's failed attempt to become emperor. Steven Au has chosen to tell Liang's story as a novel, adding additional colour to the political drama. Thus there are descriptions of Liang's life-style, including his wife and concubines. A purist might wish that Au had stuck to the known facts, but others will find this an easy way to get a picture of a Beijing that has long disappeared.

364   The China option.
Nancy Dall Milton.   New York: Pantheon Books, 1982; London; Sydney: Pluto Press, 1984. 311p.

Nancy Dall Milton taught at the Beijing First Foreign Languages Institute from 1964 to 1969, an experience that she wrote about, with her husband David, in *The wind will not subside: years in revolutionary China, 1964-69* (New York: Pantheon Press, 1976. 397p.). She clearly draws on that background in this thriller set in the China of the early 1980s, when Deng Xiaoping's reforms had begun to lead to major changes in the Chinese view of the outside world, and to new tensions in Chinese society. Her characters are rather stock: the glamorous female investigative reporter, the bright young diplomat with whom she has an affair, and mysterious Chinese and American security officials – the latter appear to owe much to Dr Kissinger – but the Chinese background against which they all operate is well-drawn, and the result is entertaining.

130

365   It happened in Peking.
Louise Jordan Miln.   New York: Stokes, 1926. 368p.
A novel set during the 1900 siege of the legations, which draws heavily on the various
diaries and other accounts of that event. It is now mainly an historical curiosity.

366   The maker of heavenly trousers.
Daniele Varè.   London: Metheun, 1935. Reprinted, London: Black
Swan, 1986. 217p.
A light-hearted novel set in Beijing in the early 1930s, by the Italian diplomat Daniele
Varè, which sketches the lives of both foreigners and Chinese against the backdrop of the
neat lanes, palaces and temples of the then former capital city. It enjoyed a huge success
when it first appeared, and by 1948 it had gone through thirteen reprints. Equally
successful were two sequels, *The gate of happy sparrows* (London: Metheun, 1937.
Reprinted, London: Black Swan, 1987. 239p.), and *The temple of costly experience*
(London: Methuen, 1939. Reprinted, London: Black Swan, 1988. 237p.). All were
translated into Italian, German and French, and were published in the United States by
Doubleday, Doran & Co. A one-volume edition, incorporating all three novels, was
published as *Novels of Yen-Ching* (London: Methuen, 1954. 647p.).

367   Peking picnic.
Ann Bridge.   London: Chatto & Windus, 1932; 19th impression,
1967. 328p.
Ann Bridge (Lady O'Malley) was the wife of a diplomat who served in the British
legation in Beijing in the 1920s. *Peking picnic*, her first novel, became well-known for its
account of the gilded life of the foreign community in the legation quarter, while its
descriptions of the city and the countryside round about seemed to contemporaries to
capture the essence of the exoticism of China. The tale is contrived – although not as far-
fetched as it might now seem – involving the kidnapping and escape of a group of
diplomats and friends on a picnic near Beijing, but is still fun to read. Ann Bridge
returned to the theme of the foreign community in Beijing in *The ginger griffin* (London:
Chatto & Windus, 1934, reprinted 1968. 378p. [The Landmark Library]), while those who
wish to trace the origins of her characters and of at least part of her plots should read Ann
Bridge, *Facts and fictions* (London: Chatto & Windus, 1968. 215p.).

368   René Leys.
Victor Segalen.   Paris: Gallimard, 1971, 1979. 239p. map.
(Collection l'Imaginaire).
Segalen was an archaeologist (see item no. 468) as well as a novelist. His story of the
mysterious involvement of a young Belgian, René Leys, in the affairs of the Manchu
imperial court in its final days of 1911 is a masterpiece of half-certainty and allusion.
Hugh Trevor-Roper, in *Hermit of Peking: the hidden life of Sir Edmund Backhouse* (q.v.),
suggests that Segalen may have based the character of René Leys on a young Frenchman
he met in Beijing, Maurice Roy, who claimed to have had similar adventures. Some may
find the tale far-fetched. In the light of the existence of a possible model, others may see
in it the recreation of a psychological type. Yet others may willingly yield to the powerful
creation of atmosphere. Segalen's novel, first published in 1922, illustrates admirably the
sense of intoxication that overcame some Western residents of old Beijing in face of what
they felt to be the riches of the hidden life of the city.

369 Le sabotage amoureux. (Loving sabotage.)
Amélie Nothomb. Paris: Albin Michel, 1993. 124p. (Le Livre de
Poche Series).

This short, amusing novel tells of life in the diplomatic ghetto of Sanlitun in Beijing, as seen through the eyes of a seven-year old in the early 1970s. As the author makes clear, the main concern of its heroine is her role as a scout in battling the enemy – first East Germans, then Nepalese – and trying to persuade the Italian Elena to be her friend. China is incidental, and yet China intrudes all around, whether as the country of cabbages and pork, or a place where the people appointed as guardians lock the fire escapes not out of malice but because it is more convenient. Anyone who lived in Beijing before the 1980s will recognize the reality behind Nothomb's small girl growing up.

370 The smile on the face of the tiger.
Douglas Hurd, Andrew Osmond.   London: Collins, 1969. 286p.

A fast-paced and amusing thriller, set in London, Beijing and a variety of other places between 1957 and the early 1970s. Both Hurd, later British Secretary of State for Foreign and Commonwealth Affairs, and Osmond, were at one time members of the British diplomatic service. The novel draws on this background, and especially on Hurd's experiences in China in the 1950s, to give an authentic feel to the places and people described.

Stories and legends

371 Beijing legends.
Jin Shoushen, translated by Gladys Yang.   Beijing: Chinese
Literature Press, 1990. 141p. (Panda Books).

Jin Shoushen (1906-68) was of a Manchu family, and originally published these stories in the 1950s. They record folk tales which the author collected from the ordinary people of the city, and while not particularly polished, they serve as an introduction to the once thriving oral story-telling tradition for which Beijing became well-known throughout China. They also bring back memories of buildings and scenic spots which have long since disappeared.

372 Inside stories of the Forbidden City.
Er Si, Shang Hongkui and others, translated by Zhao Shuhan.
Beijing: New World Press, 1986. 165p.

A collection of stories and legends about the Forbidden City, the imperial palace in Beijing, from its foundation by the third Ming emperor to the days of the last emperor at the beginning of the 20th century, which help to bring to life the inhabitants of that vast collection of buildings. There is perhaps a slight political edge to many of the stories, which emphasize the wicked ways of many of the emperors, but the tales are well told and translated. An appendix gives a brief account of each of the emperors from 1368 to 1911.

373 Sights with stories in old Beijing.
Chinese Literature Press.   Beijing: Chinese Literature Press, 1990.
189p. (Panda Books).

This is not a guidebook, although it does draw attention to some of the interesting places
to visit in Beijing; rather it is a collection of stories, magical, ghostly or merely intriguing,
about forty-seven sites popular with visitors to Beijing. As is proper, some begin with the
fairytale formula 'Once upon a time', while others plunge straight into a fantastical
account involving a dragon, an immortal or some other magical figure. A similar, smaller
collection appeared as *Legends of Beijing*, edited by Cheng Weishen (Hong Kong: China
Foreign Publishing Co. [HK]. Ltd, [c. 1990]. 61p.).

374 Traditional comic tales.
Zhang Shouchen and others, translated by Gladys Yang.   Beijing:
Panda Books, 1983. 141p.

A tradition of comic story-telling developed in North China during the late 19th century,
in cities such as Beijing and Tianjin, which became known as *xiangsheng* or 'face and
voice' performances. Despite the political upheavals of the 20th century, these remain
popular, and this little book provides a representative selection. Many of them are set in
Beijing, and most show how a smart ordinary fellow can outwit his social superiors. The
translations read easily, and make the stories readily accessible.

Translations

375 Camel Xiangzi.
Lao She, translated by Shi Xiaoqing, illustrated by Gu Bingxin.
Beijing: Foreign Languages Press, 1981, 1988. 236p.

This well-known novel, set in 1930s Beijing, describes in unsentimental fashion the lives
of the city's poor. The hero is a rickshaw-puller, and the story tells of the struggle he and
many like him face to survive against immense odds. Robbed by soldiers, despised by his
clients, Camel Xiangzi struggles on. Pleasures are few, and the novel ends with the hero
realizing that there is nothing for the likes of him but hard work and little joy. This
translation reads well enough, but is somewhat wooden in style, and ends a chapter short
of the original twenty-four chapters. There have been other translations, including Lau
Shaw (sic), *Rickshaw boy*, translated and partially rewritten by Evan King (New York:
Reynal & Hichcock, 1945. 383p.), which has a happier ending, and *Rickshaw: the novel
Lo-t'o Hsiang Tzu by Lao She*, translated by Jean M. James (Honolulu, Hawaii:
University of Hawaii Press, 1979. 249p.). The novel has been filmed, and remains very
popular in China, where it has also been turned into an opera. Lao She's work is drawn
on extensively in David Strand's *Rickshaw Beijing* (q.v.), while Ranbir Vohra, *Lao She
and the Chinese revolution* (Cambridge, Massachusetts: East Asian Research Center,
Harvard University Press, 1974. 199p. [East Asia Monographs, no. 55]), looks at his place
in modern Chinese politics.

376   Dream of the red chamber.
Cao Xueqin, continuation by Gao E., full version first published 1791, 2nd ed. 1792. 2nd ed. reprinted, Shanghai: Ya Tung Book Company, 1927.

The story of the Jia family, with its many ramifications and vicissitudes, is set in and around Beijing in the first half of the 18th century. Often described as a 'novel of manners', it can be interpreted also as an account of the passage to enlightenment of its principal character, Pao Yu. The full version of *Hung lou meng* (its Chinese title) is generally divided into 120 chapters, the first 80 of which are the work of Cao Xueqin (Tsao Hsueh-chin). The remaining 40 are said to have been 'edited', possibly written, by Gao E (Kao Ou, Kao Ngo). It is one of the best-known Chinese novels and has been translated several times into English, not always under the same title. Partial translations are by: H. Bancroft Joly, *Dream of the red chamber* (Hong Kong: Kelly & Walsh, 1892-93. 2 vols.); Wang Chi-chen, *Dream of the red chamber*, (1) preface by Arthur Waley (London: George Routledge & Sons Ltd, [n.d.]); (2) preface by Mark Van Doren (London: Vision Press Ltd, 1959. 574p.); Florence McHugh, Isobel McHugh, *The dream of the red chamber: a Chinese novel of the early Ching period*, introduction by Franz Kuhn, English translation from a German translation by Franz Kuhn of part of the Chinese original (London: Routledge & Kegan Paul Ltd, 1958. 582p.); Yang Hsien-yi, Gladys Yang, *A dream of red mansions*, abridged version of a full Foreign Languages Press translation (Sydney; London; Boston, Massachusetts: Unwin Paperbacks, 1986. 499p.). Full translations are by: Foreign Languages Press, *A dream of red mansions* (Beijing: Foreign Languages Press, 1980. 3 vols.); preface and translation by David Hawkes, *The story of the stone: a Chinese novel by Cao Xueqin in five volumes* (Harmondsworth, England; New York; Ringwood, Australia; Ontario, Canada; Auckland, New Zealand: Penguin Books, 1973, 1977, 1980. Vols. 1-3 [Penguin Classics]); and preface and translation by John Minford, *The story of the stone: a Chinese novel by Cao Xueqin in five volumes* (Harmondsworth, England; New York; Ringwood, Australia; Ontario, Canada; Auckland, New Zealand: Penguin Books, 1982, 1986. Vols. 4-5 [Penguin Classics]). The novel has attracted a large corpus of critical studies in both Chinese and Western languages.

377   Lao She.
Lao She, English translations by Shi Xiaoqing, Helena Kuo, Ida Pruitt, Don J. Cohn, Gladys Yang, Sidney Shapiro, William J. F. Jenner, Ying Ruocheng, Liao Hungying.   Nanjing, China: Yilin Press, 1992. 3 vols. (Modern Chinese Literature Library).

Lao She was the pen-name of Shu Qingchun (also styled Shu Sheyu). He was born in Beijing and spent much of his life there. The experiences of an impoverished childhood together with an intimate knowledge of the city, its people and their speech provided him with material and a style for many of his stories and plays. He died in Beijing, probably by committing suicide, after red guard persecution during the early years of the Cultural Revolution. These three volumes present some of his most important work, much of it set in Beijing: *Camel Xiangzi* (see item no. 375); *The quest for love of Lao Lee* (of which another title was *Divorce*); *Four generations under one roof* (published in an abridged version as *The yellow storm* [New York: Harcourt, Brace & Company, 1952]); *Beneath the red banner* (an uncompleted autobiographical novel); short stories; his best-known play, *Teahouse*; and the play *Dragon beard ditch*.

Works about writers

378 A pictorial biography of Lu Xun.
Compiled by Chen Shuyu, Zhang Xiaoding, Sun Ying, Ye Shuhui,
edited by Lin Wenbi, Zu Youyi, Zhang Rong, translated by Fei
Lande, Xu Meijiang, Wu Zhenchang, Jin Meifen, Xu Yeshan, Xiong
Zhenru, preface by Soong Ching Ling.   Beijing: People's Fine Arts
Publishing House, [probably 1981]. 174p.

This album, prepared for the centenary of the birth in 1881 of the great writer,
educationalist and revolutionary Lu Xun, has a section (p. 36-65) on his years in Beijing
(1912-26), where he held a post throughout that period in the Ministry of Education of the
Provisional Revolutionary Government. During that time he immersed himself in writing,
teaching, founding and editing new literary journals and societies and in support for
revolutionary groups. One of his most famous novels, *The true story of Ah Q*, was written
while he was in Beijing. He left Beijing in 1926 after being threatened by the government
of the warlord Duan Qirui. The album contains many photographs of Lu Xun and his
contemporaries. Some of his stories, including *The true story of Ah Q*, were published as
Selected stories of Lu Hsun ('Xun' in later editions), translated by Yang Hsien-yi, Gladys
Yang (Beijing: Foreign Languages Press, 1960, 3rd ed. 1972. 255p.), a small selection
from those published in *Selected works of Lu Hsun*, translated by Yang Hsien-yi, Gladys
Yang (Beijing: Foreign Languages Press, 1956-60. 4 vols.). The influence of Beijing on
his writings is briefly touched upon in William A. Lyell, Jr., *Lu Hsün's vision of reality*
(Berkeley, California; Los Angeles; London: University of California Press, 1976. 355p.
bibliog.).

**379 Wise daughters from foreign lands: European women writers in
China.**
Elisabeth Croll.   London; Winchester, Massachusetts; Sydney;
Wellington, New Zealand: Pandora, 1989. 265p. bibliog.

Professor Croll has chosen six Western women, five of them American despite the subtitle
of the book, through whom to study the responses of foreign women to life in China
between the 1880s and 1920s. Three of the six accompanied their husbands; one travelled
in a professional capacity; Nora Waln was 'adopted' by a wealthy Chinese family; and
Pearl Buck was born into a missionary family to China. All wrote of their experiences, in
the form of letters, reports, reminiscences or novels. Only one, Sarah Pike Conger, the
wife of a senior US diplomat, spent all her time in Beijing, where she endured the 1900
siege of the foreign legations, but also formed a close acquaintance with the Empress
Dowager Cixi. Her descriptions of visits to the Empress's apartments and to the homes of
noble families, *Letters from China with particular reference to the Empress Dowager and
the women of China* (Chicago: A. C. McClurg & Co., 1909. 392p.), gave some insight
into the private lives of upper-class Chinese. The journalist Grace Seton Thompson,
visiting China in 1923 to report on the 'new woman' there, spent several months in
Beijing. Her impressions of her China travels are recorded in *Chinese lanterns* (New
York: Dodd, Mead & Company, 1924. 373p.).

Arts

General

380   The British Museum book of Chinese art.
Jessica Rawson, Anne Farrer, Jane Portal, Shelagh Vainker, Carol
Michaelson, edited by Jessica Rawson.   London: British Museum
Press, 1992. 395p. maps. bibliog.

This thorough and beautifully illustrated book was prepared to accompany the opening of
a new gallery in the British Museum dedicated to the art of China and South and
Southeast Asia and takes as its starting point the Museum's collections of Chinese art.
Beijing does not receive any separate treatment, but is cited for examples of artistic styles
and practices, such as the workshops opened in the Imperial City by the Kangxi emperor
in the 17th-18th centuries. The book contains a great deal of additional information on
archaeological sites, Buddhist sites, traditional architecture, tombs and painters and has
copious notes, glossaries, chronologies and bibliographies. It is probably best to follow
up specific references to Beijing and other topics through the index.

Fine arts

381   Bertha Lum.
Mary Evans O'Keefe Gravalos, Carol Pulin.   Washington, DC,
London: Smithsonian Institution Press, 1991. 112p. bibliog.
(American Print-makers: a Smithsonian Series).

The American print-maker, Bertha Lum (1896-1954), spent many years in Japan and
China, and her prints reflect traditional images and stories, and everyday sights from both
countries. In the case of China, she made her home in Beijing initially from 1922 to 1929.

She returned there in 1933 after a spell in the United States, and remained in Beijing until forced out by the Second World War. Her eldest daughter, Catherine, married an Italian businessman based in China, Antonio Riva, while the younger, Peter, married Colin Crowe, a British diplomat. Bertha returned to Beijing in 1948, to live with Catherine and her husband, but life became increasingly difficult after the Communist take-over in 1949. Riva was arrested and eventually executed as a spy in 1951. By that time, the Crowes had joined the British embassy, then operating in a curious half-world (see item no. 143), and Bertha was eventually allowed to live with them, before leaving for Italy in 1953. She died in Genoa in 1954. This handsomely produced book, which is full of delightful reproductions of her work, tells the story of her life and her print-making, and will appeal to the general reader and specialist alike.

382 A history of Far Eastern art.
Sherman E. Lee, edited by Naomi N. Richard.   London: Thames & Hudson, 1997. 5th ed. 576p. maps. bibliog.

This large and beautiful book, first published in the United Kingdom in 1964, makes only a few brief references to Beijing, largely in the context of its importance as the centre of empire and thus as a centre for the arts. Chapter 17 in part 4, on later Chinese art, describes (p. 468-70) the plan of Beijing and particularly of the Imperial City, laid out under the Ming along lines of symmetry and balance in reflection of the overriding principle of the harmony of the universe. Michael Sullivan, in his *An introduction to Chinese art* (London: Faber & Faber, 1961. 223p. maps. bibliog.), similarly accords only brief mention to Beijing, but in more cautious tones and with a different emphasis on the tension between Chinese taste, as exemplified by the Song dynasty, and that of the alien Yuan. Ming style, as typified by the Forbidden City, is presented as unadventurous and that of the Qing as equally conservative.

383 Modern oil painting: the first oil painting exhibition sponsored by Beijing International Art Gallery.
Chief supervisor Li Kai, translated by Li Shutian, Zhang Zhe.
Beijing: Beijing International Art Gallery, 1987. 82p.

An interesting full-colour catalogue of oil paintings shown in Beijing in June-July 1986, which demonstrates the various styles and techniques in use by contemporary Chinese artists in the mid-1980s. While such works were not confined to Beijing, they were more likely to be found there than in any other city apart from Shanghai. In addition, many of the artists live and work in Beijing, which is reflected in their paintings.

384 Rong Bao Zhai: selections of Rong Bao Zhai's water and colour woodblock printings.
Rong Bao Zhai Studio.   Beijing: Rong Bao Zhai Studio, [n.d.]. 76p.

Rong Bao Zhai in Beijing, with a history of over 300 years, is one of the principal centres for the reproduction and dissemination of classical and modern Chinese paintings. The studio, now a state-owned enterprise, reproduces original works through the water-colour woodblock printing method of tracing, carving, printing and mounting. This booklet serves both as an introduction to the crafts of the studio and as a catalogue in full colour of the reproductions available in the late 1980s and early 1990s from the Rong Bao Zhai shop. Two further examples of the studio's skills are reproduced on p. 60-61 of Frances Wood's *Chinese Illustrations* (London: British Library, 1985. 80p. bibliog.). Dr Wood points out that the crafts of colour woodblock printing and decorated letter-paper had almost died out in Beijing by the 1930s, but were revived and are now perpetuated by Rong Bao Zhai.

Handicrafts

385 Ancient Chinese woodblock new year prints.
Compiled by Wang Shucun.   Beijing: Foreign Languages Press, 1985. 184p. map.

The glory of this book lies in its reproduction of 140 new year prints, nearly all in full colour, selected from the compiler's own collection. The ephemeral nature of this form of popular art – the prints were generally discarded after each lunar new year's festivities – meant that very few have survived. This album contains twelve examples dating from before the Qing dynasty (1644-1911). In his introduction, Wang Shucun distinguishes five regions of China that became flourishing centres of production for new year pictures. One was the village of Yangliuqing to the west of Tianjin, where a tradition developed, possibly influenced, Wang suggests, by artists from the former Song Imperial Academy of Painting, of finely executed woodblock prints finished by brush. About 3,000 Yangliuqing pictures are still extant. Plates 94-140 reproduce a selection of Yangliuqing prints. Descriptive notes on each plate are presented at the end of the book.

386 Chinese kites.
Wang Hongxun.   Beijing: Foreign Languages Press, 1989. 101p. (Traditional Chinese Arts and Culture Series).

Beijing and Tianjin are two of the principal kite-making centres in China. The skill is often passed down through families. This attractive book has a short section of text outlining the historical development of kites, kites and their place in folk customs, and the processes of kite-making. This is preceded by eighty pages of plates and photographs in full colour that illustrate the many types of kites, their accessories, decoration and techniques of construction, kites as subjects of paintings and drawings, and the business of flying kites. Two pages of detailed drawings depict the frame structure of one type of kite. The captions make clear the centre of production of the kite illustrated.

387 Chinese matchbox covers.
Edited by Zhou Daguang, text by Wu Zhishi, photographs by Xu Zengxiang, cover inscription by Jin Yan, design by Zhou Daguang. Beijing: Foreign Languages Press, 1989. 172p.

Perhaps matchbox covers represent a minor art form, but there is much interest in them in China, as there is in stamps, and their collection is a major hobby. This handsome volume, illustrated in full colour, is based on the collection of Ji Zhuguang, and includes specimens from both pre- and post-1949. All China is represented, but the capital, with its ancient and modern monuments, museums and galleries, features prominently.

Performing arts

388 Chinese drama: a historical survey.
Colin Mackerras. Beijing: New World Press, 1990. 274p. bibliog.

China's dramatic arts are among the finest and longest-enduring in the world. They have been so central to people's lives that during the 20th century the Communist leadership used them to convey new messages to society, without impairing the technical excellence that underpinned them. Among the forms of drama best known outside of China is Peking opera, which developed in Beijing from the end of the 18th century, based on regional styles of music, singing and acting that took root in the capital. Mackerras describes the characteristics of Peking opera on p. 60-78. He later outlines the changes forced upon it during the Cultural Revolution (1966-76) and recounts the revival of traditional forms after 1976. He also highlights the important role Beijing has played in the development of dramatic art in China, from opera to Lao She's spoken drama *Teahouse* (1957). Notes, an appendix of translated terms, a select bibliography and an ample index increase the value of this book.

389 Chinese shadow puppet plays.
Liu Jilin, translated Fang Zhenya, Fang Guoping, photographs by Wu Yinbo. Beijing: Morning Glory Publishers, 1988. 111p.

Shadow puppet theatre in China has a long history. The first reliable records of its performance, according to this attractive book, date from the Northern Song period (960-1127). It was popular through much of China and among the Mongols and the Manchus, and regional forms evolved. When the Ming dynasty moved its capital north to Beijing in 1421, the southern style of shadow puppet drama followed. Beijing developed its own style, influenced by neighbouring northern forms, which enjoyed great popularity for two hundred years during the Qing period, with over a dozen active troupes divided broadly between those in the eastern and western districts of the city. The influence of make-up and costumes from the Peking opera was discernible. Beijing had its own repertoire of plays. The book gives synopses of several representative scenarios. Its 114 colour reproductions illustrate the delicacy and at the same time the animation of the shadow puppets. Chapters on the creation and manipulation of puppets and on characters, props and scenery add to the book's interest and usefulness.

390 Paintings of Beijing opera characters by Dong Chensheng.
Introductory text by Jiang Feng, opera synopses by Bao Wenqing.
Beijing: Zhaohua Publishing House, 1981. 64p.

The most interesting aspect of this book are the paintings, which illustrate scenes from thirty-six of the best known Peking operas. They are executed in quasi-traditional style by an artist who learnt his craft while serving in the People's Liberation Army, itself an interesting comment on contemporary China. In addition to the illustrations, there is a short account of the founding and development of Peking opera, and a brief sketch of the artist's own history.

391 Peking opera.
Text by Rewi Alley, pictures by Eva Siao, Wen Naiqiang, Zhang Zudao, Di Xianghua and others.   Beijing: New World Press, 1984, 1989. 103p.

The first version of *Peking opera* was published by New World Press in 1957 with largely black-and-white photographs. The text by the late New Zealander Rewi Alley, a long-time resident of Beijing, makes some digressions into discussion of political manipulation of the opera, as at times of dynastic change and during the Cultural Revolution (1966-76), and is unstinting in his praise of the post-1949 regime's treatment of actors. He is illuminating on the training of performers from childhood onwards and in explaining gestures, characterization, acting conventions, musical accompaniments, costumes and make-up. The book concludes with brief synopses of fifteen operas. The photographs, in full colour in the latest edition, are superb, especially of children in training, and convey the skill and drama of this unique form of entertainment.

392 Peking opera.
Colin Mackerras.   Hong Kong: Oxford University Press, 1997. 72p. (Images of Asia).

In keeping with this series' style, this little book is a well-illustrated account of Peking opera aimed at the non-specialist. Mackerras has an established reputation as a historian of the Chinese theatre, and the book reflects this interest. He also considers the future of the genre, examining some of the attempts since 1949 to 'modernize' it, and concluding that it may well not survive, given the other entertainment outlets now available to the ordinary citizens of Beijing. The pictures are well chosen, and range from old black-and-white records to excellent modern colour photographs.

393 Peking opera and Mei Lanfang: a guide to China's traditional theatre and the art of its great master.
Wu Zuguang, Huang Zuolin, Mei Shaowu, with selections from Mei Lanfang's own writings.   Beijing: New World Press, 1980. 136p.

Mei Lanfang (1894-1961) was a much appreciated interpreter of *dan* or female roles in Peking opera. His name has come to overshadow those of other artists, doubtless because of his willingness to tour abroad during the 1920s and 1930s. This book gives a slightly rambling account of the nature of Peking opera and of Mei Lanfang's own art, incorporating some of his own reflections. Numerous black-and white photographs show him in famous roles and with other actors. An interesting digression compares Mei's views on theatre with those of Brecht and Stanislavsky. For the beginner, the most useful sections of this book are probably the 'Guide to Peking opera', which, with the help of attractive line-drawings, discusses types of roles, techniques of singing and declamation and of pantomime and acting, costumes, stage properties and their symbolism, and the musical instruments of Peking opera. The appendix of synopses of twenty-five Peking operas is also useful.

394 Peking opera as a European sees it.
Marie-Luise Latsch, edited by Ma Jie, translated from the German by Dora Bradenberger, Kaethe Zhao, designed by Sun Chenwu, Zhu Penghe. Beijing: New World Press, 1980. 45p.

A short account, which appeared simultaneously in German and English, of Peking opera as it began to re-establish itself after the Cultural Revolution and the triumph of the 'revolutionary operas' favoured by Jiang Qing, Mao Zedong's wife. It is thus a useful point of comparison with Elizabeth Halson's pre-Cultural Revolution work (see item no. 395). It covers very much the same ground, with descriptions of the various types of Peking opera, the main themes likely to be found and the comic interludes which are such a feature. There are descriptions of the masks, make-up, musical instruments and other features of Peking opera. Finally, there is a brief account of the training schools which now operate in China to produce new generations of performers, which are unfavourably contrasted with those of pre-1949 days. There are numerous good-quality colour illustrations.

395 Peking opera: a short guide.
Elizabeth Halson. Hong Kong; London; New York: Oxford University Press, 1966. 92p.

This account is based on personal observation of Peking opera as it was performed just before the Cultural Revolution led to its temporary eclipse. There is much detail about the musical and performing styles, together with accounts of the musical instruments used, the style of make-up and the costumes. The author provides pen sketches of some of the most prominent characters to be found in the genre, and includes a summary of a number of the best known operas. In addition, she includes a brief account of the other styles of opera still to be found elsewhere in China. There are numerous black-and-white drawings, together with a small set of colour plates illustrating the very distinctive style of make-up which is characteristic of Peking opera.

396 Salesman in Beijing.
Arthur Miller. New York: Viking, 1984. 254p.

It was a radical departure from the world of 'revolutionary operas' and other Cultural Revolution artistic endeavours when the playwright Arthur Miller agreed to direct his own *Death of a salesman* in Beijing, using Chinese actors, in the spring of 1983. Miller successfully cast the classically-trained Chinese actor, Ying Ruocheng (who later featured as the jailer in the film *The Last Emperor*, and who was for a time Vice-Minister of Culture), as Willy Lomax. Miller describes the problems of staging the play, the modifications required and developed as the production progressed, and reflects on culture and art in both countries. Since 1983, many more Western plays have been performed in China, but this pioneering venture is still worth studying.

397 The stagecraft of Peking opera from its origins to the present day.
Pan Xiafeng. Beijing: New World Press, 1995. 252p.

This is an excellent introduction to Peking opera – the author carefully explains why it should be named thus, rather than 'Beijing opera' – by a Chinese author. It begins with a brief historical background, tracing the various musical and performing traditions that came together towards the end of the 18th century to produce the genre. Pan then explains the conventions behind the various forms of make-up, the use of masks and the costumes. Along the way, he provides much information about famous opera performers, some of the stories used in traditional operas, the music and the instruments used, and gives details of customs and superstitions associated with Peking opera. The outcome is a work that will appeal to specialist and generalist alike.

398   Le théâtre chinois. (Chinese theatre.)
Roger Darrobers.   Paris: Presses universitaires de France, 1995.
126p. (Series Que sais-je?).

A brief, but comprehensive, account of all aspects of the Chinese theatre. Peking opera, its origins and its current state receive much attention, making this a good introduction for the general reader. As with many French books, the absence of an index is an inconvenience, only partially redeemed by a detailed description of each chapter.

Tianqiao of old Beijing.
See item no. 56.

Architecture

399 Ancient pagodas of China.
Luo Zhewen, translated by Wang Yueying, preface by Jiang Bo,
photographs by Ding Jiao and seventy-three others.   Beijing: Huayi
Publishing House, 1990. 155p.

As well as opening up to the outside world since 1978, China has been exploring and
recording its own cultural heritage in comparative freedom and with the benefits of
modern research and photographic techniques. This beautiful album of full-colour plates
of pagodas throughout China is a good example of the approach of recent years. A parallel
text in Chinese and English makes it accessible to a wide readership. An introduction by
Professor Luo Zhewen emphasizes the intimate connection between Buddhism and
pagoda construction, traces the introduction of Buddhism into China from India around
the beginning of the common era and with it the pagoda, and describes its development
into a peculiarly Chinese architectural form. Because the pagodas are categorized and
described by type, those from the areas in and around Beijing and Tianjin are scattered
throughout the book, but this gives the reader a good reason to look at every page!

400 The best specimens of imperial garden of the Qing dynasty.
Edited by the Department of Architecture of Tianjin University,
Municipal Bureau of Park Administration Beijing.   Tianjin, China:
Tianjin University Press, 1990. 192p. (Beijing's Gardens and
Ancient Buildings).

A meticulously produced book with numerous plans, sections, elevations, line drawings,
black-and-white photographs and colour plates illustrating the concept of the 'garden
within a garden' as developed during the Qing period (1644-1911). Four examples are
studied, two in Beihai park in Beijing (the Garden of Mental Peace and Huapujian
waterside garden), one at the Summer Palace (the Garden of Harmonious Interest) and
one at Chengde (Misty Rain Garden). The introduction first outlines the general
development of Chinese gardens from early times and sketches the four main types:
imperial, private, temple and public. It then discusses the concept and varying designs of
'gardens within a garden' before examining in detail the characteristics of each garden.

The book is best suited to those with a special interest in the philosophy and construction of Chinese gardens and would benefit particularly those able to visit the four gardens in question.

401 Chinese architecture.
Laurence G. Liu. London: Academy Editions, 1989. 297p. maps. bibliog.

This is a magnificent volume, full of breath-taking photographs, and filled with plans and sketches of all aspects of Chinese architecture. The whole of China is covered, but the importance of Beijing as a centre of architecture is such that the author regularly returns to the capital and its surrounding area, and the many architectural treasures to be found there. The book will appeal to both scholar and amateur alike.

402 Chinese architecture and town planning 1500 BC-AD 1911.
Andrew Boyd. London: Alec Tiranti, 1962. 166p. map. bibliog. (Chapters in Art, volume 36).

While Boyd deals with all aspects of Chinese architecture, which he notes at the beginning is more remarkable for its continuity than for its antiquity, he takes Beijing as typical of Chinese town planning. Much of the book, therefore, is concerned with the development and layout of Beijing over the centuries. Many of the plans that dot the text and the numerous black-and-white plates grouped at the end also refer to Beijing. The text itself is clear and full of throwaway insights; these include explanations of the lack of kitchens and bathrooms on most plans of Chinese houses and the role of the privy in providing manure for the fields. While there have been a number of more recent books on Chinese architecture, and several which give more detail specifically on Beijing, this remains a valuable introduction for both the specialist and non-specialist.

403 The Chinese garden: history, art and architecture.
Maggie Keswick, contributions and conclusion by Charles Jencks. London: Academy Editions, 1978. 216p. map. bibliog.

Maggie Keswick's pleasing study of the history, development and significance of the Chinese garden has a certain amount to say about gardens in the Beijing area, but largely in the context of imperial gardens, which are the subject of chapter 3 of her book. Other chapters on 'Architecture in gardens' and 'Flowers, trees and herbs' draw on details of the imperial gardens for examples. The book is an attractive introduction to Chinese traditions of garden-making, with ground plans, line drawings, reproductions of Chinese paintings and photographs. The only irritation is the poor standard of proof-reading.

404 The Chinese house: craft, symbol and folk tradition.
Ronald G. Knapp. Hong Kong; Oxford; New York: Oxford University Press, 1990. 87p. map. bibliog. (Images of Asia).

Although neither Beijing nor Peking appears in the index of this little book, Knapp, Professor of Geography at the State University of New York, does give some account of the typical North China houses found in and around the capital. In particular, he describes the development of the courtyard house, one of the most typical styles in use in Beijing. He also provides general information about matters such as decoration and the traditional site selection system of *feng shui*, here somewhat detached from the semi-mystical sense it has acquired in the West. As with all the books in this series, there are numerous illustrations, many in colour, which add to its usefulness for the non-specialist reader.

405 The garden as architecture: form and spirit in the gardens of Japan, China, and Korea.
Inaji Toshiro, translated and adapted by Pamela Virgilio. Tokyo; New York; London: Kodansha International, 1998. 204p. bibliog.

This handsome book by an eminent Japanese scholar, with its profusion of line drawings, ground plans, illustrations and black-and-white photographs, examines the functions and aesthetic qualities of the garden in the three East Asian societies. In chapter 4 (p. 83-102), the traditional Beijing *siheyuan*, the four-sided courtyard, is taken as an example of one form of treatment in Chinese architecture of the relationship between covered interior spaces and open exterior spaces. (The southern Huizhou style of housing provides a second, contrasting approach.) The text shows, as might be expected, a thoroughly Asian understanding of the principles involved.

406 Gardens of longevity in China and Japan: the art of the stone raisers.
Pierre Rambach, Susanne Rambach, translated from the French by André Marling. Geneva: Editions d'Art Albert Skira S. A.; New York: Rizzoli International Publications, Inc., 1987. 231p. bibliog.

This lavishly produced book is translated from the authors' original *Les jardins de longévité: l'art des dresseurs de pierres en Chine et au Japon* (Geneva: Editions d'Art Albert Skira S. A., 1987). Two-thirds are devoted to the place that ornamental stones have always occupied in the Chinese garden. The concepts behind the incorporation of stones into garden design are familiar to the Japanese, but can be difficult for other foreigners to comprehend and appreciate. The authors, through patient and unhurried discussion and the use of many illustrations, endeavour to explain for Western readers the importance of stones as elements of cosmic forces that can bring vital strength into the human environment. Beijing, as the seat of imperial power, accumulated massive stones in the palace gardens. Yangzhou and Suzhou further south were the other great centres for the cultivation of stone compositions. The book has a useful annotated index.

407 Historic Chinese architecture.
Compiled by the Department of Architecture, Qinghua University, photographs by Lou Qingxi, Zuo Chuan, Xu Bo'an. Beijing: Qinghua University Press, 1985. 146p.

Qinghua University's Architecture Department in Beijing is among the leading schools of architecture in China. Possibly because of its location, it has selected the greater number of its examples from within and around Beijing. That said, many of the surviving structures of types of architecture such as palace and tomb design were erected by emperors of the Ming and Qing dynasties and are thus clustered around the capital. The book approaches its subject in terms of basic types of design and structural elements, both in the clear and carefully illustrated introduction and in the order of the photographs. The Forbidden City is discussed and illustrated at some length as the largest and most complete surviving example of palace architecture. Other Beijing monuments are chosen to illustrate different principles of design: the Altar and Temple of Heaven; the Ming and Qing tombs; temples in and near Beijing and at Jixian (Hebei province) and Chengde; the

Niujie mosque; lamaist pagodas; the gardens and structures of the Summer Palace; and stone and wooden gates and archways. This is a helpful and attractive introduction to the subject.

408 Hsi yang lou: untersuchungen zu den 'europäischen bauten' des kaisers Ch'ien-lung. (Hsi yang lou: examination of the 'European buildings' of the emperor Ch'ien Lung.)
Alexander Schulz.   Isny im Allgäu, Germany: Alexander Schulz, 1966. 98p. bibliog.

This scholarly work on the Qianlong emperor's 'European buildings' was submitted in 1966 as a doctoral dissertation to Julius-Maximilian University in Wurzburg, Germany. It is a detailed account of the two projects (1749-52 and 1755-59), undertaken principally by Giuseppe Castiglione (1688-1766), aided by other Jesuit missionaries in Beijing, such as Michel Benoist (1715-74), to construct a complex of buildings and gardens in the European style at the Yuanmingyuan, Qianlong's pleasure park to the north of Beijing. A final project was launched in 1767. In a preliminary section, Schulz outlines the fortunes of the Jesuit missionary community at the imperial court from the early 17th century, their introduction of European religious paintings and thus of European taste and technique, their construction of churches in Western style, and the influence of drawings of European garden and architectural design on the Chinese emperor's curiosity. Etchings from a set of twenty produced in 1783, illustrating the complex, and photographs from 1880 and 1915, are reproduced, adding greatly to the interest of this work.

409 Imperial China.
Charis Chan.   London: Viking, 1991. Reprinted, London; New York: Penguin Books, 1992. 164p. maps. bibliog. (Architectural Guides for Travellers).

This work is aimed at the interested but non-expert reader, who wishes to know more about the principles and practices of Chinese architecture. Much of the text is taken up with Beijing, and with the areas particularly associated with the city, such as the Ming Tombs and the various summer palaces, including that at Rehe (Jehol or Chengde), although the introductory sections cover more than just the capital. It is clearly written, with numerous illustrations. These include black-and-white photographs and a wealth of drawings to illustrate particular aspects of architecture. It admirably meets the needs of the general reader and the traveller who wishes to know a little more than is provided by orthodox guidebooks.

410 Imperial gardens.
Cheng Liyao, English translation by Zhang Long, prefaces by Ye Rutang, Lothar Ledderose.   Vienna; New York: Springer, 1998. 193p. maps. (Ancient Chinese Architecture, vol. 3).

The third volume in a projected series of ten, originally published in Chinese by the China Architecture and Building Press. The other two volumes already published in this series are *Imperial mausoleums and tombs* (q.v.) and *Palace architecture* (q.v.). This volume traces the development of gardens in China from earliest times before leading to a discussion of Qing gardens, the culmination of the imperial tradition of garden-making. Ninety colour plates illustrate the text, of which seventy-one are studies of the imperial gardens in and around Beijing; the remainder are of the park and surrounding views at the

Qing summer resort of Chengde. Appendices show the layout of the most important
gardens and buildings in Beijing and Chengde and supply elevations and details of
construction and design. There are notes to the photographs and a chronology.

411 Imperial mausoleums and tombs.
Wang Boyang, English translation by Liu He, prefaces by Ye
Rutang, Lothar Ledderose.   Vienna; New York: Springer, 1998.
188p. maps. (Ancient Chinese Architecture, vol. 2).

Like the two other volumes that have already appeared in this series, *Imperial gardens*
(q.v.) and *Palace architecture* (q.v.), all three of which were originally published in
Chinese by the China Architecture and Building Press, this volume is beautifully
produced and illustrated. The text discusses the evolution of tomb and mausoleum design
from the 3rd century BC, when the Qin emperor ordered construction of his vast burial
chambers, and examines the siting, construction and decoration of tombs, including those
of the Ming and Qing dynasties. Plates 17-35 and 53-90 illustrate respectively the Ming
Tombs, near Beijing, and the East and West Qing tombs, which are located in the Beijing
region. Appendices detail the layout of some of the Ming and Qing mausoleums. There
are notes on the photographs and a chronology.

**412 Klassische chinesische baukunst: strukturprinzipien und soziale
funktion.** (Classical Chinese architecture: structural principles and
social function.)
Thomas Thilo.   Vienna: Edition Tusch, 1977. 252p. map. bibliog.

The emphasis in Thilo's work is on principles of structure and function in classical
Chinese architecture. The opening section on the organization and dynamics of
construction examines the ancient principles of symmetry, of the arrangement of
buildings in groups rather than individually, of the use and enclosure of space, of
alignment and axis, and of the dynamics of weight and proportion and horizontality and
verticality. The Imperial City in Beijing is taken as the finest exposition of these
principles (p. 18-51). Other monuments in the capital provide further examples. A
discussion of large-scale architectural forms such as terraces, walls, gates, bridges and
vaulted buildings illustrates its points with examples in and around Beijing (p. 80-108).
A later section outlines the development of the city and of its parks and gardens (p. 178-
99). Many of the plates show details of the architecture of Beijing, complemented by line
drawings and ground plans.

**413 The landscape of man: shaping the environment from prehistory
to the present day.**
Geoffrey Jellicoe, Susan Jellicoe.   London: Thames & Hudson,
1975. 3rd ed., revised and enlarged, 1998. 408p. maps. bibliog.

Although the Jellicoes never visited China, the country and its architecture clearly
intrigued them, and it makes regular appearances in this volume. As well as describing
Beijing from the point of view of landscape designers, they trace the influence which
travellers' accounts of the city had on the development of garden and park design in the
West. In particular, they note the linkage between the Chinese use of space and the
development of imperial summer palaces in and around the capital, and its effect on
similar developments in 18th-century Europe, with its vogue for Chinoiserie. There are
numerous black-and-white illustrations.

414 The monuments of civilisation: China.
Text by Gildo Fossati, translated by Bruce Penman, foreword by
Anthony Burgess. London: New England Library, 1983. 191p.
bibliog.

Originally published in Italian (Milan: Arnaldo Mondadori Editore, 1982), this is a
magnificent collection of colour photographs, with linking texts, of the main monuments
(statues, buildings) in China. Many of the photographs are of buildings in and around
Beijing, including the Great Wall, the tombs and the Old Summer Palace. Appendices
include a chronology from 5000 BC to the 1980s, and a guide to the pinyin and Wade-
Giles systems of transliteration.

415 New China builds.
Academy of Building Research, State Capital Construction
Commission. Beijing: China Building Industry Press, 1976.
unnumbered (approx. 150p.).

This collection of pictures of new buildings in China from 1949 to the mid-1970s includes
many of those in Beijing, from the massively rebuilt Tiananmen Square to more humble
power stations. Various Beijing sports buildings are included, as are the new Soviet-style
housing blocks that sprang up on the edge of the city in the 1950s and 1960s. There is
minimalist text, usually little more than the name of the building.

416 Oriental architecture.
Mario Bussagli, with contributions by Paola Mortari Vergara, Chiara
Silvi Antonini, Adolfo Tamburello, translated by John Shepley.
London: Faber & Faber Ltd, 1989. 2 vols. bibliog.

Originally published in Milan by Electa in 1979, this work was immediately translated
into English and published by Academic Editions of London the same year. This revised
edition has a long chapter on China (vol. 2, p. 46-138), with much of the attention focused
on Beijing. Beijing also features in the introductory chapter, in which Mario Bussagli
links the city which developed after Beijing became China's capital under the Mongols
with its several predecessors. This theme is also taken up in the main chapter, which notes
that in the view of many architects and historians, the Ming and Qing city which has come
down to us often represents a debased form of architecture. There are excellent
photographs, mostly in black-and-white, but also including a few in colour. One of these,
of the Temple of Heaven, also features on the cover of vol. 2. The bibliography includes
works in Chinese and Japanese, as well as in European languages.

417 Palace architecture.
Ru Jinghua, Peng Hualing, English translation by Zang Erzhong, Cui
Sigan, Ling Yuan, Liu He, prefaces by Ye Rutang, Lothar Ledderose.
Vienna; New York: Springer, 1998. 193p. maps. (Ancient Chinese
Architecture, vol. 1).

This sumptuously produced volume, the first in a projected series of ten, was originally
published in Chinese by the China Architecture and Building Press. Fellow volumes are
Imperial gardens (q.v.) and *Imperial mausoleums and tombs* (q.v.). It takes the Forbidden
City in Beijing and the Imperial Palace in Shenyang, the early capital of the Manchu Qing
dynasty, as the chief focus of its study of palace architecture. Forty-seven colour plates,

supplemented by notes, are devoted to the Forbidden City. The accompanying twenty-three pages of text discuss the philosophical concepts embodied in its creation, its design, details of construction and decoration, and techniques and organization of its building. Appendices supply plans, elevations and details of design. The volume is augmented by a chronology and glossary.

418   Quadrangles of Beijing.
Ma Bingjian, translated by Mai Yangzeng, photographs by Ma Bingjian, Zhang Zhaoji, Tian Yunjing, Zhang Zhenguang, Zhang Chengzhi, Huang Lukui.   Beijing: Beijing Arts and Photography Publishing House, 1994. 90p.

The use of the word 'quadrangle' to translate the phrase *siheyuan* – four sides enclosing a courtyard – of the original Chinese is perhaps confusing, since the Chinese term connotes no more than a structural arrangement shared at the most by several families. The book itself, however, with a text in Chinese and English, line drawings and many colour photographs, is a useful and charming introduction to the single-story courtyard dwellings still characteristic of Beijing, despite much demolition and new building. Six chapters outline the principles of construction and basic design; the gates and screen walls that ensure privacy, together with their knockers and clasps; the internal gates that divide larger courtyard complexes into outer and inner spheres; the construction and internal fittings of the inner rooms; the carving and decoration of the courtyards; and the gardens that lie within them. The examples chosen range from the fairly simple to the grandiose.

419   6000 years of housing.
Norbert Schoenauer.   New York; London: Garland STPM Press, 1981. 3 vols. maps.

This is a major survey work on the history of housing throughout the world, based on a course taught by the author at McGill University, Canada. Volume 2, subtitled 'The oriental house', includes a chapter on the Chinese house, of which a major sub-section is devoted to a study of the Beijing house. Schoenauer describes how Beijing developed as a city, noting the emergence of specialized shopping and residential areas, traces of which can still be found, although the external face of the city has been much altered. He describes the highly private nature of the traditional house, which was designed to seclude its inhabitants, especially the women, from the world outside, and which gave little indication from the street of what lay beyond the high exterior walls. The text is simple and straightforward, and is accompanied by good clear drawings, while each chapter has its own short bibliography. On a sad final note, the author writes that there is little in the post-1949 development of Beijing reflecting the influence of traditional housing styles.

420   The temples of the western hills.
G. E. Hubbard.   Beijing; Tianjin, China: La Librairie française, 1923. 76p. map.

The Western Hills, due west of Beijing, house a large number of Buddhist temples, endowed in past centuries by the rich and pious. By the early 20th century many had seen a falling away in support and had become dilapidated, tended by only a few monks. There was little objection to renting them out to foreigners as retreats from city life in the hot summer months. The author of this work was clearly among those taking advantage of such an arrangement, and his book has a discursive, anecdotal touch to it. He does, however, make a systematic grouping of the temples, describes them carefully and sympathetically, provides a map and routes and adds a note on temple worship. Line drawings and fine black-and-white photographs, some taken by Messrs. Hartung of Beijing, add to the book's interest.

421 A treasury of Chinese watercolor paintings of Beijing's ancient city gates.
Zhang Xiande, Fu Gongyue, Li Yancheng, Yuan Xuejun, painter and editor Zhang Xiande, translated by Yang Shaoping, inscription by Ai Xinjueluo Pu Jie, forewords by Hou Renzhi, Wang Jinglu, postscript by Li Qi.   Beijing: Beijing Yanshan Publishing House, 1990. 82p. map.
This collection of eighty-four watercolour views of the sixteen gates of Beijing, reproduced in full colour, fulfils several functions. It provides a record of how these gates once looked, for many of them have now been destroyed. It recreates the ambience of the old Beijing. It is a work of piety, but also a very attractive album. Its association with past grandeur is emphasized by the inscription by Pu Jie, brother of the last Qing emperor and admired for his calligraphy. Zhang Xiande started making these paintings in the 1950s, when rather more of the gates were still standing, and appears to have resumed in the late 1970s. Several paintings show the gates at dates in the past and are clearly based on archival photographs, which are here reproduced. A map showing the walls and gates of the Yuan and Ming periods helps to relate these to the later gates. The text and captions are in Chinese and English. An earlier account, from a time when the walls were complete, can be found in Osvald Sirén, *The walls and gates of Peking, researches and impressions. Illustrated with 109 photogravures after photos. by the author and 50 architectural drawings made by Chinese artists* (New York: Orientalia, 1924. 239p. map).

Home tuning.
See item no. 23.

Chinese imperial city planning.
See item no. 177.

Food and Drink

422 Celebrated Chinese dishes in Beijing.
Chief editor, Yu Tianwei, photographed by Chen Shubo, Liu Yingjie, translated by Dao Yongbao, Yang Aiwei, Wu Zhaojun.   Beijing: China Travel and Tourist Press, 1982. 192p. maps.

The rapid opening up of China during the 1980s and 1990s has perhaps left this book as something of a period piece. Nevertheless, because many of the most famous of Beijing's old restaurants have survived the changes, it is still of interest to those who wish to seek out good food. There is virtually no text, and the bulk of the book is made up of photographs of dishes produced in what were the main Beijing restaurants c. 1980, together with pictures of the restaurants themselves and simple sketch maps of how to find them. Most of the pictures have rather basic recipes attached, so that it should be possible to produce an approximation of the dishes concerned.

423 Chinese cooking.
Frank Oliver.   London: Andre Deutsch, 1955. 4th impression, 1960. 232p.

A straightforward collection of recipes, drawn from the author's experience of cooking in Beijing before the Second World War. He notes that the recipes come from all over China, but also that they have been adapted and modified in the kitchens of the capital, where the best of all Chinese food was obtainable. The recipes themselves are clear and easy to follow, and there are the usual sections on Chinese cooking methods, utensils and a guide to serving.

424 Chinese cooking.
Edited by Wang Yanrong, Yu Shenquan, photographs by Wu Yinbo, Yan Zhongyi, illustrations by Li Shiji.   Beijing: Zhaohua Publishing House, 1983. 2nd, rev. ed., 1986. 189p.

Another standard cookery book, produced in China, which contains detailed descriptions of utensils, condiments, Chinese cuts of meat and nutritional tables. The specifically Beijing angle is that the eighty-three colour plates show dishes as prepared in two well-known Beijing restaurants, that of the Minzu (Minority Peoples) Hotel and the Hongbinlou Restaurant.

425   The Chinese festive board.
Corrine Lamb.   Shanghai: Henry Vetch, 1933. Reprinted, Hong Kong: Oxford University Press, 1985. 2nd impression, 1986. 153p. map.

A pleasing mixture of reminiscences about food, restaurants, recipes and general information about food in China, which provides a good introduction to the subject. While by no means solely concerned with Beijing food, many of the dishes described come from that city, or the surrounding area. The reprint includes reproductions of the original photographic illustrations which add a certain period charm, even if they are not very useful as illustrations. There are also a number of attractive line drawings.

426   Chinese imperial cuisines and eating secrets.
Translated by Zhang Tingquan.   Beijing: China Literature Press, 1998. 360p. (A Panda Book).

This bilingual work (in English and Chinese) offers a general account of the eating traditions of the imperial court, especially during the Qing dynasty (1644-1912). As well as stories of how certain dishes found their way to the imperial table, there are accounts of some of the great banquets of the past, and a selection of recipes for dishes which can easily be reproduced in more humble surroundings.

427   Food and drink in China: a visitor's guide.
Gong Dan, with photographs by Wu Yinbo and others.   Beijing: New World Press, 1986. 95p. map.

As the PRC opened up more and more to foreign visitors in the 1980s, there was a clear need for guidance on what a visitor might expect to eat during a Chinese meal in China, rather than in a Chinese restaurant in the West. This little book is one of those issued to meet such a need. It explains how a Chinese banquet is constructed, and has short pieces on the various regional styles of cooking, including that of Shandong province, which, the author claims, is the source of much Beijing cooking. There are also descriptions of what the visitor might drink with a meal, remarks on table manners and a special section on Peking duck – the duck, like Peking Man and Peking opera, having kept the traditional English name of the city.

428   Imperial dishes of China.
Edited by Liza Wong, translated by Dao Yongbao, section entitled 'Stories from "Celebrated Dishes and Legends" ' by Tang Keming, translated by Gong Lizeng, Yang Aiwen.   Hong Kong: Tai Dao Publishing Co., 1986. 160p.

A handsomely illustrated book, which blends reminiscences by the brothers of the last emperor, an account of the Fangshan restaurant in Beijing's Beihai park, legends about court food, and a series of lavish, but workable, recipes derived from the palace kitchens. The Fangshan restaurant, which still functions, was founded in the 1920s by staff expelled from the Forbidden City together with the last emperor. The result is a good introduction to the more exotic side of Beijing cooking. The illustrations show both the imperial personages and the food they ate.

429 Peking cooking.
Kenneth Hsiao Chien Lo, foreword by William Empson.   London: Faber & Faber, 1971; New York: Pantheon Books, 1973. 176p.

This short book combines an interesting and well-written account of the development of the Beijing style of cooking, tracing the influence of the court and the large Muslim community, for example, with a series of easy-to-follow recipes. Lo shows how particular restaurants have introduced the cooking of other regions of China to the capital, and modified the local cuisine as a result. The recipes are often accompanied by anecdotes about their origins or about those with whom they were associated in the past. Lo has written a number of other Chinese cookery books, but none deals in such detail with the Northern, or Beijing, style. Less detailed, but still useful, is Helen Chen, Simon de Courcey Whelan, *Peking cuisine* (London: Wiedenfeld & Nicholson, 1997. 39p. [Classic Cooking Series]), which provides a well-illustrated collection of classic Beijing-style dishes, for preparation in Western kitchens.

Libraries and Museums

Libraries

430 The Beijing library.
Edited by China Pictorial Publications. Beijing: China Pictorial
Publications, 1989. 12p. (Pictorial China, no. 113).

A short illustrated pamphlet describing the capital's main library, completed in 1987 (not
to be confused with the National Library), and its contents. Most foreigners will only visit
the library for special exhibitions, although access to such institutions has become easier
in recent years.

Museums

431 Art treasures of the Peking museum.
Text by François Fourcade, translated by Norbert Couterman. New
York: Harry H. Abrams Inc., [n.d.]. 177p.

After introductory essays on the history of the museum and its collection, this work
divides into sections covering paintings, sub-divided into landscapes, figure paintings,
flora and fauna, and ceramics. There are eighty-seven colour plates, fifty of paintings and
the rest of ceramics, together with a chronology of the paintings.

432 A catalogue of various clocks, watches, automata.
Simon Harcourt-Smith. Beiping [Beijing]: Palace Museum, 1933.
32p.

Timepieces of various sorts formed an important part of China's trade with the West from
the 17th century onwards, and were frequently given to emperors as presents. This little

catalogue, which has thirty-six pages of plates in addition to the text, shows the imperial collection as it was soon after the Forbidden City had become the Palace Museum. War and revolution have taken their toll, and it is now a record of what once was, rather than a current catalogue.

433 Chinese paintings in the Palace Museum, Beijing, 4th-14th century.
Dickson Hall.   Hong Kong: Joint Publishing Company, 1989. 175p.

A well-illustrated account of the early paintings held in the Palace Museum (the Forbidden City). Although the collection is good, connoisseurs should be aware that many of the best items from the museum were taken to Taiwan by the retreating Chinese Nationalists at the end of the Civil War in 1948-49.

434 Dragons and silk from the Forbidden City.
Teresa Coleman.   Hong Kong: Odyssey Publications, 1999. 2nd ed. 32p.

The author is a specialist in Chinese textiles. This collection of her photographs shows some of the many imperial costumes from the Forbidden City/Palace Museum in Beijing. Silk refers of course to the material used, while the dragon was a symbol uniquely associated with the emperor.

435 Mei Lanfang memorial museum.
Edited by the Mei Lanfang Memorial Museum.   Beijing: China Printing Corporation, 1988. 24p.

Mei Lanfang (1894-1961) was probably the most famous exponent of Peking opera in the 20th century (see item no. 393). In 1986, his former residence was turned into a museum which celebrates both his life and the genre. This booklet gives a brief description of his life, shows some of the rooms, kept as they were when he was alive, and reproduces some of the pictures found in the museum.

436 Museums in Beijing.
Edited by China Pictorial Publications.   Beijing: China Pictorial Publications, 1989. 24p. (Pictorial China, no. 117).

This is essentially a folding sheet, divided into twenty-four panels. The panels contain descriptions and colour photographs of forty museums in Beijing. Although the descriptions are very brief, they provide adequate information about each museum, and the accompanying colour photographs are good. Another in the same series, *The palace museum*, edited by China Pictorial Publications (Beijing: China Pictorial Publications, 1989. 12p. [Pictorial China, no. 116]), concentrates on the contents of the Palace Museum (the Forbidden City), rather than on the architecture. While it is no substitute for a guidebook, it provides a useful, easily absorbed introduction.

437 A variety of museums.
Edited by Jiang Jialin, Zhang Jinming, picture editor Wang Guizhen, layout Han Fengze, translated by Fu Guiyun, Jiang Chengzhen, Ma Xiuzhi, Ran Xiancui. Beijing: China Reconstructs Press, 1989. 56p. (What's New in China, no. 39).

Designed to introduce the growing number of Chinese museums to foreigners, this little book provides brief accounts of museums throughout China. As far as Beijing is concerned, it covers the Palace Museum (the Forbidden City), the Bell Museum, and the Stamp Museum. In addition, there is a section on the Drama Museum in Tianjin. The descriptive text reads well but the photographs, all black-and-white, are a disaster. Readers actually wanting to visit any of the museums will need to consult a conventional guidebook, since no details about access or opening hours are provided.

438 Xu Beihong museum.
Edited by the Xu Beihong Museum. Beijing: Xu Beihong Museum, [c. 1976]. 36p.

Xu Beihong (1895-1953) was a well-known painter, famous for his pictures of horses. His works were popular with Mao Zedong and after 1949, he became president of the Central Academy of Fine Arts and chairman of the Chinese Artists' Association (see item no. 156). After his death, his former residence became a museum in 1954 but the museum was moved to a new site in 1967 because of the construction of the Beijing subway. Apart from a brief sketch of his life, in English and Chinese, this booklet consists of reproductions of over thirty of his paintings and drawings, showing the various styles which he used. The pictures are captioned in Chinese only, but there is a bilingual list at the end.

Xu Beihong: life of a master painter.
See item no. 156.

Peking opera and Mei Lanfang: a guide to China's traditional theatre and the art of its great master.
See item no. 393.

The Media

Publications

439 Arts of Asia.
Hong Kong: Arts of Asia Publications, 1971- . bimonthly.
This high-class, glossy magazine, with profuse illustrations, is similar to *Orientations* (q.v.) in its approach. Its target audience is both the collector of Asian art and the general reader. It carries occasional pieces about art in Beijing or about aspects of the city.

440 Asiaweek.
Hong Kong: Asiaweek, 1975- . weekly.
A journal similar in coverage to the *Far Eastern Economic Review* (q.v.), but with rather more emphasis on picture and human interest stories, which regularly features developments in China and Beijing. It also carries book reviews and reviews of films and videos.

441 Beijing Review.
Beijing: Pai Wan Chuang, 1958- . weekly.
From 1958 until January 1979, this weekly news magazine, which replaced the English-language version of *People's China* (q.v.), was known as *Peking Review*. It is primarily a source of official views on domestic and foreign affairs, publishing many government documents in translation. However, there are regular articles and illustrations about the capital. In addition to the English edition, the journal also appears in French, Spanish, Japanese, Russian and Esperanto.

442 China Aktuell: Monatszeitschrift. (China Today: Monthly.)
Hamburg: Institut für Asienkunde, 1971- . monthly.
This is an invaluable journal, which chronicles developments in the PRC, Hong Kong, Macau and Taiwan. It charts the appearances and disappearances of Chinese leaders both in central and provincial governments, derived from the study of a wide range of

157

publications and media sources, and it also carries articles about political and economic changes. In addition, each issue carries a detailed bibliography of articles in Western languages that have appeared in the previous month. Most of the material refers to China generally, but there is also much about Beijing.

443 China Daily.
Beijing: China Daily, 1981- . daily.
Although the *China Daily* is a national newspaper, and, like all such newspapers in China, reflects the government line on important domestic and international issues, its arrival has been a great boon to foreigners in that it provides a ready access to most major news stories. The paper proper occasionally carries items about Beijing, and provides listings for theatres and other entertainment centres, as well as carrying advertisements for housing and other things foreigners might need. In addition, there is a weekly supplement *Beijing Weekend*, which is packed full of information likely to interest foreign residents and visitors. *China Daily* is also available on-line at http://www.chinadaily.net/cndy/cd_cate1.html. In theory, both newspaper and supplement are commercial enterprises, but in practice, both can be found freely available in major hotels. Outside Beijing, however, they will often be several days late. Since the late 1980s, a number of other free newspapers and magazines have become available in Beijing, including *Beijing Scene* (Beijing: Beijing Scene, 1995- . weekly), and the oldest one, *Welcome to China – Beijing* (Hong Kong: Ismay Publications, 1988- . monthly), a glossy production under the auspices of the Beijing Tourist Administration. All have much practical and tourist information. An annual edition of *Welcome to China* first appeared in 1990 (Hong Kong: Ismay Publications, 1990- . annual), containing chapters on Beijing and Tianjin. *Gourmet World* (Hong Kong: Doshu AGC Co., 1994- . quarterly), a glossy publication heavily reliant on advertising and promotional features, has a Beijing section.

444 China Information.
Leiden, Netherlands: Documentation and Research Centre for Contemporary China, 1986- . quarterly.
A scholarly journal covering all aspects of modern China, similar to the *China Quarterly* (q.v.). It carries articles and reviews which from time to time include material about Beijing. There is a strong emphasis on the contemporary, in both articles and book reviews.

445 China Pictorial.
Beijing: Foreign Languages Press, 1951- . monthly.
A glossy general magazine, designed for distribution overseas, and thus often widely available outside China. It is concerned with all aspects of China, but has regularly carried features about Beijing and Beijing life.

446 China Quarterly.
London: Congress for Cultural Freedom, 1960-68; Contemporary China Institute, School of Oriental and African Studies, 1968- . quarterly.
The *China Quarterly* is probably the world's leading academic journal on things Chinese. As well as high-quality articles by leading scholars, there is an extensive book review section, and each issue contains a 'Quarterly Chronicle and Documentation', providing a

detailed and classified chronology, together with policy texts, speeches and other useful material. Although articles on the capital are relatively rare, the book reviews and the other regular features provide much information on developments in and affecting Beijing.

447 China Review.
London: Great Britain-China Centre, 1995- . three times a year.

The Great Britain-China Centre was established in 1974 to provide a forum for developing links between Britain and China. Although funded in part by the British Foreign and Commonwealth Office, it operates independently. From 1974 to 1995 it produced *Britain-China: Magazine of the Great Britain China Centre,* which was essentially a members' newsletter. From summer 1995, this was replaced by *China Review,* aimed at a wider audience. Both journals carry occasional articles about developments in Beijing, as well as book reviews and other studies, including texts or summaries of talks given at the centre. The style is more informal than that of strictly scholarly journals such as *China Quarterly* (q.v.), and still partly reflects its 'house magazine' origins.

448 China Review International.
Honolulu, Hawaii: Centre for Chinese Studies, University of Hawaii, 1994- . quarterly.

A journal designed to bring to the attention of the China academic community the range of books being published on China. The aim is to be both international and comprehensive, avoiding the temptation to concentrate on one category of books. This includes, inevitably, a number of books relating to Beijing and its inhabitants. Thus the first issue (Spring 1994), had reviews of Bickers, *Ritual and diplomacy: the Macartney mission to China 1792-94* (see item no. 239), several other books on late imperial China, and a number on the events of June 1989, making this a useful source for anybody wishing to be aware of leading academic work relating to China's capital city.

449 China Today.
Beijing: Foreign Languages Press, 1952- . monthly.

Formerly *China Reconstructs.* Like *China Pictorial* (q.v.), this illustrated journal aims to present 'New China' in the best possible light, and is widely available abroad. It also has occasional articles about Beijing, although it is primarily concerned with China as a whole.

450 Far Eastern Economic Review.
Hong Kong: Review Publishing Company, 1946- . weekly.

Since its establishment, the *Review* has covered all aspects of development in China, and has counted many distinguished China experts among its staff. It is thus a good source for information about Beijing and its history and development since 1949, particularly at historic moments or times of crisis. Its coverage of the Cultural Revolution and the events of June 1989, for example, were particularly good. An annual index is a useful research aid.

159

451 Journal of Asian Studies.
Ann Arbor, Michigan: Association for Asian Studies, 1941- .
quarterly.

Originally entitled *Far Eastern Quarterly*, this is probably the premier journal of Asian studies in the West. It regularly includes articles and reviews on all aspects of China's history, culture, literature and society, including Beijing. Its annual review of the scholarly literature on Asia is particularly valuable.

452 North China Star.
Tianjin, China: North China Star, 1928-41. daily.

This is a foreign-language treaty port newspaper, published in Tianjin, but covering developments in North China and the rest of the country in some detail, unlike its 19th-century predecessors, which tended to be somewhat preoccupied with the doings of the small foreign communities. Normally this would now only be found in specialist libraries, but a version on microfilm, based on the Library of Congress holding, is available from Norman Ross Publishing Inc., 330 West 58th Street New York, 10019 (e-mail inquiry@nross.com).

453 Orientations: the Monthly Magazine for Collectors and Connoisseurs of Oriental Art.
Hong Kong: Orientations Magazine, 1971- . monthly.

A lavishly illustrated journal, which is essential reading for those interested in all aspects of Asian art. It regularly carries articles about art exhibitions in Beijing, and other aspects of artistic development in the capital.

454 Peiping Chronicle.
Beijing: Peiping Chronicle, 1932-42. daily.

This typical China coast or treaty port newspaper catered for the interests of the foreign residents of Beijing during the 1930s. Unlike their 19th-century predecessors in Shanghai, Guangzhou and Tianjin, however, by the 1930s, such newspapers had begun to devote considerable space to developments in China, were far less concerned with the minutiae of lives of the foreign community, and were taking an active interest in Chinese social, political and economic affairs. The *Peiping Chronicle* is normally only available in major libraries, but a version on microfilm, covering the years 1932-42, based on the Library of Congress holding, is available from Norman Ross Publishing Inc., 330 West 58th Street New York, 10019 (e-mail inquiry@nross.com).

455 People's China.
Beijing: Foreign Languages Press, 1950-57. weekly.

A journal established soon after the foundation of the PRC in 1949, as one of the new government's earliest attempts to provide views and information to the outside world. This included regular information about the capital and developments there, making it an important source for understanding the Communists' approach to the improvement of the city. In 1958, the English-language edition was replaced by *Beijing Review* (q.v.), but *People's China* has continued to appear in other languages, including Japanese and Korean.

456   South China Morning Post.
Hong Kong: South China Morning Post Company, 1903- . daily.
The *South China Morning Post* (*SCMP*) is now the last of the original China coast newspapers. While its main concern for many years has been with developments in Hong Kong, it also has extensive coverage of China, including Beijing, especially as far as political, economic and cultural issues are concerned. It is also a good source for reviews of books about China. A CD-ROM version is available from Norman Ross Publishing Inc., 330 West 58th St., New York, 10019 (or website http://www.nross.com/checklists/ckasian.htm).

457   Summary of World Broadcasts (SWB): part 3: Asia-Pacific.
British Broadcasting Corporation (BBC) Monitoring Service.
Reading, England: BBC, 1939- . daily.
Since 1939, the BBC has provided daily translations of Chinese media material. Originally, its sources were confined to radio broadcasts and wire services, but as the nature of broadcast media has changed, so has the range from which the BBC draws its material. Given Beijing's major role in China, it is hardly surprising that there is much information on the capital and its affairs. A weekly supplement is devoted to economic matters, though there is also economic information in the daily reports. Much of the material is used by the BBC's own staff in the preparation of news bulletins. From 2000, the SWB will only be available to subscribers on-line. The same fate has already overtaken the more extensive US government production, the *Foreign Broadcasting Information Service* (FBIS) (Washington, DC: Department of Commerce, 1941- . daily), which has abandoned paper and only been available on-line since 1997.

Media studies

458   China turned on: television, reform and resistance.
James Lull.   London; New York: Routledge, 1991. 230p.
This interesting study on television and its impact in China is obviously not confined to the capital. However, there is sufficient in it about the role of Beijing in television matters, and also much relating to the lead up to the military suppression of the demonstrations in Beijing in May-June 1989, to justify its inclusion here. Chapter 9, for example, on 'Tiananmen Square and beyond' shows how the events of 1989 have had a lasting impact on Western perceptions of China, however distorted the actual television pictures broadcast might have been. There is also much casual information about how people live in Beijing.

459   Reporting the news from China.
Edited by Robin Porter.   London: Royal Institute of International Affairs, 1992. 127p.
Based on a series of seminars held at London's Royal Institute of International Affairs in 1990, following the events of June 1989, this collection of essays looks at how news is reported from China. Most of the participants were Western journalists who at one time

or another were posted to Beijing, though not always as news journalists. Kelly Haggart and Robin Porter, for example, both worked at different periods for the New China News Agency (Xinhua) in Beijing, and help to explain both how that organization functions as a work unit, and how it handles news. John David was in Beijing in the mid-1980s as an adviser from the Thomson Foundation to Xinhua, then setting up its International Journalism Training Centre. Several of the papers deal with the events of June 1989 and how both Chinese and foreign journalists handled the developing news stories. The result is an important contribution both to our understanding of what happened in Beijing in June 1989 and how China's media operate.

Associated Areas and Places

The Great Wall

460   The great wall.
Texts by Luo Zhewen, Di Wenbao, Dick Wilson, Jean-Pierre Dreze,
Hubert Delahaye, foreword by Jacques Gernet, designed by Emil
Bührer, edited by David Baker.   London: Michael Joseph, 1982.
191p. maps. bibliog.

This is a magnificent picture book, full of diagrams, maps, drawings, reproductions and
photographs of the Great Wall. The text explains the historical background to the
construction of the Ming-dynasty wall, which has become 'the Great Wall', and then
concentrates on the latter. The book as a whole is a most entertaining account of the wall
and its history, with considerable detail on matters such as building techniques. While the
wall is seen as an important element in Chinese history, the authors maintain a degree of
scepticism about the wilder claims of its importance.

461   The great wall near Beijing.
Luo Zhewen, edited by He Shiyao, designed by Xiao Shuyin, with
photographs by Zhang Changjiang and twenty-two others.   Beijing:
China Pictorial Publishing Co., 1989. 127. map. (Beijing Scenes
Series).

This short book gives a reasonable account of the origins and history of the Great Wall,
especially in the areas near the capital, filling in details such as the architects' names,
where known. The main interest, however, lies in the very good colour photographs.
These depict the wall in all seasons, and from a variety of different perspectives. As well
as the wall itself, the photographers have sought out curiosities associated with it, which
other photographers sometimes miss. Autographed bricks are one example, and a
discarded millstone another. Modern developments such as the cable-car at the Mutianyu
section also feature. While the quality of reproduction is perhaps not as good as the best
found in Japan or Hong Kong, it is good enough to make this an interesting book to
acquire. It certainly compares well with the quality of the photographs in another booklet

which appeared about the same time, *The Great Wall and the Imperial Palace*, edited by the Foreign Languages Press (Beijing: Foreign Languages Press, 1990. 20p. [China – Facts and Figures]).

462   The great wall of China.
L. Newton Hayes.   Shanghai: Kelly & Walsh, Ltd, 1929. 56p. map.

This short work, first presented in 1927 in Shanghai as a lecture given to the North China branch of the Royal Asiatic Society (and printed in the 1928 volume of the Society's Journal), gives a rather too straightforward account of the history and construction of the wall, which is described as Qin Shi Huang Di's achievement. There are references to the wall north of Beijing, but only as part of the general story.

463   The great wall of China.
Jonathan Fryer.   London: New English Library, 1975. 207p. maps. bibliog.

Presents a rapid run through the history of China in terms of the rise and fall of dynasties and the part that various walls played in protecting, or failing to protect, imperial fortunes. The ease with which rebel troops broke through the wall northwest of Beijing in 1644 to help in the overthrow of the Ming dynasty in the capital is made clear. Chapter 9, on Westerners' impressions of the walls from early times, is interesting. The quality of the black-and-white plates is disappointing, but is compensated for by the clearly drawn maps and attractive line illustrations.

464   The great wall of China.
Photographs by Daniel Schwartz, texts by Jorge Luis Borges (translated by James E. Irby), Daniel Schwartz, Luo Zhewen. London: Thames & Hudson Ltd, 1990. 224p. maps.

In this superb collection of 159 duotone photographs by the Swiss photographer Daniel Schwartz, the Great Wall is invested with poetic, even metaphysical dimensions. Schwartz speaks of his travels along the various walls as an experience he cannot readily express. This mood is heightened by a musing, entitled 'The wall and the books', by Borges on the motivations of Qin Shi Huang Di, who was credited with building the first wall and with burning the scholars' books (extract from Borges' *Labyrinths* [New York: New Directions Publishing Corporation, 1962, 1964]). Maps and a note by Professor Luo Zhewen on 'The Great Wall in history' provide a factual counterbalance. Part 1 (sections 1-4) of the book covers the portions of the wall closest to the capital. Those who have visited the Great Wall from Beijing will appreciate Schwartz's studies of this amazing construction. Others may be strengthened in their resolve to see it.

465   The great wall of China: from history to myth.
Arthur Waldron.   Cambridge, England; New York; Oakleigh, Victoria, Australia: Cambridge University Press, 1990. 296p. maps. bibliog.

For many this will be a book full of disillusionment, since Waldron effectively shows that there is in reality no one 'Great Wall' but several walls, and that none of them are visible from the moon. Yet at the same time it is a most illuminating and well-written account of the origins and significance of the Great Wall. Waldron describes the Chinese tradition of wall building, and links it to Chinese foreign policy over many centuries. He then shows how the symbol of the wall, and what lies inside and outside, have come to play an important part in Chinese state building. In addition, there is much interesting information about China and its traditions. The bibliography covers a wide range of Chinese, Japanese and Western sources, and the illustrations and maps are all well chosen. The result is a book which will be of interest to both specialists and general readers.

466   The great wall of China in history and legend.
   Luo Zhewen, Zhao Luo.   Beijing: Foreign Languages Press, 1986.
   61p. maps. bibliog. (Traditional Chinese Arts and Culture).

Offers an informative guide to the history of the Great Wall, making it clear that far more was involved than the wall visible today, which was built by the Ming towards the end of the 16th century. It describes the attempts of succeeding dynasties from the state of Chu in the 7th century BC onwards to construct walls as a means of deterring invaders. The purpose, functions and construction of a 'great wall' are all discussed. Colour and black-and-white photographs illustrate the remains of earlier walls and the best-known spots on the present Great Wall. These include Shanhaiguan just north of Beidaihe, where the wall meets the sea, and popular locations in the Beijing municipality and nearby. Four appendices list stories that have grown up about the Great Wall, chronological and dynastic tables, and the units of measure of each dynasty.

Chronicle of the Chinese emperors: the reign-by-reign record of the rulers of imperial China.
See item no. 178.

Imperial China.
See item no. 409.

The Imperial Tombs

467   Aerial image map of Ming tombs.
   Edited by Zhong Shi'an, Chen Ligen, photographs by Zong
   Tongchang.   Beijing: China Map Publishing Co., 1987. Two-sided
   single sheet.

Like the companion aerial map to the Palace Museum (see item no. 63), this map carries on one side an aerial view of the Ming Tombs and the surrounding area, full of fascinating detail, and on the other a text in Chinese and English giving a brief introduction to the tombs, together with a small map and photographs of details. The maps are intended for tourists, but can also serve as souvenir posters.

468 Chine, la grande statuaire, suivi de Les origines de la statuaire de Chine. (China: the great statuary, followed by The origins of Chinese statuary.)
Victor Segalen. Paris: Flammarion, 1996. 237p. maps.

The French archaeologist and writer Victor Segalen undertook considerable field research into Chinese statuary in the years before the First World War. His death in 1919, together with wartime disruption, prevented the comprehensive publication of his investigations. The two parts of this book have been published separately: *Chine, la grande statuaire* (Paris: Flammarion, 1972, 1996); *Les origines de la statuaire de Chine* (Paris: Editions La Différence, 1976; Flammarion, 1996) before being reunited in this text. Segalen had strong preferences, which were for the ancient statuary of the Han, Liang and Tang dynasties; what followed, from the Song onwards, he dismissed as decadence. His views on the statuary of the spirit way leading to the thirteen Ming Tombs outside Beijing are thus predictably scornful, but he admires the siting and design of the tombs themselves (Chapter 11 of *Chine, la grande statuaire*), arguing that the setting of a statue is as important as the aesthetic qualities of the statue itself.

469 The Chinese spirit road: the classical tradition of stone tomb statuary.
Ann Paludan. New Haven, Connecticut; London: Yale University Press, 1991. 290p. map. bibliog.

In this finely produced book, Ann Paludan examines the history of the spirit road and its statuary, the 'classical non-Buddhist tradition of Chinese sculpture', from the earliest known statue found at a Western Han tomb dated to 117 BC. Examples of this enduring tradition have been identified all over China. In the area around Beijing, the spirit roads and attendant statuary of the Ming and Qing imperial tombs offer the best ensembles but also close the tradition. In chapter 7 the author shows how the Ming dynasty revived what was felt to be an essentially Chinese practice after a century of foreign rule. The succeeding Qing, another foreign dynasty, maintained the pattern in the Eastern and Western Qing tombs in Hebei province, but without the same philosophical commitment. Tables and charts give summary details of the spirit roads, tombs and statuary discussed and of the location of tomb complexes. The bibliography is very full. The photographs, all by the author, are excellent.

470 The imperial Ming tombs.
Text and photographs by Ann Paludan, foreword by L. Carrington Goodrich. New Haven, Connecticut; London: Yale University Press; Hong Kong: Hong Kong University Press, 1981. 251p. map. bibliog.

During her stay in Beijing from 1972 to 1976, when the trip to the Ming Tombs was one of the few then permitted to foreigners residing in the capital, Ann Paludan had the opportunity to study all of the thirteen tombs, and her photographs record their appearance as they were in 1975. Comparing her observations to those of earlier scholarly studies, such as those by Georges Bouillard – for example, Georges Bouillard, *Les tombeaux impériaux: Ming et Ts'ing: historique, cartes, plans etc* (Beijing: A. Nachbauer, 1931. 560p. maps) – she was able to estimate the extent of restoration work carried out by the Chinese authorities. Her descriptions of the tombs, supplemented by ground plans and by superb black-and-white and colour photographs, include a brief note on their occupant(s). Additional chapters discuss the Ming dynasty and the origins of the tombs, the approach to the tombs, the spirit road leading to them, general principles of Chinese architecture and of tomb architecture, and administration and ritual sacrifices. The tomb of the founder of the Ming dynasty at Nanjing and Prince Jingtai's tomb in the Western Hills are also described. Appendices on the 'four intelligent creatures' and on birds of the Ming valley and an ample bibliography increase the book's usefulness. In 1991, Ann Paludan published a concise version: *The Ming tombs* (Hong Kong; Oxford; New York: Oxford University Press, 1991. 69p. maps. bibliog. [Images of Asia]), which contains some new material.

471 Imperial tombs of the Ming and Qing dynasties.
Text by Shi Yongnan, Wang Tianxing, Li Yin, Wei Yuqing, edited by Wang Tianxiang, Shi Yongnan, translated by Liu Zhongren.
Beijing: China Esperanto Press, 1995, second printing 1997. 159p. maps.

This handsomely produced book, which is full of photographs and diagrams, provides a brief introduction to the various sets of Ming and Qing tombs. Most attention focuses on those near Beijing, but there are also brief accounts of the first Ming tomb near Nanjing, and the early Manchu tombs near Shenyang. The authors admit in a postscript that there is a fair degree of similarity between the various tombs, but in fact they have managed to show the different characteristics and styles by a judicious selection of photographs. The same publishers have also produced separate volumes on *The eastern Qing tombs* and *The Ming tombs* (Beijing: 1997), which draw on the same material.

Chronicle of the Chinese emperors: the reign-by-reign record of the rulers of imperial China.
See item no. 178.

Imperial China.
See item no. 409.

Imperial mausoleums and tombs.
See item no. 411.

Chengde: the summer capital

472 Cheng De.
Foreword translated into English by Hsu Pang-hsin. Hong Kong: Polyspring, 1987. 61p.

This is one in a series of picture books widely available in China, which cover a number of scenic spots. The foreword, in Chinese, English and Japanese, contains the briefest of introductions, but the pictures are captioned and provide a comprehensive indication of what to see. The only map is a reproduction of a mid-Qing dynasty panoramic guide to the 'Mountain resort to flee the heat', Chengde's somewhat poetic name in the Qing period (1644-1911).

473 Jehol: city of emperors.
Sven Hedin, translated from the Swedish by E. G. Nash.   New York: Dutton, 1933. 278p. map.

An account of the Qing dynasty summer resort, situated some 150 miles north east of Beijing, to which the imperial court would depart to escape the summer heat in the capital. It was here that Lord Macartney was received by the Qianlong emperor in 1794. Hedin, a well-known Swedish explorer of the 1920s and 1930s, produced what remains the most comprehensive account of the city, its temples and palaces.

474 One's company: a journey to China.
Peter Fleming.   London: Jonathan Cape, 1934. 319p. map.

In 1933, Peter Fleming travelled in various parts of China, in search of adventure. As he wrote at the beginning of this book, he was twenty-six years old, spoke no Chinese and was in the country for a mere seven months. But the book has excitement and a freshness that make it still worth reading. One of his sketches recounts a visit to Chengde (then known as Jehol), which was newly occupied by the Japanese. He and his companion had planned to spend a day there, but were forced to spend three. This gave them time to view the temples and the other sights of the city, and to get to know a group of American missionaries who sound very grim. Fleming's account of them also appears in *China's treaty ports: half love and half hate*, selected and edited by Chris Elder (Hong Kong; Oxford; New York: Oxford University Press, 1999. 258p. map. bibliog.).

475 Summer palace and lama temples in Jehol.
Sekino Tadashi.   Tokyo: Kokusai Bunka Shinkokai (Society for International Cultural Relations), 1935. 50p. map. (K. B. S. Publication Series – B. no. 9).

Sekino (1868-1935) was known for his pioneering studies on the architecture and monuments of Japan, China and Korea. This short paper, based on a lecture he gave in 1935 in Tokyo, is, however, disappointingly uninformative on the sites in Jehol (Chengde). The thirty black-and-white plates that accompany the text are of a high quality and somewhat compensate for the paucity of research. The chief interest of the paper for the present-day reader is political. It was presented against the background of Japan's annexation and creation in 1932 of the puppet state of Manzhouguo (Manchuria) in northeast China. The new state was protected by a buffer zone reaching as far as Chengde, and Sekino makes much of the new government's determination to preserve and restore the monuments there, which had been allowed, under Chinese rule, to fall into decay.

Chronicle of the Chinese emperors: the reign-by-reign record of the rulers of imperial China.
See item no. 178.

Cherishing men from afar: Qing guest ritual and the Macartney embassy of 1793.
See item no. 203.

The collision of two civilisations: the British expedition to China 1792-94.
See item no. 207.

Imperial China.
See item no. 409.

Imperial gardens.
See item no. 410.

Beidaihe: the beach resort

476   Near to heaven: Western architecture in China's old summer resorts.
Tess Johnson, Deke Erh.   Hong Kong: Old China Hand Press, 1994. 135p. maps.

Tess Johnson is an American foreign service officer, who has spent many years in Shanghai, where she became interested in the surviving Western-style architecture. To record this before it disappears, she teamed up with a Shanghai photographer, Deke Erh (Erh Dongqiang). Together they have produced a series of books full of splendid photographs and sufficient text to provide historical background and an account of the present-day condition of buildings and areas once important to foreigners in China. Pages 40-53 of the present work deal with Beijing's beach resort, Beidaihe, once the favourite haunt of diplomats and missionaries in the summer, and now the place where China's senior leaders spend their summer. As a result, many old buildings have survived, although relatively few are now accessible to foreigners. The clear, sharp pictures, however, give some idea of the resort's former glory, and it is interesting to compare the general air of well-being that seems to mark Beidaihe with the more run-down air of the four other summer resorts featured.

477   Shells of Peitaiho.
Amadeus W. Grabau, Sohtsu G. King.   Peking [Beijing]: Peking Laboratory of Natural History, 1928. 2nd ed., revised and enlarged. 279p. (Peking Society of Natural History, Hand-Book no. 2).

This reference book on the shells to be found on the shores at Beidaihe (Peitaiho), on the Bohai Gulf, is indicative of the range of scholarly activity supported by the foreign community in Beijing in the early decades of the 20th century. Printing houses such as the Peking Leader Press, which produced this volume, allowed a diversity of books to be published, principally in English. This one discusses the means of collecting shells, describes the types to be found at Beidaihe and presents them systematically by family and genus. An index and eleven black-and-white plates aid identification. Beidaihe was a popular seaside resort for the foreign community living in Beijing, who thus had access to a beach and to the shells it produced. The first handbook in the series (see items nos. 160, 162-63), by D. R. Wickes, was entitled *Flowers of Peitaiho* (Beijing: Peking Natural History Bulletin, 1926. 88p.).

478 **Tourism and local economic development in China: case studies of Guilin, Guizhou and Beidaihe.**
Xu Gang.   Richmond, England: Curzon Press, published in association with the Institute of Asian Affairs Hamburg, 1999. 200p.

Studies of tourism in China are relatively rare, and so this is something of a pioneering work. Beidaihe, the seaside resort nearest to Beijing, first popularized by Western missionaries, merchants and diplomats in the late 19th century, is probably the oldest resort in China. Lacking the grand scenery of the other two resorts studied, it has developed since the Communist take-over in 1949 as a centre for rest and recuperation for both ordinary Chinese and for the party and government leadership, which has traditionally retired there for the month of August to discuss matters of importance. Xu also examines Beidaihe's attempt to attract customers from China's newly wealthy groups.

The Grand Canal

479 **China's imperial way: retracing an historical trade and communications route from Beijing to Hong Kong.**
Kevin Bishop, additional text by Annabel Roberts.   Hong Kong: The Guidebook Company Limited, 1997. 240p. maps.

The imperial way was the waterborne route linking the Chinese capital in the north with the south of the country by means of the Grand Canal from Beijing to Hangzhou, and then of rivers. The second chapter (p. 29-55) of Kevin Bishop's account of his and Annabel Roberts' journey by bicycle along the length of this route is devoted to the northern end of the canal and describes the stretch along the Tonghui canal that joins the Beijing waterways to the Grand Canal near Tongzhou, and thence to Tianjin. The whole of the book, illustrated with superb photographs by Kevin Bishop, is worth reading for the way it conveys the manner in which the needs of the imperial household and the capital impinged on the rest of the country.

Chronicle of the Chinese emperors: the reign-by-reign record of the rulers of imperial China.
See item no. 178.

Tianjin: the port of Beijing

480 Britain in China: community, culture and colonialism 1900-49.
Robert Bickers. Manchester, England; New York: Manchester
University Press, 1999. 276p. map. bibliog. (Studies in Imperialism).

Bickers' theme is what he calls the informal imperialism of China's treaty ports and
foreign settlements, rather than the formal imperialism of colonies such as Hong Kong
and Singapore. In the treaty ports, foreign control was more indirect, even though, as he
makes clear, it was no less real. There is much about Tianjin, even though the main focus
is, inevitably, on Shanghai, the great port and largest foreign settlement in the East. He
notes that Tianjin had really suffered, during the Boxer incident of 1900, the siege that
Shanghai was always expecting but did not experience, and that Tianjin also proved more
adept than Shanghai and some of the other concessions in removing formal barriers
between Chinese and foreigners before these became an issue. As well as the treaty ports,
there is also more general information about the British diplomatic community, which
casts light on behaviour and attitudes in Beijing.

481 Business guide to China's coastal cities.
Zheng Yiyong. Beijing: Foreign Languages Press, 1988. 347p.
maps.

This general guide to doing business in China, written by an experienced Chinese
manager who also holds a Master of Arts degree from the University of Nebraska,
contains much of the usual material found in such works, and in some guidebooks, from
accommodation to tax issues. In addition, however, it contains sections each of which is
devoted to a specific open zone or city. The one on Tianjin gives practical information
about transport conditions, the size of the city, and similar information, together with an
account of the city's planned economic development. A series of appendices covers
matters such as statistics, the laws and regulations governing foreign trade as they were
in 1988, details of the major Chinese organizations dealing with foreign trade, and
addresses and telephone numbers for travel agencies and hotels.

**482 China and Christianity: the missionary movement and the
growth of Chinese anti-foreignism, 1860-70.**
Paul A. Cohen. Cambridge, Massachusetts: Harvard University
Press, 1963. 392p. bibliog. (Harvard East Asian Series, no. 11).

Cohen traces the growth and development of a strong anti-Christian tradition in China
from the Ming onwards, noting how this tradition intensified as the Western powers
forced China to open up to foreign trade from 1842 onwards. The treaties allowed
missionaries access to the interior and as Chinese contact with them increased, so did
tension. In 1870, matters came to a head in Tianjin, where Chinese and foreign relations
had been poor since 1860, and where the French were particularly prominent. Allegations
that Roman Catholic missionaries had been kidnapping Chinese children escalated into a
furious anti-foreign riot in June 1870, which left between thirty and forty Chinese
converts and twenty-one foreigners dead. Cohen describes how this came about, and how
the issue was eventually resolved. He also notes (in an extended footnote on p. 344-45)
how the incident became an important factor in the Chinese Communists' view of
imperialism.

483 China dreams: growing up Jewish in Tientsin.
Isabelle Maynard, foreword by Albert E. Stone. Iowa City, Iowa: University of Iowa Press, 1996. 166p. (Singular Lives: The University of Iowa Series in North American Autobiography).

China's once large foreign Jewish community is now mainly forgotten, but before the Second World War, it formed a sizeable portion of the population in several of the Chinese foreign settlements, and like most of the foreign community, it kept itself apart from the Chinese. There are few accounts of this community, and this one of a Russian Jewish family settled in Tianjin is therefore part of the very small literary record that exists. The author was born in Tianjin in 1929 and lived there until her family left for the United States in 1948. Although the reader may have some doubts about her apparent ability to recall conversations and thoughts some sixty years after the event, she provides a vivid account of a world long gone, when foreigners lived in, but not with, China. The author does not claim accuracy of history, only accuracy of the heart. There are numerous black-and-white photographs recalling her lost world.

484 China: Tianjin.
Edited by Lu Niangao, Li Tiefei, art design by Song Xiangning. Beijing: China Travel and Tourism Press, 1983. 62p. map. (China City Guide Series).

This brief guide to Tianjin is well-written and clear, though the map is rather poor. Its contents cover all the usual tourist sites in and around the city proper, as well as one or two schools and other educational institutes that now probably seldom figure on tourist itineraries. Such guides were once rare and the visitor was grateful to find anything, but since the expansion of tourism in the 1980s, they are more common. Visitors should therefore seek out the latest possible edition.

485 The ford of heaven.
Brian Power. London: Peter Owen, 1984. 192p.

Brian Power was born in Tianjin (literally 'ford of heaven' in Chinese), where his father worked for the Chinese Maritime Customs, in 1918. He lived there until 1936. In this delightful memoir, he recalls treaty port life as it was before the outbreak of the Sino-Japanese War in 1937 destroyed it forever. In his case, there was an added twist to living in the British-dominated world of Tianjin, in that he was of Irish Catholic origin, which carried its own tensions. Perhaps the total recall conversations are unlikely, but there is a general feeling of authenticity about the book. The photographs help to recall a world long since gone.

486 The growth and changes of Tianjin.
Edited by the Tianjin Historical Museum, translated by Zhang Maopeng. Tianjin, China: Tianjin Historical Museum, 1985. 95p.

As the introduction says, this is not a guidebook. Rather it is a distillation of the exhibits in the Tianjin Historical Museum, as they were in the mid-1980s. This was a time of China's major opening up to the outside world, and so it is revealing to see how history was viewed in Tianjin, one of the first ports opened to foreign trade after 1842, but a port with links to earlier attempts to establish trade. Anybody hoping to find a new liberal spirit abroad would be disappointed, for the account given is one of unremitting hostility by foreign powers, met with equally unremitting Chinese hostility. While unsubtle, and even crude, this is a useful insight into what China officially thinks of foreigners and their policies towards China, whether missionaries, diplomats or traders.

487 Household durable goods ownership in Tianjin, China.
Hu Teh-wei, Li Ming, Wei Shangjin. *China Quarterly*, no. 120 (Dec. 1989), p. 787-99.

An interesting study of the effect of increasing incomes on the pattern of purchasing in Tianjin in the early 1980s. The authors draw on a 1984 household survey to show how quantity – the sheer wish to have certain types of goods, whether bicycles or, increasingly, washing machines – was gradually giving way to demands that such goods should also meet acceptable standards. There are many statistical tables, which indicate that this is an article primarily aimed at specialists, but the work also throws light on life in one of China's major industrial and trading cities at a time of far reaching changes.

488 Little foreign devil.
Desmond Power. West Vancouver, Canada: Pangli Imprint, 1996. 264p. map.

The author, the younger brother of Brian Power (see item no. 485), was born in 1923 in Tianjin, into a family rooted in expatriate society. He remained in the city until early 1942, by which time Westerners were classed as enemy nationals by the occupying Japanese, and was then interned in camps in and near Shanghai and at Weixian (Shandong). His mother remained in Tianjin. His breezy style is at its most successful when he relates the events of a childhood spent in the international society of a treaty port, with summertime escapes to the resort at Beidaihe. His account is not without perspective and balance, for example, when he presents the Chinese case against extraterritoriality through the mouth of a Chinese schoolmate, but these passages, possibly reconstructed with hindsight, sit uncomfortably in the general flow of the narrative. The book is illustrated with family and other photographs and with lively line drawings, some by the author.

489 Marriage and fertility in Tianjin, China: fifty years of transition.
Burton Pasternak. Honolulu, Hawaii: East-West Centre, 1986. 76p. (Papers of the East-West Population Institute, no. 99).

Pasternak's fieldwork was conducted from September 1981 to January 1982 in a single neighbourhood in Tianjin, largely inhabited by factory workers. From modest industrial beginnings in the 1920s-1930s, followed by a period of great deprivation under the Japanese occupation, Tianjin achieved rapid population growth and industrialization after 1949 and became a socially integrated city. The city has been exposed to the same modernizing tendencies that have affected the rest of China. The changes in fertility that Pasternak discerned in his fieldwork reflect the general pattern of changes caused by modernization, but he also argues that fertility in Tianjin, as in China as a whole, has been responsive to political shifts and that demographic data can provide an objective indicator and measure of social and political change. The book has no bibliography but carries ample references.

490 Revolution and tradition in Tientsin 1949-52.
Kenneth Lieberthal. Stanford, California: Stanford University Press, 1980. 231p. bibliog.

Although by 1949 Tianjin was well prepared for the eventual Communist take-over, since the Chinese Communist Party (CCP) had been actively working towards revolutionary power since at least 1945 (see item no. 264), there was nevertheless resistance to some of the changes, especially from existing organizations. Lieberthal deals with these two themes, showing how by a mixture of compromise and ruthlessness the CCP achieved its aims. He has examined one aspect of this policy in more detail in an article entitled 'The suppression of secret societies in post-liberation Tientsin' (*China Quarterly*, no. 54 [June 1973], p. 242-66).

491 Tianjin opening to the world.
Compiled by the Editorial Board of 'Tianjin opening to the world'. Tianjin, China: Red Flag Publishing House, 1985. 376p. (Reform in China's Cities Series).

This glossy production, full of photographs, deals with all aspects of contemporary Tianjin. Although the stress is heavily on the city's manufacturing and commercial development, there is also information on Tianjin as a cultural centre, and on the historical and scenic sites to be found in the Tianjin Municipal Area, which covers a much wider area than the city proper.

492 Tianjin sceneries.
Hong Kong: Polyspring Co. Ltd, [n.d.]. 64p. map.

At the beginning of this work, there is a short introduction in Chinese, English and Japanese, which sketches the history of Tianjin, but this is mainly a collection of good-quality photographs of the city of Tianjin and the surrounding countryside. The photographs reflect to a certain extent Tianjin's past role as one of China's foreign settlements. In addition, there is a note in Chinese listing the city's twinning arrangements with cities in the United States, Japan, France and Australia.

493 Tianjin Yangliuqing art society.
Tianjin Yangliuqing Art Society. Tianjin, China: Tianjin Yangliuqing Art Society, [n.d.]. 22p.

Although basically a catalogue of the Society's main products and activities in the late 1980s, this booklet contains a brief introduction to the new year pictures for which it is most famous. These colourful woodblock prints, originating in the early 17th century in the village of Yangliuqing to the west of Tianjin, have a distinctive style within the genre of pictures traditionally produced in China to mark the lunar new year. The catalogue shows some typical prints. The Society also reproduces paintings and calligraphy in traditional styles using the water-colour woodblock printing technique. An album commemorating thirty years (1958-88) of activity by the Art Society (Tianjin, China: Tianjin Yangliuqing Art Society, [n.d.], but presumably 1988. 90p.), with a text in Chinese only, offers a wider range of examples of the Society's skills.

494 Treaty ports.
Hallett Abend. New York: Doubleday, Doran, 1944. 271p. map.
Abend's descriptive account of China's treaty ports appeared when the majority, including Tianjin, were under Japanese occupation in the Second World War. In theory, by then Japan, Britain and the United States, the three principal treaty port powers, had all restored them to Chinese sovereignty. The book, in a sense therefore, provides an epitaph on a way of life that had already disappeared and would not be restored after 1945.

495 The workers of Tianjin 1900-49.
Gail Hershatter. Stanford, California: Stanford University Press, 1986. 313p. maps. bibliog.
While much work has been done on the development of Shanghai as an industrial centre after the 1895 Sino-Japanese treaty of Shimonoseki allowed industrial development in the treaty ports, similar developments in Tianjin have not received the same attention. This detailed academic study, which is likely to appeal mainly to specialists, redresses the imbalance, and gives an account of the development of a working-class community in the city of Tianjin from the end of the Boxer rebellion to the eve of the Communist take-over of China in 1949. The author outlines the modern history of Tianjin, and then describes how the very varied workers of the pre-industrial period were gradually welded into a coherent class, mainly as a result of the development of factories, which steadily undermined, if they did not entirely destroy, the old craft industries. She describes the various types of occupation of this new working class, showing in particular how women were brought into the workforce, and examines the social consequences of the new ways of working, and the attempts by workers to resist the tight social control which the factory owners tried to impose on them both inside and outside the factory.

No dogs and not many Chinese: treaty port life in China 1843-1943.
See item no. 28.

Beijing-Tianjin.
See item no. 78.

China: a tourist guide.
See item no. 85.

Vanished China: Far Eastern banking memoirs.
See item no. 122.

Death throes of a dynasty: letters and diaries of Charles and Bessie Ewing, missionaries to China.
See item no. 212.

The foreign establishment in China in the early twentieth century.
See item no. 220.

Associated Areas and Places. Tianjin: the port of Beijing

The international relations of the Chinese empire.
See item no. 227.

The lion and the dragon: British voices from the China coast.
See item no. 263.

Making urban revolution in China: the CCP-GMD struggle for Beijing-Tianjin 1945-49.
See item no. 264.

Pekin: ses palais, ses temples, & ses environs: guide touristique illustré. (Peking: its palaces, temples and surroundings: a illustrated tourist guide.)
See item no. 267.

Stilwell and the American experience in China, 1911-45.
See item no. 276.

A history of Chinese currency: 16th century BC-20th century AD.
See item no. 355.

A variety of museums.
See item no. 437.

A research guide to China-coast newspapers 1822-1911.
See item no. 507.

Reference Works

496 Beijing address and telephone handbook.
Compiled by Gao Min.   Hong Kong: Hai Feng Publishing
Company, 1981. 317p. maps.

The general, if not universal, availability nowadays of addresses and telephone numbers
for Beijing offices and institutions is one result of twenty years of growing openness in
daily life, but in 1981, this handbook would have been an extremely useful innovation.
Information of such a basic kind was woefully short in the years before 1978. The
handbook, with facing pages of names of organizations and addresses in English and
Chinese, is designed for both foreign and overseas Chinese tourists and business people.
It lists the type of business, institution or amenity likely to be frequented by such visitors.
The expectation in 1981 was that most visitors would enter China from Hong Kong and
travel to Beijing via Guangzhou (Canton), so an appendix of Guangzhou addresses was
included. This is now of limited usefulness, though some offices have not moved.

497 Complete guide to Peiping [Peking] streets and alleys.
Compiled by Beijing Public Security Bureau, translated and
prepared by United States Joint Publications Research Service.
New York: CCM Information Corporation, [n.d.]. 2 vols.

This guide was originally compiled in 1958 by the Beijing Public Security Bureau as
Beijingshi jiexiang mingcheng lu, and its claim to completeness is doubtless exact, since
it represents the police register of all the capital's streets with earlier names and means of
access. The list is arranged according to the number of strokes in the first character of the
name of a street. There is no map. The real puzzle is why an English translation running
to 921 pages was made and published. Until recent years a foreign visitor poking about
in the back streets of Beijing, particularly one carrying a printed list, would have been
challenged as very suspect. A Taiwan agent would not have needed an English-language
guide. The use of Peiping in the title is also strange, though it reflects the usage both in
Taiwan and the United States until the 1970s. The whole production has the air of a
provocation to the Chinese authorities, to show that their security had for once slipped.

Bibliographies

498 Bibliotheca Sinica.
Henri Cordier.   Paris: E. Guilmoto, 1904-08, 1924. Reprinted,
Taipei: Ch'eng-wen, 1965-66; New York: Burt Franklin, 1968.
5 vols.

This comprehensive collection covers some 18,000 European-language books and articles published before 1922. It has become the standard guide to such material, and is often used by booksellers and others to identify early publications on China. The reprint edition includes an author index. A supplement, covering books published from 1922 to 1957, can be found in Yüan T'ung-li, *China in Western literature: a continuation of Cordier's* Biblioteca Sinica (New Haven, Connecticut: Far Eastern Publications, Yale University, 1958. 802p.), while articles published between 1920 and 1957 are listed in John Lust, compiler, *Index Sinicus: a catalogue of articles relating to China in periodicals and other collective publications, 1920-55* (Cambridge, England: Heffer, 1964. 663p.). In addition, publications on art and archaeology, following on from those in Cordier, can be found in *The T. L. Yuan bibliography of Western writings on Chinese art and archaeology*, edited by Harrie A. Vanderstappen (London: Mansell Information/Publishing, 1975. 606p.). All contain many items relating to Beijing.

499 China.
Charles W. Hayford.   Oxford; Santa Barbara, California; Denver,
Colorado: ABC-Clio Press, 1997. rev. ed. 601p. map. (World
Bibliographical Series, vol. 35).

A bibliography for the general reader which lists and annotates over 1,500 works on China, and which replaces an earlier edition in the same series, edited in 1983 by Peter P. Cheng (Oxford; Santa Barbara, California; Denver, Colorado: Clio Press, 1983. 390p. map). Curiously enough, neither volume pays much attention to the literature relating to Beijing, despite the generally acknowledged role of the capital in most aspects of China's political and cultural history since the 13th century. There is inevitably some overlap between the two volumes, but on the whole, the edition by Hayford has the more detailed entries. Cheng has also published *Current books on China, 1983-88: annotated bibliography* (New York; London: Garland, 1990. 268p. [Garland Reference Library of Social Science]), which follows the same pattern as his ABC-Clio volume.

500 China bibliography: a research guide to reference works about China past and present.
Harriet Thelma Zurndorfer. Leiden, the Netherlands: New York; Cologne, Germany: E. J. Brill, 1995. 348p. (Handbuch der Orientalstik, no. 4).

A very comprehensive guide to finding information on all aspects of China, which lists Chinese and Japanese works as well as those in Western languages. There is an introductory essay on Chinese studies and Sinology, followed by listings of newspapers, journals, dictionaries and books. Zurndorfer includes information on yearbooks and statistics.

501 Chinese drama: an annotated bibliography of commentary, criticism and plays in English translation.
Manuel D. Lopez. Metuchen, New Jersey: The Scarecrow Press, 1991. 525p.

A detailed bibliography of English-language works covering all aspects of Chinese drama from the Yuan (Mongol) court dramas onwards. The author covers a wide range of subjects, including stagecraft and theatre construction, as well as types of drama. There is much on specifically Beijing styles of theatrical performance, including Peking opera.

502 The cultural revolution: a bibliography 1966-96.
Compiled by Song Yongyi, Sun Daijin, edited by Eugene W. Wu. Cambridge, Massachusetts: Harvard University Press, 1998. 521p. (Harvard-Yenching Library Bibliographical Series no. 6).

Although the Cultural Revolution affected all of China and not just Beijing, the capital was the major centre for the playing out of the drama, especially in the early years, and it features prominently in this bibliography which covers a huge range of material. It concentrates on material published outside China after 1966 on the subject in Chinese, Japanese and English, but does include some material from China published after 1976.

503 Doctoral dissertations on China and Inner Asia, 1976-90.
Frank Joseph Shulman, with contributions by Patricia Polansky, Ann Leon Shulman. Westport, Connecticut; London: Greenwood Press, 1998. 1,055p.

Frank Shulman's contribution to scholarship on East Asia is by now a well-established one, as his series of dissertation bibliographies grows longer. This one, which covers over 10,000 theses submitted between 1976 and 1990, like the others, gives the author's name, title and type of thesis, date and place of submission, availability and details of related publications. It follows on from Leonard H. D. Gordon, Frank Joseph Shulman, *China: a bibliography of doctoral theses in western languages* (Seattle, Washington; London: University of Washington Press, for the Association for Asian Studies, 1972. 317p.), which listed some 2,000 theses, and Frank Joseph Shulman, *Doctoral dissertations on*

China, 1971-75 (Seattle, Washington; London: University of Washington Press, 1978. 329p.), covering about 3,000. All three works contain much about Beijing.

504   A guide to manuscripts and documents in the British isles relating to the Far East.
Compiled by Noel Matthews, M. Doreen Wainwright, edited by J. D. Pearson.   Oxford: Oxford University Press, 1977. 182p.

Provides details of all the archives, both public and private, in England, Scotland, Wales and Northern Ireland, which hold manuscript material relating to China, Japan and Korea. There is a surprising amount involving Beijing, from occasional letters from the Jesuits, to the papers of Lord Macartney, and various later diplomats, together with military and naval records of regiments and ships involved in events such as the forced opening of Beijing in 1860, the siege of the legations and garrison duty at the British legation/embassy from 1900 onwards. Additional information about some of those who appear in Matthews and Wainwright can be found in Royal Commission on Historical Manuscripts, *Private papers of British diplomats 1782-1900* (London: Her Majesty's Stationery Office, 1985. 80p. [Guides to sources for British history based on the National Register of Archives, no. 4]); this includes records that have been exported abroad and others that can no longer be traced. British official papers on China, including correspondence to and from the legation/embassy in Beijing, are detailed in Michael Roper, *The records of the Foreign Office 1782-1939* (London: Her Majesty's Stationery Office, 1969. 189p. [Public Record Office Handbooks, no. 13]), and Louise Atherton, *'Never complain, never explain': records of the Foreign Office and State Paper Office 1500-c.1960* (London: PRO Publications, 1994. 189p. [Public Record Office Readers Guide, no. 7]).

505   Modern Chinese society: an analytical bibliography.
Edited by G. William Skinner, assisted by Deborah B. Honig, Edwin B. Wincke.   Stanford, California: Stanford University Press, 1973. 3 vols.

The first volume of this work is subtitled 'Publications in Western languages 1644-1972', and is some 802 pages long. It provides the most detailed survey available of all types of writing about China from the beginning of the Qing dynasty (1644) to the end of the more extreme phase of the Cultural Revolution in 1972. There is a comprehensive explanation of the methodology used and the sources consulted, and while there is no annotation for individual entries, they are carefully cross-referenced across the various categories. One useful feature is that the reader is introduced to much work produced in Russia/Soviet Union and in Eastern Europe, which is often little known in Western Europe and the United States. While the work is clearly aimed at scholars, the interested amateur might also find useful references, especially on more esoteric areas. Volumes 2 and 3 cover works in Chinese and Japanese, and have somewhat different time-scales; the Japanese volume is the shortest of the three, and only covers works produced between 1944 and 1971.

506 Premodern China: a bibliographical introduction.
Chang Chun-shu.   Ann Arbor, Michigan: Centre for Chinese
Studies, 1971. 183p. (Michigan Papers in Chinese Studies, no. 11).

This remains a useful short bibliography of Western-language works on China from the
prehistoric past until the early 19th century. There are three broad categories: an
introduction to the field of Chinese studies; details of Western-language bibliographies;
and the bibliography proper. In the last section the works described are broken down into
standard categories such as politics, economics, religion and travellers' tales. Some of the
entries are annotated. There is no special section on Beijing, but given its importance after
the founding of the Ming dynasty in 1368, many of the works listed inevitably cover
aspects of the city and its development.

507 A research guide to China-coast newspapers 1822-1911.
Prescott Clarke, edited by Frank H. H. King, foreword by John King
Fairbank.   Cambridge, Massachusetts: East Asian Research Centre,
Harvard University, 1965. 255p. (Harvard East Asian Monographs,
no. 18).

China coast newspapers are an invaluable, if often under-used, resource for the historian
of modern China. Not only are they essential for an understanding of the foreign
communities in the open ports and cities of China, but they also contain much information
about political, economic and social developments in China. This book provides a history
of the development of the China coast press, from its beginnings in Macau to the end of
the Qing dynasty in 1911. It lists all the newspapers known to have been published, even
when they no longer survive, as well as providing details of the people who worked on
them whether in editorial or other capacities. Foreigners published newspapers in both
Beijing and Tianjian, which are fully described (p. 102-03, and 98-101 respectively), but
those published elsewhere also contain information about the capital and about North
China generally. Those who wish for more details should consult Prescott Clarke's 1961
University of London MA thesis, 'The development of the English-language press on the
China coast, 1827-1881'.

**508 Western books on China published up to 1850, in the Library of
the School of Oriental and African Studies, University of
London. A descriptive catalogue, with author, title and
supplementary subject indexes.**
John Lust.   London: Bamboo Publishing Ltd, 1987. 352p.

This bibliography is surprisingly important for the history of Beijing. Listed are many
hundreds of books ranging from encyclopaedias to the Jesuit letters from the Ming and
Qing courts, to travel accounts from expeditions such as that of Lord Macartney. About
half the works listed here, including many of those relating to Beijing, are available on
microfiche from Inter Documentation Company bv, PO Box 11205, 2301 EE Leiden, The
Netherlands.

Indexes

There follow three separate indexes: authors (personal or corporate); titles; and subjects. Title entries are italicized and refer either to the main titles, or to other works cited in the annotations. The numbers refer to bibliographical entry rather than page number. Individual index entries are arranged in alphabetical sequence.

Index of Authors

Bredon, J. 33, 223
Bretschneider, E. 187
Bridge, A. 122, 367
British Broadcasting
    Corporation (BBC) 457
Brodie, P. 263
Brook, T. 311
Brooke, P. 68
Broomhall, A. J. 331
Bruner, K. F. 223
Bührer, E. 460
Bullock, M. B. 350
Bullock-Webster, G. R.
    328
Burgess, A. 414
Burgess, J. S. 340, 342
Burrows, J. 14
Bussagli, M. 416
Butterfield, F. 286
Bywaters, N. 118

C

Cai, Rong 48
Cail, O. 88
Cameron, J. 141
Cameron, N. 44, 184
Cammann, V. R. S. 93
Cantacuzène, M. 54
Canterbury, Archbishop of
    328
Cao, Xueqin 376
Capdeville, C 54
Carl, K. A. 113
Carrington, G. W. 248
Cartographic Publishing
    House 67
Cassidy, A. 45
Chan, C. 409
Chan, Chor Keung 102
Chan, R. 26
Chance, N. A. 339
Chang, Chun-shu 506
Chao, A. 170
Chapnick, H. 281
Che, Muqi 283

Chelminski, R. 145
Chen, Dezhen 50
Chen, Gengtao 64
Chen, H. 429
Ch'en, J. 174, 279
Chen, Lie 165
Chen, Ligen 63, 467
Chen, Ruilan 169
Chen, Shubo 230, 422
Chen, Shuyu 378
Chen, Xiafu 223
Chen, Xitong 64, 169
Cheng, J. Y. S. 285
Cheng, Lingfang 14
Cheng, Liyao 410
Cheng, P. P. 499
Cheng, Weishen 373
Chia, Lan-po see Jia
    Lanpo
Chin, Annping 43
China Handbook Editorial
    Committee 61
China International Travel
    Services 103
China People's Publishing
    House of Fine Arts 100
China Photo Library 45
China Pictorial
    Publications 430, 436
China Review Press 345
China Travel and Tourism
    Press 69
China Travel Service Head
    Office 359
Chinese Literature Press
    373
Chou, Shu-ch'un 160
Chow, Hang-fan 162
Chow, Tse-tsung 265
Chu, C. C. 342
Chua, M. 315
Chun, Baohui 64
CIA see United States
    Central Intelligence
    Agency
Clarke, A. B. 176

Clarke, P. 507
Coates, P. D. 214
Coggan, D. 331
Cohen, P. A. 224, 482
Cohn, D. J. 79, 377
Coleman, T. 434
Collis, M. 250
Coltman, Jr., R. 197
Colville, G. A. 183
Committee on Scholarly
    Communication with
    China 83
Compilation group of the
    'History of Modern
    China' series 251
Cong, Shi 349
Conger, S. P. 379
Constantini, O. 183
Cook, C. 263
Copeland, G. 313
Cordier, H. 104-05, 498
Costa, F. J. 5
Cottrell, R. 317
Couling, S. 19
Courtauld, C. 179
Couterman, N. 431
Cradock, P. 135
Cranmer-Byng, J. L. 237
Croll, E. 379
Cronin, V. 193
Crouel, W. 249
Crow, C. 257
Crowe, C. 248
Cui, Fengxia 64
Cui, Sigan 417

D

Danby, H. 234
Daniel, J. 49
Dao, Yongbao 422, 428
Darcy, Y. 267
Darrobers, R. 398
Davin, D. 14
Dawson, R. 37
Dehergne, J. 208

188

Pu, Yi *see* Aisin-Gioro Pu
Yi
Pulin, C. 381
Purcell, V. 200
Putnam Weale, B. L. *see*
Simpson, B. L.

Q

Qi, Fang 51
Qi, Jiren 51
Qi, Xing 85
Qian, Gang 22
Qian, Hao 58
Qian, Jinkai 70
Qin, Shi 7
Qin, Yin Pan 90
Qin, Zhou 300
Qiu, Ke'an 99
Querbeuf, P. de 229

R

Rambach, P. 406
Rambach, S. 406
Ran, Xiancui 437
Rao, Fengqi 60
Rawson, J. 165, 380
Redesdale, Lord *see*
Freeman-Mitford, A. B.
Reed, L. A. 83
Reichenbach, T. 294
Reinsch, P. S. 114
Ren, Ying 60
Rennie, D. F. 235
'Resident in Peking' 269
Ribaud, M. 49
Rice, D. 295
Richard, N. N. 382
Richter, U. 301
Rickett, Adele 146
Rickett, Alleyn 146
Robards, B. 152
Roberts, A. 479
Roebuck, P. 237
Rogaski, R.-A. 140

Romano, K. M. 131
Ronan, C. 68
Rong Bao Zhai Studio 384
Roper, M. 504
Rose, A. 47
Rosner, C. 250
Rothschild, J. 207
Rowe, P. G. 35
Royal Commission on
Historical Manuscripts
504
Ru, Jinghua 417
Ru, Shichu 98
Ruoff, E. G. 212
Rutherford, S. 73
Ruxton, I. C. 107
Ryckmans, P. *see* Leys, S.

S

Saich, T. 289
Salisbury, H. 316
Sanders, R. M. 323
Sang, Yangsen 351
Sang, Ye 14
Satow, E. M. 107
Schell, O. 281, 303
Scherer, J. L. 346
Schoenauer, N. 419
Schulz, A. 408
Schupbach, W. 47
Schwartz, D. 464
Scotland, T. 132
Scott, Robert 243
Scott, Rosemary 211
Seagrave, S. 215
Segalen, V. 368, 468
Segonzac, A. de 155
Sekino, Tadashi 475
Service, J. S. 20
Shan, Guoqiang 249
Shang, Hongkui 372
Shapiro, H. L. 166
Shapiro, S. 125, 377
Shaw, Yu-ming 352
She, Lao *see* Lao, She

Shen, Caibin 85
Shen, Honglei 87
Shen, Lixin 169
Shen, Ping 100
Shen, Yantai 48
Shepley, J. 416
Shi, Tianjian 310
Shi, Xiaoqing 375, 377
Shi, Yongnan 471
Shipley, E. 211
Shu, Qingchun *see* Lao,
She
Shu, Sheyu *see* Lao, She
Shulman, A. L. 503
Shulman, F. J. 503
Siao, E. 308, 391
Silber, C. 22
Simon, R. 208
Simpson, B. L. ('Putnam
Weale, B. L.') 226
Singer, A. 207
Sirén, O. 421
Sit, V. F. S. 3, 12
Sivin, N. 68
Skinner, G. W. 505
Smedley, B. 218
Smith, P. C. *see* Hooker,
M.
Smith, R. J. 223
Snow, E. 262, 270
Sobin, J. M. 20
Song, Xiangning 484
Song, Yongyi 502
Soong, Ching Ling 378
Spence, J. D. 6, 15, 43,
110, 179, 185, 193, 205
Spender, S. 130
Spurling, R. 73
Stalberg, R. H. 97
State Statistical Bureau of
China 348
Steel, R. A. 248
Steinhardt, N. S. 177
Stent, G. C. 324
Stone, A. E. 483
Strand, D. 271

Index of Titles

Index of Subjects

B

Backhouse, Edmund 198,
200, 261
Baliqiao 233
Ball, James Dyer 36
Banks 71, 355
Bao Ruo-wang (Jean
Pasqualini) 145
Baptist Missionary Society
118
Barbican Arts Centre,
London 49
BBC (British Broadcasting
Corporation) 132, 302,
361, 457
World Service 316
Beggars 232
Behaviour, advice on 83
Beidaihe see Associated
areas and places:
Beidaihe
Beihai Park 67, 79, 400,
427
Beijing Administrative
Bureau of Cultural
Relics 169
Beijing airport 66
Beijing area state protected
historical sites 169
Beijing Children's
Hospital 338
Beijing dialect see
Language
Beijing First Foreign
Languages Institute
364
Beijing Jeep Company
354, 356-57
Beijing Language Institute
301
Beijing Lay Buddhist
Association 325
Beijing Library 430
Beijing Movie Studio
140

Beijing Municipal
Government
Information Office 76
Beijing Municipality
protected historical
sites 169
Beijing Public Security
Bureau 127, 497
Beijing Review 455
Beijing Shifan University
129
'Beijing spring' (1979)
186
Beijing This Month 76
Beijing/Tianjin region 59
Beijing/Tianjin/Tangshan
economic region 12
Beijing Tourist
Administration 76,
443
Beijing University
(originally Imperial
University) 148, 186,
243, 293, 296, 301,
306, 351-52
and Mao Zedong 270
Beijing YMCA 342
Beijingren 14
Beiping (Peiping) 46, 118,
150, 254, 259, 262,
271, 276, 278, 497
Beiping (later Beijing)
Private Children's
Hospital 338
Beitang Cathedral 240
Bell museum 437
Benoist, Michel 408
Berne 151
Bertolucci, Bernardo 45
Bertram, James 150
Bewicke, Alice (Mrs
Archibald Little) 222
Bibliographies 498-508
Bicycling 81, 479
Birth ceremonies 26, 273
Bishop, Kevin 479

'Black hands of Beijing'
284
see also Tiananmen
incident (1989)
Bland, John Otway Percy
261, 269
Blind musicians 273
Blowfeld, John 254
Bodde, Derk 120
Bodo, Uhse von 308
Borges, Jorge Luis 6, 464
Bowra, Cecil 205
Bowra, Edward 205
Boxer uprising (1900) 37,
50, 108, 112-13, 171,
182, 195-202, 204, 210,
212, 218, 220, 223-24,
241-45, 248, 251, 279,
331, 334
Chinese Christians and
242
indemnity funds 298
see also History; Siege
of the legations
Boyarsky, A. E. 41
Brecht, Bertold 393
Bredon, Juliet 33
Bredon, Robert 33
Bridge 152
Bridge, Ann 122, 367
Britain 153, 171, 494, 504
diplomatic relations 154
British and German trade
rivalry 269
British Broadcasting
Corporation *see* BBC
British China consular
service 21, 108, 111,
116, 214, 223, 243,
245-46, 321
British colonial
administration Malaya
256
British forces (1860) 44,
98-99, 194, 225, 233,
235

Crowe, Peter *see* Lum,
Peter (Lady Crowe)
Cultural Revolution (1966-
76) 11, 16, 49, 96, 103,
125, 133-35, 137, 140,
142, 148, 151, 153,
287, 288, 291, 293,
298-99, 301, 306-07,
311, 326, 335, 377,
388, 391, 394, 396,
450, 502, 505
see also History
Culture 64, 170
Currency 355

D

Dadu
(Cambalac/Kambalac –
the Mongol capital) 5,
104, 170, 178, 188-90,
355
Dagu forts 44, 233
Dan Pao Tchao 93
Dancers 308
David, John 459
Death of a salesman 396
Dehergne, Joseph 208
Democracy Wall (1979)
186, 290, 360
Democratic People's
Republic of Korea
(North Korea) 280
Demonstrations 271
Deng Xiaoping 26, 132,
135, 286, 290, 315, 364
'Diary of Chin-Shan' 200,
261
Diplomats and diplomatic
community 19, 106-07,
109, 114, 116-17, 135,
138-39, 141, 171, 186,
194, 201, 219, 235,
257, 280, 290, 478, 504
Dissertations 503
Dragons 434

Drama 388, 396, 398, 501
see also Peking opera;
Puppet theatre
Dress 236, 434
Duan Qirui 378
Dule temple 100
Durham, University of 9

E

East India Company 207
Eastern Qing Tombs *see*
Associated areas and
places: Imperial tombs
Economic reforms (1978)
26, 35, 40, 94, 132,
135, 315, 353, 364
see also Deng Xiaoping
Economy 20, 59, 95, 142,
154-55, 182, 353-58,
457
Edinburgh 209
Education and educational
institutions 20, 64, 72,
142, 152, 350-52
Eight-Power Allied Forces
(1900) 50, 52, 98
see also Boxer uprising
(1900)
Elgin mission (1860) 233,
246
Embassies 70-71, 74, 85,
101-02
see also Diplomats and
diplomatic
community
Emperors 3, 12, 19
see also individual
emperors by name
Engst, Fred 339
Entertainment 67
Environment 3, 349
Erh, Deke (Erh
Dongqiang) 476
European publications on
China 498, 500, 505

European style and design
408
Ewing, Bessie Smith 212
Ewing, Charles Edward
212
Executions 43, 232, 241
see also Boxer uprising
(1900)

F

Fahai temple 95
Fairbank, John 115
Fangshan caves 86
Fangshan restaurant 428
*Far Eastern Economic
Review* 440
Far Eastern Quarterly 451
Favier, Alphonse 182
Fayuan temple 326
Feminism 152
Feng shui (wind and
water) 404
Festivals 259, 362
Films and film industry 17,
31, 152
First World War 114, 272
Chinese Labour Corps 363
Fisher, Lois 144
Fleming, Peter 241, 474
Flora and fauna 157-63, 182
Fokkema, D. W. 312
Folklore 36, 255, 335
Food and drink 15, 18,
236, 422-29
see also Restaurants
Footbinding 222
Forbidden City (Imperial
City) 42, 67, 79, 89, 95,
112-13, 121, 136, 168,
178-80, 211, 213, 215,
217, 230, 249, 252, 256,
260, 308, 372, 380, 382,
407, 412, 417, 428
see also Imperial court;
Palace Museum

Mongol dynasty *see* Yuan (Mongol) dynasty
Mongolia 41, 160, 260
Mongolian emissaries 232
Montaubon, General (Count of Palikao) 233
Montreal 148
Monument to the People's Heroes 169
'Morgan' *see* Chua, Morgan ('Morgan')
Morrison, Alastair 55
Morrison, George E. 55, 209, 231
Morrison (Hammer), Hedda 55, 57, 93
Moslems *see* Muslims
Mosques 332, 407
'Mountain resort to flee the heat' *see* Associated areas and places: Chengde
Museums 72, 90, 169, 259, 431-38
see also Palace Museum; Prince Gong's mansion and gardens; Xu Beihong Memorial Hall and Museum
Music 325
Muslims 232, 332, 429
see also Islam
Mutianyu cablecar 461

N

Nanjing 191, 470-71
treaty of (1842) 26
National Library 430
Natural resources 64
Nature reserves 157
Neighbourhood committees 341
Neill, Desmond 256

New China News Agency (NCNA-Xinhua) 295, 459
New York Times 286
New Yorker 124
Newsweek 281
Night-spots 101
1911 Revolution 43
1990 Asian Games, Beijing 60
Niujie mosque 407
Novels 71, 181, 222

O

Observatory 100, 186
Old Summer Palace (Yuanmingyuan) 44, 186, 194, 225, 232-34, 246, 408, 414
see also Palaces; Summer Palace
Oliphant, David 108
Oliphant, Nigel 108
O'Malley, Lady *see* Bridge, Ann
Opium smokers 254
Opium trade 269
Opium Wars
First (1839-42) 13, 28, 194
Second (1856-60) 194, 246
Orientations 439
Osmond, Andrew 370
Overseas Missionary Fellowship 331
Oxford, University of 115

P

Pagodas 399, 407
Paintings 383, 431, 433
Palace Museum 63, 100, 179, 181, 431-34, 436-37, 467

Palaces 69, 92, 105, 113, 123, 195, 237, 267, 407, 409-10, 413, 417
see also Palace Museum; Old Summer Palace; Summer Palace
Palikao *see* Baliqiao
Palikao, Count of *see* Montaubon, General (Count of Palikao)
Panikkar, Kavalam Madhava 138
Papal States 193
Paper gods 335
Paris 213
Parkes, Harry S. 216, 246
Parks 69, 408, 412
see also Gardens; Palaces
Pasqualini, Jean *see* Bao Ruo-wang (Jean Pasqualini)
Patten, Chris 135
Pearl Harbour 277
Peiping *see* Beiping
Peking Chronicle 362
Peking duck 427
Peking Leader Press 477
Peking Man 14, 86, 100, 164-70
Peking Natural History Bulletin 162
Peking opera 45, 291, 296, 388-95, 397-98, 435, 501
Peking picnic 122, 367
Peking Review 441
Peking Union Medical College 118, 350
social services department 11
Pekingese 161
People's Bank of China 355
People's China 283, 441, 455

People's Liberation Army
281
Peru 116
Peyrefitte, Alain 207
Photographs 2, 38-58, 194,
196, 204, 210, 212,
219, 223, 225, 230,
243-44, 263, 269, 273,
281, 286, 295, 300,
308, 318, 378, 386,
391-92, 399-400, 402,
408, 410-11, 414-18,
431-32, 434, 437, 460-
62, 464, 466, 469-71,
475-76, 479, 483, 492
Photographers 44, 195,
420, 464, 476
see also Hartungs
Photograhpic Studio;
Morrison (Hammer),
Hedda
Pinyin transliteration 28
Plain tales from the Raj
263
Plant life 32
Police 247
see also Beijing Public
Security Bureau
Political activism 310
Polo, Marco 6, 10, 28-29,
105, 187-89, 278
Population and population
control 20, 32, 64, 337
Porter, Frank 111
Porter, Robin 459
Portisch, Hugh 134
Post Office transliteration
28
Power stations 414
Prehistory and archaeology
164-67, 380, 498
Prince Gong's mansion
and garden 86
Prince Jingtai's tomb 470
Princeton University
Centre 342

Prints and print-making
381, 384-85, 493
Prisons 141, 146, 292
Pronunciation 71
Prostitution 242
Proverbs 93
Provinces, municipalities
and autonomous
regions 61
Pruitt, Ida 119
Pu Jie see Aisin-Gioro Pu
Jie
Pu Yi see Aisin-Gioro Pu
Yi
Public health 64
see also Medicine
Puppet theatre 308, 389
Putonghua see Language
Pyasetsky, P. Y. 41

Q

Qianlong emperor 24, 110,
186, 225, 234, 408, 473
Qin emperor 411, 463-64
Qing (Manchu) dynasty
44, 50, 56, 110, 121,
169-70, 172, 176, 178-
79, 185, 192, 206, 209,
211-12, 215, 219, 227,
230, 232, 236, 247,
269, 276, 279, 382,
385, 389, 400, 407,
410-11, 414, 421, 426,
469, 471-73, 475, 505,
507-08
see also History
Qing Tombs see
Associated areas and
places: Imperial tombs
Qinghua University 27,
124, 146, 298
faculty of architecture
27, 407
Qinhuangdao 222, 260
Queen Elizabeth II 11

R

Rae Yang 151
Rear lakes area 79
Red Army (later People's
Liberation Army) 116
see also People's
Liberation Army
Red guards 135, 137, 140,
151, 301, 377
Re-education from the
peasants 151
Reference works 496-97
Rehe see Associated areas
and places: Chengde
Religion 18, 36, 93, 236,
260, 267, 325-36
official religious
organizations 72
see also individual
religions by name
Rennie, David F. 235
Residential areas see
Houses and housing
Restaurants 67, 71-73, 79-
80, 90, 101, 102, 422,
424-25, 428-29
Reuters News Agency 137
Revolutionary operas see
Peking opera
Ribaud, Marc 49
Ricci, Matteo 15, 193,
229, 327, 333
Rice, David 295
Rickett, Adele 146
Rickett, Alleyn 146
Rickshaws 40, 271, 375
Rightists 153
Riva, Antonio 143, 381
Riva, Catherine see Lum,
Catherine (Riva,
Catherine)
Robards, Brooks 152
Roberts, Annabel 479
Rockefeller Foundation
350

Waseda University 96
Watches 432
Water supplies, decline of 59
Weihaiwei 121
Weixian 488
Wellcome Institute for the History of Medicine, London 47
Werner, E. Chalmers 36
Western Han dynasty 469
Western hills 109, 117, 420, 470
Western Qing Tombs see Associated areas and places: Imperial tombs
Wet collodion process 47
White Dagoba (Beihai park) 100
White Peking duck 158
Wittfogel, Karl 6
Women 337, 343
Wong, Jan 148
Woods, Grace 118
Work 1, 305
Workers 289, 314
see also Tiananmen incident (1989)
Wright, G. N. 13

Wright, Stanley F. 223
Wu Liangyong 27, 35
Wu'er Kaixi 315
Wuxing (five essences) 330

X

Xiamen (Amoy) 256
Xiangsheng ('face and voice performances') 374
Xinjiang province 62
Xinjiang villages 62
Xu Beihong 156, 438
Xu Beihong Memorial Hall and Museum 156, 438

Y

Yan'an 262, 277
Yangliuqing 385, 493
Yangzhou 406
Yanjing (Yenching) University 277, 293, 334, 352
sociology department 341

Yearbooks 500
Yenan see Yan'an
Yijing (Book of Changes) 330
Ying Ruocheng 396
Yin-yang 330
Yonghegong (Lama) temple 95, 326, 336
Yongle emperor 179, 372
Yongzheng emperor 225
Yuan (Mongol) dynasty 5, 170, 172, 178, 187-91, 355, 382, 416, 421, 501
see also History
Yuan Shikai 269, 279, 363
Yuanmingyuan see Old Summer Palace

Z

Zeng Nian 54
Zhang Xiande 421
Zhao Ziyang 318
Zhihua monastery 86
Zhou Enlai 138, 270, 360
Zhoukoudian 86, 100, 164-69

ALSO FROM CLIO PRESS

INTERNATIONAL ORGANIZATIONS SERIES

Each volume in the International Organizations Series is either devoted to one specific organization, or to a number of different organizations operating in a particular region, or engaged in a specific field of activity. The scope of the series is wide ranging and includes intergovernmental organizations, international non-governmental organizations, and national bodies dealing with international issues. The series is aimed mainly at the English-speaker and each volume provides a selective, annotated, critical bibliography of the organization, or organizations, concerned. The bibliographies cover books, articles, pamphlets, directories, databases and theses and, wherever possible, attention is focused on material about the organizations rather than on the organizations' own publications. Notwithstanding this, the most important official publications, and guides to those publications, will be included. The views expressed in individual volumes, however, are not necessarily those of the publishers.

VOLUMES IN THE SERIES